Readers' praise for *Finding Your Roots*

"It's the best book I've found to assist me in my research. A most invaluable tool."

—B.W., SYRACUSE, NEW YORK

"At the time I got your book I had twenty-three ancestors on my family tree. I now have fifty-four. Your book helped me work out many, many dead ends in my research. I have set my goal at tracing at least one of my lines back to the eleventh century. I'm fourteen now and I think I can do it by the time I am fifty-five."

—M.V., OMAHA, NEBRASKA

"I am employed in the Local History and Genealogy Department of our local library. Our staff teaches a beginning genealogy class twice a year and your book Finding Your Roots is our main text. We find it to contain material that is hard to find in just one book."

—P.H.L., ANDERSON, INDIANA

"I recently found in the library, and have since purchased, a copy of your excellent text on genealogical research. I'm writing in the hope that your research on the Bigler line might help me."

—F.W.H., SARATOGA, CALIFORNIA

"Your information was very helpful."

—W.J.K., ST. LOUIS, MISSOURI

"I read your book Finding Your Roots with great interest, and was amazed to find that we have two common ancestors."

—M.B.C., TEMPE, ARIZONA

"When I read your chapter on the LDS church records, I looked them up in the phone book and found a branch library five blocks from my house."

— D.F., ORLANDO, FLORIDA

"I'm glad you told me to tape my great-grandfather. His dialect speech led me to my ancestor's birthplace in Germany."

— G.W., SAN ANTONIO, TEXAS

"You told me wonderful surprises were in store, but I didn't quite believe it until we took a family vacation and were passing through Petaluma, California, where my grandfather was born. I begged my husband and kids to let me run into the library, leaving them in a hot car. I literally had five minutes, so I rushed up to the librarian and asked if he had any books on the Dilling family. He said that his great-grandmother was a Dilling and he'd researched that line. His family chart was waiting for me when I got home."

— B.D.T., GLENDALE, CALIFORNIA

Finding Your Roots

Finding Your Roots

*How to Trace Your Ancestors
at Home and Abroad*

Jeane Eddy Westin

FOREWORD BY JOHN J. STEWART
Founder and Past President, Genealogy Club of America

JEREMY P. TARCHER / PUTNAM
a member of Penguin Putnam Inc. *New York*

Most Tarcher/Putnam books are available at special quantity discounts for bulk purchases for sales promotions, premiums, fund-raising, and educational needs. Special books or book excerpts also can be created to fit specific needs. For details, write Putnam Special Markets, 375 Hudson Street, New York, NY 10014.

Jeremy P. Tarcher/Putnam
a member of
Penguin Putnam Inc.
375 Hudson Street
New York, NY 10014
www.penguinputnam.com

Library of Congress Cataloging-in-Publication Data

Westin, Jeane Eddy.
Finding your roots: how to trace your ancestors
at home and abroad / Jeane Eddy Westin.
p.   cm.
Includes bibliographical references and index.
ISBN 0-87477-943-X (acid-free paper)
1. Genealogy.   2. United States—Genealogy—Handbooks, manuals,
etc.   I. Title.
CS16.W46   1998   98-22244 CIP
929'.1'072073—dc21

Printed in the United States of America
1   3   5   7   9   10   8   6   4   2

This book is printed on acid-free paper. ∞

BOOK DESIGN BY LEE FUKUI

Acknowledgments

MANY PEOPLE deserve thanks for helping make this book possible—so many that I cannot mention them all, which in no way lessens my gratitude to them.

A special word of thanks must go to those who made significant contributions: Cheri R. Smith, managing editor of the *Genealogy Digest*, whose expertise is matched by her unending enthusiasm for family history; Shirley Linder Rad, who gave special insights for the chapter on family associations, Effingham P. Humphrey, Jr., former editor of the *Pennsylvania Genealogical* magazine, and Jimmy B. Parker, of Utah, who helped with sources on American Indians; Dr. Mary Matossian of the University of Maryland for her kind permission to quote from her research into psychohistory; and William D. Rowe at the Library of Congress Local History and Genealogy Reading Room and James D. Walker of the National Archives in Washington, D.C., who helped me see into the hearts of those two exciting institutions; and Norman Dawson, who taught me the importance of names.

I would also like to thank dozens of reference librarians, who never once refused my seemingly endless requests for information; the staff at the LDS (Mormon) Genealogical Library in Salt Lake City and at the branch library in Sacramento, California; and the many ancestor hunters who allowed me to study their personal family history books and handle their precious photographs.

The illustration in chapter 11 of the heraldic components, plus the pedigree chart, family group record, family inquiry sheets, and the

United States Census Summary Chart, are reproduced by permission of the Genealogy Club of America and *Genealogy Digest.*

The illustration in chapter 12, which originally appeared in *Science Digest,* May 1976, is reproduced with the permission of Dr. Mary K. Matossian.

Dedicated to my ancestors,
the saints and the scamps;
and to my husband, Gene,
a bit of both

Contents

Journey to Your Past

A MONG MY FONDEST childhood memories is a marvelous train trip I took with my mother to visit my grandparents in a far-distant city. I remember especially my excitement at arriving at our destination, and the warmth and affection that grew stronger in all of us as we became familiar with one another once again. *Finding Your Roots* is much like that childhood experience. By starting out with your mother and father, you embark on a journey to meet your ancestors. As you travel back into your family history, you are bound to experience the pleasure and excitement of discovering warm and fascinating characters whose blood flows in your veins.

Genealogy is one of the oldest pursuits of mankind—and possibly one of the most interesting. (The Bible itself is a monumental genealogical record.) You are fortunate to have in your hands an excellent guidebook for this pursuit. Jeane Westin's *Finding Your Roots* will help you take an enjoyable and challenging journey into the past. The author is a skillful writer, well acquainted with her subject. She has prepared a practical and easy-to-follow, step-by-step itinerary of where to go, how to do it, and what to do when you get there.

As one of the founders of the Genealogy Club of America, I have seen that many people in all walks of life are eager to pursue their family biography but have no idea how or where to begin. Jeane Westin's book will provide anyone interested in undertaking this search with concise and invaluable information.

There are many rewards to be derived from your ancestral quest. One is the sheer pleasure and excitement of engaging in this fascinating hobby. As moving as it is to read about the journey of immigrants from all over the world to this country, consider how much more poignant it would be to find the story of a great-grandparent's hazardous, months-long voyage across continents and oceans to reach America. And especially when you yourself have discovered that story on the pages of a yellowed diary while digging through an old family trunk.

Another reward for investigating your family's past is this: The better you get to know your forebears, the better you will come to know yourself. Through a genealogical search you can come to a much more complete understanding of who and what you are. What worthier effort, then, can we make than to seek out the story of our ancestral past and record and preserve it for future generations in a Family History Book? The benefits are first your own, but the legacy to your children and grandchildren will be priceless.

One final thought: When you and I and a sufficient number of other people start finding our roots, the whole world may recognize at last that we are all one family, and that it is time we learned to live in love and peace and goodwill toward all mankind.

John J. Stewart
Founder and past president,
Genealogy Club of America

Introduction

WHENEVER I HEAR someone bemoaning the lack of family values in this country, I remind them that today more than forty-two million Americans are tracing their ancestors. What is this explosion of interest in genealogy but the inherent idea of *families valued?* And these family historians don't just value past generations and the times in which they lived, but their living families. Today's genealogists are intent on leaving a history of family heritage for their children and grandchildren. It's never been easier or more exciting to do.

Twenty years ago when I wrote *Finding Your Roots,* I thought the fascination with where we came from had peaked. I didn't know then, nobody did, that the personal computer would change the face of genealogical research, and change the way you could use this book. How could anyone have predicted that one day in the late 1990s amateur genealogists could get on the World Wide Web in their own living rooms and search tens of thousands of different family history sites and databases all over the world? Yes, you still have to do the careful basic records search in family interviews and census rolls and courthouses which I describe in the first few chapters, but after that you'll find countless Web sites available to help you expand your discoveries along with inexpensive CD-ROM programs to help you organize your findings and get them ready for publication. (See chapter 10 to learn more about CD-ROM programs and how to get started on the World Wide Web.) Now, that doesn't mean you can't dig for your roots the old-fashioned way without a computer and do it well, too; what it means is that today you have more options than you ever had.

Other changes have taken place in genealogy in the past few years, all to the good. Almost every public library, even small local ones, now has its genealogical collection (sometimes even a genealogical librarian to help you), and welcomes patrons who want to do re-search. Many libraries are set up with their own Internet access and make it available to you. The big genealogy libraries of two decades ago are now even larger and the largest of them all, the Mormon Family History Center in Salt Lake City (see chapter 5), has *two billion* names in their computerized searchable files and many dozens of new library branches, a total of over 2,000 in all.

Genealogical societies have also proliferated with hundreds of new organizations and some of them, like ComputerRooters in my own hometown, specializing in cyberspace genealogy. Many more family groups, or one-name societies as they're called, have formed and pub-lish newsletters. There are an estimated 200,000 family reunions in this country every summer! But a particularly gratifying change in the last twenty years is the dramatic increase in the numbers of Latin-American, Asian-American, Jewish- and African-American family his-torians, along with a huge growth in the numbers of resources for them to search. I've listed many of them in this major revision, plus hundreds of new addresses, toll-free numbers, and Web site addresses to make every family historian's search easier and quicker and yes, more fun.

So there you have it—more help, more resources, indeed more of everything you need to find your roots. Remember, if you go back twenty generations (that's about 700 years), you'll find more than 37,000,000 ancestors, and back one more generation that figure dou-bles. Perhaps you'll discover, as many family historians do, that we all belong to the same human tribe, and that this sense of belonging in-creases our love of the human family as well as of our own. Not a bad result for pursuing the world's most interesting hobby.

Happy hunting.

Jeane Eddy Westin
Sacramento, California, 1998

P.S. Although I can't do genealogical research for you, I would like to hear about how you found your roots. You can write to me c/o Jeremy P. Tarcher, Inc., Penguin Putnam Inc., 375 Hudson Street, New York, NY 10014 or at *www.findingyourroots.com.*

Genealogy – Your
Greatest Adventure

TODAY MILLIONS of Americans of all kinds are searching for their forebears—from American Indians to those whose English ancestors stepped off the *Mayflower* to those whose African, Asian, Latin-American, and European ancestors arrived much later. These searchers have been gripped by one of the oldest and now fastest-growing avocations: genealogy, tracing your roots and making a family history.

The word *genealogy* is fast losing its stuffy association with elderly aunts, upper-class statesmen, and cobwebbed scholars. In fact, ancestor hunting has become one of the most democratic and popular pursuits around, one of the greatest forms of collecting except that, instead of acquiring Indian-head pennies or first-day covers, you are collecting the historical pieces of yourself.

Genealogy is truly for every American—as much for those of eastern- and southern-European, American-Indian, Asian, African, or Spanish-speaking descent as it is for those of Anglo-Saxon or northern-European heritage, with which it has been traditionally associated. There are family records of nearly all cultures, and much of the past is recoverable.

Moreover, to be a successful family historian you don't have to identify all your forebears back to the beginning of time. Just recovering the three or four generations to which almost any of us can trace back provides a world of enjoyment for you and your family. You may trace them only as far as you want. You can choose to seek out living relatives rather than long-gone ones. The idea is to learn more about your larger family and to have some fun doing it. The promise of ancestor hunting is not only in the finding but also in the looking. As one fan of detective stories told me, "Trying to solve mysteries in your own family is more fun than seeing them solved in Agatha Christie or John D. MacDonald." In addition, it need not be expensive; most of it can be done from your home with letters or on your personal computer. Yet if you want, it can carry you to new towns and new countries in an ever-widening search.

Is ancestor hunting important, considering all the other things we could do with our time? I think so—and so do 42 million other Americans joining in the search. Americans are *hungry* to uncover the buried secrets of their heritage. Most of us live far from the homes that our ancestors—even our parents—established. Many of us don't know much about our grandparents, let alone our great-grandparents. The freedom of mobility in our society takes its toll in that many of us feel rootless and yearn for a wider sense of family. As you begin to understand who your forebears are, you begin to understand who you are.

But perhaps best of all is the fun of it and where it can lead you. My story is typical of what you will hear from thousands of others who have joined in the ancestor hunt.

I began to explore my ancestral past by talking with older relatives. (Indeed, this can be one of the most pleasant aspects of searching for family roots.) One of my earliest talks was with Great-uncle Joseph, who sometimes thought I was my mother but remembered every detail of events that occurred seventy-five years ago. He was able to give me dates, names, and anecdotes about long-dead ancestors, important to every family historian, but best of all, he mentioned that his grandfather, Thomas Moffitt, had come from northern Ireland in the 1850s.

After interviewing all my living relatives, in person and by mail, I sought access to family Bibles and other records that many families had stored away in attics and basements. After that, I turned to library, government, and other public records to search for my ancestors, Thomas Moffitt in particular.

Acting on advice from a librarian, I went to the local branch of the Mormon library in Sacramento, California, where I live. The staff there ordered for me the 1880 federal census for Harrison County, West Virginia. It showed that Thomas Moffitt had married and had eight children. The Harrison County library in turn answered my request for information about my ancestor with a photocopied sheet from a printed 1890 county history, which listed his birthplace as County Fermanagh, Ireland. It did not, however, list where in County Fermanagh.

Great-uncle Joseph had told me that Thomas had arrived in New York City on a ship from Belfast in the summer of 1852, but he did not know the name of the ship or exactly when it reached port. While on a business trip to Washington, DC, my brother Dick took up the search and spent three hours in the National Archives scanning passenger list microfilms. Finally, there he was, on the manifest of *Sea Nymph*, captained by L. B. Hale: *T. Moffitt, arrived in America, July 11, 1852.* Most exciting of all, this record listed his point of origin: *Enniskillen, County Fermanagh.*

My search for Great-great-grandfather Thomas led me to a summer reunion with Moffitt cousins in Ohio, and eventually to northern Ireland. During a long-saved-for European vacation, my husband and I drove from Belfast about eighty miles across a moss-green Irish landscape to Lough Erne and the island town of Enniskillen.

It had been well over a century since my ancestor lived there, and no one alive remembered him or knew about his family.

"Never mind," Patrick and Joanna Moffitt, owners of the Guards Inn, told me over a glass of Guinness stout. "While you're here, we'll be your family."

Who knows? Maybe they were. They *felt* like family.

Alex Haley, in *Roots*, has told perhaps the most sensational genealogical story of our time, but he is far from being the only African-American to have traced his ancestors. The Vaughn family in Chicago has charted its past back six generations to a slave ancestor named Scipio. Using census and country historical records, a slave inventory, family Bibles, and interviews, Mrs. Aida Stradford, born a Vaughn, was able to piece together an epic tale. Born in 1784, Scipio was a member of the Ega family of the Yoruba tribe in Nigeria. He was captured and sold to a South Carolina planter named Wilie Vaughn. After becoming a valued ironworker, Scipio eventually helped two of his thirteen children buy their freedom in 1853 and return to Nigeria. With this background, the Vaughn family has been able to trace and contact Scipio's descendants—their relatives—on two continents.

Another story: Orphaned in this country in 1930, Helga Pehrson had not even known her own middle name and very little of her Danish immigrant family's history. She wrote to many parish *Folkregisters* in Denmark, until she made a contact. The clerk at Norup recognized the family name and took the letter to her father's sister. Five days later Helga got an airmail letter from an aunt she had never heard of, inviting her to come to Denmark and meet her family. The result of her trip was that she met an unknown half brother and two half sisters—and was reunited with her past.

Charles Wing of Honolulu had a similar kind of experience. After tracing an immigrant forebear through early Episcopal missionary registers and Oahu island tax records to the province of Canton, he wrote to a public official in his ancestral village. To his astonishment, several weeks later he received a large package wrapped in rice paper from mainland China. In it was the Wing clan genealogy, meticulously hand-copied from ancient temple tablets.

The element of surprise in genealogy is never far away. While most immigrants to America were not from the noble classes, genealogical tracing sometimes comes up with wonderful exceptions. While researching his great-great-great-grandfather's ties, Kerry Ross Boren found that he had Irish royalty hanging all over his family tree back to A.D. 347. When the chief herald of Ireland confirmed the discovery, Boren caused to be posted on the walls of Dublin Castle this rather grand public notice:

THAT I, Kerry Ross Boren, by right of title and blood, do hereby proclaim my rightful ascent to the throne of Eir, through the gracious blood of my ancestor, Brian Boru, 175th Monarch of Erin, and by right of whole blood I descend into the 29th generation, and whose proof of lineage is hereby attached, do hereby declare that I am herewith and for all time PRINCE KERRY OF IRELAND.

Quite often genealogy is the joy of finding the unexpected. Almost all ancestor hunters can tell you about an experience in which a seemingly blocked channel in their search was suddenly opened up by a chance conversation with someone, by a comment from a relative passing through town who knew of the connecting link, or by the unexpected gift of a family diary or Bible. These are occasions of *serendipity*—fortunate discoveries made quite by accident. It happened to the John Lindholm family of Denver when the succeeding owners of a former Lindholm family home told them they had found an old ironing board, on the back of which on March 18, 1899, Mrs. Augusta Lindholm, for some unknown reason, had written her thirteen-member family's names and birth dates.

Perhaps you, too, will thrill to see the names and birth dates of a long-dead forebear and all his family flash across the screen of a microfilm reader or computer screen. Maybe you will conjure up a mental image from 1908 immigration records of a frightened Polish girl in a white babushka alone in the giant halls of Ellis Island. Perhaps you will feel rage at finding the name of one of your forebears in a North Carolina slave sale record. Or maybe you'll feel shame upon discovering an ancestor who mistreated a slave, as I did. This pulling together of your family's history is something like presiding at your own reincarnation—finding little pieces of yourself in the past that make up the total of who you are today.

In this book, I deal with all the major ethnic groups that provided America with immigrants. You will learn about fascinating sources for all your forebears, sources that are more than just written records of the past. They will lead you to all the romance, adventure, humor, and pride that is your hidden family treasure. It will also draw the bonds of your own family unit closer together. Enlist your children in the search, for they are likely to be interested. My daughter recently asked me why her hair had a reddish cast. I told her that her great-great-grandmother was an Irish redhead. My response brought a flurry of interest in things Irish even to the baking of soda bread for the next family reunion. The enthusiasm of others can enrich the search for family history, especially if it leads to a vacation visit to the ancestral hometown or homeland.

The Irish and the Welsh had oral accounts of their ancestors covering 1,500 years, the Elizabethans painted their heritage on their ceilings, and the emperor of Japan can trace a 2,600-year family history. Historians will write the biographies of famous families, but possibly no one but you will trace your family history. The story of your family—a family whose experiences helped build the world we live in today—must be written by you. And with each passing year, as older family members die, you risk losing some part of your heritage forever.

You can't start a moment too soon.

CHAPTER 2

What's in a Name?
A First Clue to Your Roots

W HEN YOU BEGIN your search for where you came from, you start with the obvious: your name.

Your name is your most personal possession. It defines to the world who you are. As psychologists point out, a name can predispose others to like or dislike us. Indeed, even today, some primitive tribes keep their names secret to prevent enemies from acquiring power over them. In terms of history, your name is a fingerprint, perhaps the first clue of who you are. Some knowledge of naming practices in your ancestral country could help you trace your early ancestors to a town, an occupation, or give you a clue to their physical characteristics.

NAMING NAMES — FIRST AND MIDDLE

First names, of course, are called "given," or "Christian," names, after early Christians who converted their pagan first names to Christian ones after baptism. Most of the first names in use in the United States today come from five languages: Hebrew, Teutonic (which includes Germanic), Greek, Latin, and Celtic (which includes Irish, Welsh,

Scottish). No matter what their ethnic background, these are the names most immigrants have given their children. The reason? To "Americanize" them. A second-generation Japanese, for example, might be named not, say Masa, but David, which is Hebrew.

Hebrew contributed biblical names and accounts for about a quarter of all first names (see the box on pages 9–11). The Teutonic tongues gave us names associated with warlike characteristics.

The Greek, Latin, and Celtic languages often gave us names for personal characteristics and abstract qualities.

The origin of many first names is in the Bible. In A.D. 325, the Church outlawed the use of pagan names (like Marcus or Diana, which referred to pagan gods) and much later, in 1545, made the use of a saint's name mandatory for Catholic baptism. As a result, in all Western countries during the Middle Ages, there were only about twenty common names for infant boys and girls. John and Mary led the name parade.

In the 1600s, Protestants, rejecting anything Catholic, turned from the saint names of the New Testament to Old Testament names, such as Elijah, Joshua, Patience, Priscilla, Rejoice, Truth—even He-Soundeth-the-Trumpets-for-Jehovah (imagine a child going through school with *that* tag).

As any parent who has struggled with choosing a name for the baby can attest, there is far more choice in girls' names than in boys'. As name authority Elsdon C. Smith points out, this is because a boy's name can be made feminine by putting a feminine ending on it: Christina for Christian, Charlotte for Charles, Juanita for Juan. Because of the ancient cultural bias against applying feminine names to males, however, it doesn't work the other way around.

Middle names, usually a second "first" name, were first used as a status symbol by German nobility in the fifteenth century. They did not come into widespread use until several hundred years later and were not common in the United States until after the Revolutionary War, when the fashion was to use the mother's maiden name as a middle name. Remember this when you come across an unusual middle name in your search. It could be a valuable clue to a foremother.

COMMON AMERICAN FIRST NAMES AND THEIR ORIGINS AND MEANINGS

Names of Hebrew origin:	Meaning:
Adam	Earth
Ann	Grace
Dan	He judged
David	Beloved
Elizabeth	Oath of God
Eve	Life
James	May God protect
John	Gracious gift of Yahweh
Joseph	He shall add
Judith	Praised
Mary	Bitter
Samuel	Name of God
Thomas	Twin

Names of Teutonic (including Germanic) origin:	Meaning:
Amelia	Industrious
Arnold	Strong as an eagle
Arthur	Fearless
Charles	To become adult
Edward	Guardian of property
Ethel	Noble
Francis	Free
William	Resolute protector

Names of Greek origin:	Meaning:
Andrew	Manly
Barbara	Stranger
Basil	Most noble ➤

COMMON AMERICAN FIRST NAMES AND THEIR ORIGINS AND MEANINGS

(continued from page 9)

Names of Greek origin:	Meaning:
Cynthia	Of the moon
Dorothy	Gift of God
Eugene	Well born
Eunice	Fair victory
George	Tiller of the soil
Peter	Rock
Philip	Lover of horses
Sophia	Wisdom

Names of Latin origin:	Meaning:
Camilla	Free-born
Clarence	Famous
Claude	Limping
Emily	Industrious
Florence	Flower
Laura	The air
Genevieve	White enchantress
Martin	Warlike
Patricia	Noble
Paul	Small
Rufus	Red
Sylvia	Of the woods
Victor	Victory in battle
Virginia	Pertaining to spring

Names of Celtic origin (including Irish, Scotch, and Welsh):	Meaning:
Alistair	Defender of men
Brian	Strong

➤

Names of Celtic origin (including Irish, Scotch, and Welsh):	Meaning:
Donald	A lord
Douglas	Dark-complexioned
Duncan	Brown warrior
Eileen	Light
Kevin	Gentle and beloved
Leslie	From the gray stronghold
Morgan	Sea dweller
Owen	Well-born

Highly unusual first names may be of some use in tracing family history, but valuable, tantalizing clues are often found in last names. This is one of the aspects of family tracing that makes it a great adventure.

According to the 1990 U.S. Census, first names haven't changed drastically over the years. The most common female names today are Mary, Patricia, Linda, Barbara, Elizabeth, Jennifer, Maria, Susan, and Margaret. The most common male names are James, John, Robert, Michael, William, David, Richard, Charles, Joseph, and Thomas.

LAST NAMES: TWO HUNDRED YEARS OF SMITH

There are over 1,500,000 family names (surnames) in the United States today. Although enormous numbers of German, Italian, Polish, Russian, Asian, Mexican, and other immigrants brought their own surnames to this country during the last two centuries, the predominant family names in America are still very close to what they were in Revolutionary times. The first federal census, taken in 1790, listed the most common surnames as follows: Smith, Brown, Johnson, Jones, and Davis. Today the five most common are (see the chart on page 13): Smith, Johnson, Williams, Jones, and Brown. Americans no longer need to try to keep up with the Joneses, but with the Smiths (all 2.2 million of them).

Why have the predominant family names changed so little in 200 years? The answer is that many of the people whose names mean "blacksmith"—Schmidt from Germany, Kuznetzov from Russia, Ferraro from Italy, and so on—simply "Americanized" their names and disappeared into these 2.2 million Smiths we now have. And many other names were similarly translated, such as Woods from the German Holtz, the Dutch Bos, the French DuBois, the Polish Borowski, and the Spanish Silva. Or Hills from the German Buehler, the French Dumont, the Italian Costa, the Hungarian Hegy, the Irish Bryant, the Czechoslovakian Kopecky, the Polish Zagorski, and the Scandinavian Berg.

Some of the ethnic groups in our country have not, in general, Americanized their last names. The Chinese are an example. Surnames first appeared in China in 2852 B.C. when the emperor decreed that all families were to choose a name from a sacred poem (Po-Chia-Hsing). Since the poem contained only 438 characters, the result is that today there are only about 1,000 Chinese surnames and only sixty are common. Chew ("mountain"), Chan ("old"), Fu ("teacher"), and Wing ("warm") are four of the most common Chinese surnames in America. Because the Chinese have extremely strong family and ancestral ties and because the names are short and easy to pronounce, very few Chinese family names have changed.

In Europe only noble families had surnames until medieval times. Surnames were first used by the nobles of Venice, and from there the practice spread to France, England, Germany, and then the rest of Western civilization.

But since only 1 percent of the population was wellborn, the rest—an estimated 60 million—answered to John and Mary, or Hans and Maria. If there were three Johns in the same village, one would be John Will's son, another John the Miller, another John One-Ear, and so on.

The general practice of using surnames was not adopted in Western countries until well after A.D. 1000, when the growth in population

THE FIFTY MOST COMMON SURNAMES IN AMERICA*

1. Smith	18. Clark	35. Mitchell
2. Johnson	19. Lewis	36. Campbell
3. Williams	20. Walker	37. Phillips
4. Brown	21. Hall	38. Carter
5. Jones	22. Robinson	39. Evans
6. Miller	23. Allen	40. Turner
7. Davis	24. Young	41. Collins
8. Wilson	25. King	42. Parker
9. Anderson	26. Nelson	43. Murphy
10. Taylor	27. Wright	44. Rodriguez
11. Moore	28. Baker	45. Edwards
12. Thomas	29. Hill	46. Morris
13. Martin	30. Scott	47. Peterson
14. Thompson	31. Adams	48. Cook
15. White	32. Green	49. Rogers
16. Harris	33. Lee	50. Stewart
17. Jackson	34. Roberts	

* From the records of the Social Security Administration.

and commerce caused average Europeans to take them up (merchants needed to know which William owed them money). Experts generally agree that family names originated in all Western countries in much these same ways: according to place, patronymics (son of), occupation, or nicknames. In the United States, surveys show the percentage of descent to be:

place names	43.13%
patronymics	32.23%
occupational	15.16%
nicknames	9.48%

In England, to which William the Conqueror brought the custom of family names from Normandy, nobles usually took their surnames from the names of their estates (Somerset, for example), then passed both estate and name on to their sons. But by the end of the thirteenth century, the peasants, who made up about 70 percent of the population, had begun to imitate their manor lords and adopt the use of family names.

Quite often the common people took the name of their village or a distinguishing geographical feature. When the local priest wanted to differentiate among the many Samuels on his parish rolls, he would write "Samuel atte [at the] water" or "Samuel river" or "Samuel near the mill" or "Samuel by the [village] green"—which of course eventually became Atwater, Rivers, Mills, and Green.

Occupational names are, of course, based on trade or occupation, such as Miller or Farmer (see the box on page 15).

One of the most common ways of forming surnames in many Western languages is by means of patronymics. Williamson in English means "son of William," Petersen in Danish means "son of Peter," O'Brien is Irish for "descendant of Brien," MacGregor is Scottish for "son of Gregory," Janowicz is Polish for "son of Janos," Pieterzoon is Dutch for "son of Peter," Mendelssohn is German for "son of Mendel," Antonescu is Romanian for "son of Anton," Sanchez is Spanish for "son of Sancho," Bertucci is Italian for "son of little Berto," Mohammed ibn Ali is Arabic for Mohammed, "son of Ali," and Isaac ben Jacob is Hebrew for "Isaac, son of Jacob."

It took a few centuries for the patronymic as we know it to stabilize. At first, in England, Robert the son of Peter became Robert Peterson. His son John would not be John Peterson but John Robertson, and so on, changing the surname every generation. Then, in 1413, Henry V decreed that the surname of an individual be listed on every official paper, and this tended to start the legal process of standardizing family names, which was completed when parish registers were established in 1538.

Nicknames form the last class of words from which surnames are derived. If your family name is Stout, it is possible that centuries ago you can claim an ancestor who was more than a little overweight; if Little, a forebear who was small of stature; if Reid, a red-haired ancestor; if Longfellow, a person who was tall or long legged; if Goodman, a man kind to his neighbors.

THE ORIGIN OF OTHER LAST NAMES

Although most Western countries formed surnames in the four ways I have mentioned—place names, patronymics, occupation, nicknames—some countries had slightly different methods. If your heritage can be found among any of the following, this section will be of interest to you: African, American Indian, Chinese, German, Japanese, Jewish, Russian, Scottish, Spanish and other Spanish-speaking nationalities, Norwegian, Swedish, Greek, Arabic, Indian.

OCCUPATIONAL NAMES AND THEIR TRANSLATIONS

English:	German:	French:	Italian:	Polish:
Archer	Reisman	Flèche	Battaglia	Luczak
Baker	Becker	Boulanger	Fornari	Piekarz
Carpenter	Schreiner	Charpentier	Martello	Cielak
Coward (cowherd)	Schweiger	Bouvier	Vaccaro	Krowa
Farmer	Bauer	Gagnon		Kmiec
Fisher	Fischer		Pisciolo	Ryback
Miller	Müller	Meunier	Farina	
Miner		Mènier	Carbone	Weglarz
Priest	Pabst		Prete	Kaplan
Shepherd	Schaefer	Berger	Pecora	
Taylor	Schneider	Tailleur	Sartori	Krawczyk

African

African naming customs vary from tribe to tribe, but most are descriptive. For example, the children of some western African tribes receive what amounts to a name based on the order of their birth ("first born," "second born," and so on). The Ashanti tribes of Ghana name their children for the day of the week on which they are born and give them a second name which further pinpoints their birth order. For example, "Kofi" means Friday, but if you are the second child born on Friday your name would be "Kofi Buo," meaning "Friday who has come again."

During the two centuries during which blacks were brought to this hemisphere as slaves, except in the West Indies, they rarely kept their African tribal names. Usually the slave's owner arbitrarily picked a first name (such as Toby, which was forced on Kunte Kinte, *Roots* author Alex Haley's Mandinka ancestor), often a fancy classical name such as Cicero, Scipio, or Caesar. Then the slave owner often ignored even this name in his property records, listing instead "a male Negro, strongly made." No surname was allowed until the slave was freed. And, contrary to popular belief, it is not true that most freed slaves took the names of their former masters. Although some did, many wanted no reminder of their days in slavery.

Freed slaves generally chose familiar or prestigious family names from the South, and since these names were primarily English, Scottish, Welsh, and Irish in origin, that is why the most common are patronymical—such as Johnson, Jackson, and Robinson. But black family names were often changed until the northern migration, World War I draft, and Social Security made change more difficult.

American Indian

Among Native Americans, names generally described traits of character. The Shawnee, for instance, had a "name giver" (a man often as important as the tribal chief) who gave each child a name never used before. Other tribes simply called all first sons a name that translated as "First Son" and first daughters "First Daughter," and the same with second sons and daughters. Later, this name was replaced when the child had a unique experience or acquired a distinctive personality trait. Most tribes had a manhood initiation ceremony for boys at puberty, requiring them to choose their own adult names based on a spirit vision during a fast in the wilderness. (The Dakota chief Crow-Flies-High, for example, received his name from a spirit disguised as a crow.) The initiation rites for women often accompanied the first menses, after which the girl could choose an adult name.

Most tribes allowed for name changes throughout life, and so surnames were not needed until Indians ran up against the white man's passion for record keeping. Then Indian names that were lyrically beautiful in their native tongues defied English phonetic spelling. Or their translation proved to be too unwieldy (such as "Buffalo-Bulls Back-Fat" or "She-Who-Bathes-Her-Knees"). And so, on most reservations the surname that was assigned was often ignored by Indian families. This produced such great confusion in record keeping that in 1903 President Theodore Roosevelt urged Dr. Charles Eastman, a Sioux, to rename every person on a large Sioux reservation. The result was a codifying of family names, and today American Indians researching their ancestry have some records through which to start searching.

Chinese

Traditional Chinese placed their surname first (Chiang Kai-shek, for example, is really Kai-shek, a member of the Chiang family).

Usually of one syllable, a few are place names such as Chew, after the province, and Pei, meaning "north." The most common, however, are descriptive, such as Chan ("old"), Chang ("draw-bow"), Fu ("teacher"), Gee ("well-mannered"), Li ("plum tree"), Moy ("plum flower"), Wang ("yellow"), Wong ("field" or "wide water").

Chinese-Americans no longer place their surname first but follow the Western custom.

German

Unlike English surnames, which are predominantly derived from place names, German family names most usually come from occupations, such as Schmidt ("smith"), Kaufman ("merchant"), or Richter ("judge").

Among other German names, colors predominate, such as Schwarz ("black"), Weiss ("white"), Roth ("red"), Braun ("brown"), Grün ("green"), Silber ("silver"), Gold ("gold"), and Rosen ("rose").

Other name forms are descriptive, such as Gross ("big"), Klein ("little"), Baum ("tree"), and Blume ("flower").

Location names account for the last definable group of German surnames, such as Wald ("Forest"), Brück ("bridge"), Sachs ("Saxony"), Hess ("Hesse"), Schlesinger ("Silesian").

Japanese

The nobility had surnames as early as the fifteenth century, but most common Japanese surnames (taken primarily from locations) were assumed late in the 1800s when Emperor Mutuhito declared that everyone must take a family name. Whole villages took the same name, so that there are only about 10,000 surnames in Japan today. Examples of such names taken from locations are Takahashi ("high bridge"), Nakagawa ("middle river"), Nakamura ("middle village"), and Yamashita ("mountain below").

Other Japanese family names are descriptive, such as Suzuki, which means "bell tree," and Matsumoto, "pine origin."

Another group of surnames is composed of two words, usually taken from nature but seemingly not related to each other—for example, Ito ("only, wisteria"), Kato ("add, wisteria"), Sato ("help, wisteria"), and Saito ("festival, wisteria").

Jewish

For most of their history, Jews favored patronymics, but during the early 1800s persecution forced them to abandon their own system and adopt permanent family names.

The Jews in Germany were made to take surnames by law. Those who were willing to pay the officials were allowed to choose names for their natural beauty, such as Blumberg ("flower mountain") or Rosenthal ("rose valley"). Those who refused to pay off were purposely assigned contemptuous or silly names such as Ziegellaub ("back branch"), Bettelarm ("destitute"), Durst ("thirst"), Eselskopf ("ass's head"), Saumagen ("hog's paunch"), and even plain Stinker.

In Bohemia, Jews were restricted by law to Hebrew names, which accounts for the prevalence of Levy ("priestly tribe"), Cohen ("priest"), Isaacs ("he who laughs"), Rubin ("behold a son"), and Abrams ("high father").

Other distinctive Jewish names are occupational, although they are few because Jews were limited by most European countries to a few professions. Some examples are Perlman ("dealer of pearls"), Dayan ("rabbinic judge"), Chalfen ("money changer"), and Lehrer ("teacher").

Place names were also favored, such as Rothschild ("at the sign of the red shield"), Moscovitz ("son of Moscow"), Dávila ("one from the Spanish city of Avila"), and Sacks ("one from Saxony").

Russian

When researching a family tree that includes Russian ancestors, one should be aware of the masculine and feminine endings of the second name. Each child receives three names at birth: first name, followed by a second derived from the father's name (for example, the son of Ivan would be Ivanovich, the daughter, Ivanovna), and the surname. After the revolution of 1917, many former peasants changed their last names, since they were often offensive or derisive names given their grandfathers as serfs. Many a Durakov ("fool") changed his name to

Umnov ("wise"). At the same time, religious names were changed to ones more appropriate for Communist revolutionaries. After the fall of the Soviets and the resurgence in religious interests, these naming practices may have reverted.

As in other countries, many Russian families have surnames derived from places where the ancestors were born: Minsky ("from Minsk"), Tchaikovsky ("from Czajkowo"), Umansky ("from Uman").

Scottish

During the late Middle Ages in Scotland, because of infant mortality, it was not uncommon to give two or even three brothers the same first name. It's possible to trace a family line back to a James Campbell and then find there were three in the family. One might also find that the Campbells were really MacDonalds or Frasers, for it was a common practice back then to change surnames with every change of residence in order to "please the laird." Finally, until the last century many good Scottish wives did not take their husbands' surnames on marriage but retained their own—a remnant of an even older custom according to which men took their wives' surnames after marriage.

Spanish (Including Mexico, Latin America, the Caribbean, and the Philippines)

Legend says that family names in Spain actually began as cries of Christian families to one another, warning of approaching Moors. If this is so, the cries have long since disappeared into the common patronymic so popular in Spanish-speaking countries, such as Rodríguez, Fernández, González, Martínez, Pérez, López. The unusual Spanish system calls for the giving of two surnames, the first from the father's family, the second from the mother's, sometimes (but not always) connected with a y, meaning "and." For example, a former president of Mexico was named Adolfo Ruiz Cortines—Ruiz from his father and Cortines from his mother. A woman named Maria Teresa de la Fuente y Fernández inherited de la Fuente from her father and Fernández from her mother.

Other common Spanish surnames are place names such as Acota ("long coast"), Alvara ("from Alvado"), Aguilar ("from Aguilas"), Cardoza ("from Cardoso"), Contreras ("from Cuevas Contrerias"), Cortez ("cour" or "town"), Espinosa ("thorny thicket"), Estrada ("paved road"), Vargas ("steep hill"), and Silva ("thicket of briars").

Other Nationalities

Norwegians quite often have farm names. Family farms have been important enough to carry names since A.D. 1100, so tradition is very old. Some examples are Eggerud ("ridge farm"), Bjornstad ("Bjorn's farm"), and Askeland (ash tree farm").

Swedish surnames are of recent origin and are usually patronymic. Because of the confusion when everyone in a country is named "son," for the last century the Swedish government has encouraged Swedes to manufacture new family names. The *Släktnamns-kommitté*, or national Family Name Committee, has approved 56,000 new names, usually combining two nature words, such as Bergstrom ("mountain, stream"), Blomberg ("flower, mountain"), Holmgren ("river island, branch"), Strandberg ("shore, mountain"), and Skoglund ("forest, grove").

The most popular Greek surname is Pappas, which indicates descent from a priest. (The Greek Orthodox Church allows its priests to marry.) Other Greek names are descriptive, such as Makris ("long") and Mavros ("dark skinned"). Patronymics such as Demetriou ("son of Demetrius") and place names such as Vlahos ("from Wallachia") are also common.

The patronymic predominates for Arab names, such as Ahmed ibn Hassan which is "Ahmed son of Hassan." There is no such name as

Abdul; it is a Western contraction of Abd al, meaning "slave of Allah"—for example, Abd al-Nasir ("slave of Allah of Nasir"), whom the West knew as Nasser. Many Arabs, especially in small villages, do not have surnames at all but carry nicknames (often unflattering) which do not stick from generation to generation.

In Indonesia, there is the curious custom of having only a surname, no first name at all—for example, ex-President Sukarno. Since in a country undergoing modernization—which implies keeping records—this creates confusion in families with more than one child, the custom is already giving way to the use of two names.

In modern India (as in Russia during its industrializing era), many lower-caste people are choosing such names as Vikas ("development"), Yojana ("plain"), and Pragati ("progress").

How Your Family Name Varies

It would make family tree tracing a lot easier if our last names were distinctive, and spelled the same way our ancestors spelled them hundreds of years ago, but that probably isn't so.

In England, for instance, most records were kept by churchmen—and they were sometimes kept in Latin, sometimes in Norman French, and finally, toward the end of the Middle Ages, in English. The result was a wide variation in spellings of family names, sometimes even on the same piece of paper. In one 1623 document described by English genealogist L. G. Pine, the name Pierce was spelled Peirs, Pearce, and PeerS—all on the same page.

Of course, it wasn't always officialdom that mutilated your ancestors' names. Sometimes your forebears did it to themselves. A famous Kentucky pioneer of the late 1700s, for instance, sometimes signed his name Bone or Boon as well as Daniel Boone. The famous maker of Levi's jeans often spelled his name Levy.

And for some of us, our most recent family baptism may have been at the hands of United States immigration officials who couldn't understand our foreign names and so changed the spelling completely or gave up and changed the name into the nearest English sound. Thus, some Polish forebears arrived at New York's Ellis Island—the processing center for millions of immigrants—bearing the name Wallachinsky, and left it with the name Wallace. Among them was the father of novelist Irving Wallace. The father of Senator Edmund Muskie was originally Marciszewski, and my own husband's ancestors became Westins because a clerk didn't want to bother with Westinetsky.

Because of this lack of standardization, there are now thirteen versions of Smith, thirty-one different Snyder spellings, thirty-seven ways to write Burke, and forty-six ways of spelling Baer. And there are 400 possible spellings of Shakespeare. Canooles, Knowles, and Knolles are all names on one family tree, which demonstrates that there have been changes both in spelling and pronunciation over the centuries.

Knowing different possible spellings of your name is important, because otherwise you could miss a significant branch of your family tree. The information will be helpful later when you begin your search through public records. The real challenge, of course, is figuring out what these different spellings are. Here are some tips:

1. Sit down and list every possible spelling you can think of. (My own list includes Eddy, Eddie, Ede, Eddye, Edde, Edy, Eddi, Edie, Edye.)

2. Say your name out loud, and see if this brings to mind other possibilities.

3. List the way other people frequently mispronounce your name; you can be sure that somewhere on your family tree it is spelled that way.

4. Next try pronouncing your name several different ways—for example, "Ride" for Reid. Next change the soft consonants to

hard ones and vice versa. For instance, if your name is Keegan, pronounce it "Seegan" or "Keejan."

One woman whose maternal name was Crockett made a list of her ancestors as follows: Crocket, Crockette, Crokit, Crockitt, Cruckett, Crucket, Crukett, Cruket. She found most of these spellings before her search ended with an English gentleman born in 1271, Thomas de Cruket.

While at first it might seem that making a list of all the possible spelling variations would make your ancestor hunt more difficult rather than less so, actually it won't. After all, you will not be searching for a name alone but a name coupled with a birth date or a birthplace or both.

When you have listed the possible spellings for your family name, you may also want to check them in a surname encyclopedia to discover their origin and probable meaning. They will help convey the fascination and adventure that you will encounter as you search for your family's roots.

Now let's look at where your ancestors came from and how they got here. Doing so will determine in good part where and who *you* are.

CHAPTER 3

The American Family History: How Our Ancestors Got Here

Throughout history, in good times and bad, most of the world's population has stayed right where it was. Your forebears did not. Historian Arthur Schlesinger uses the phrase "the choosing people" to describe Americans, and except for those who were already here or who came as slaves, the expression is apt.

For 375 years people have chosen America—50-plus million of them. Although often compelled to do so by religious and political oppression and economic hard times, still they chose the difficult course of leaving their homes. As you retrace your immigrant ancestors and chart their progress from their homeland and through America, perhaps some of their brave spirit will be rekindled in you.

WHERE THEY CAME FROM

It is impossible to do justice to 50 million people, but let me briefly describe in the next few pages the major immigration tides, for some of your ancestors may very well have been part of those waves. The first immigrants—the ones who stepped off the *Mayflower* in 1620 and thereafter—were overwhelmingly English. Then in 1700 Germans and Scotch-Irish also began to emigrate. After the Revolutionary War, when the first census was taken in 1790, there were about 5 million people in the United States and, except for 750,000 black African slaves, most were descended from these three original groups. During the next fifty years, a million more immigrants arrived, again most of them from England and Germany. Although thousands more black Africans were brought in as slaves, they were not even considered immigrants. (Only 104,000 Africans—both black and white—have emigrated, in the choosing sense of the word, since 1820.)

In the middle of the nineteenth century, the tide of immigration became a virtual flood. Between 1841 and 1860 nearly 3.5 million people came from Ireland and Germany. Another million came from England, Scandinavia, France, and Switzerland. And, beginning in 1850, thousands of Chinese began arriving in California, and later Japanese also. From 1880 until World War I, the growth of American industry attracted more than 15 million southern and eastern Europeans—Italians, Russians, Poles, and Hungarians.

Most European immigrants, no matter what their country of origin, left from one of two German ports, Bremen or Hamburg. And while waiting to board ship they usually stayed in inns especially designed to house them and their families. If they wandered around the evil port cities, they would most likely be bilked of whatever money they had—which is one reason why the average immigrant arrived in America with less than twenty dollars. Because steamship companies had to bring rejected immigrants back to Europe at company expense, everyone had to undergo a medical inspection. This was not always thorough. One of my husband's aunts, a twelve-year-old girl, was forced to return from Ellis Island to Hamburg with her younger brother and remain with him until his eye infection healed, returning the following year. I've often wondered at the courage of this young girl all alone in a strange country with a sick child.

The ocean voyage for most immigrants, of course, was not quite up to the glowing advertisements. Your ancestor was probably assigned a six-by-six-foot cabin with triple-decker bunks and five other passengers who were sick all the way. Sometimes mothers were too ill even to care for their children.

Immigrants who made the Atlantic crossing after 1855 were processed through Castle Garden, a converted amusement park on the tip of Manhattan. This was replaced in 1892 by Ellis Island, which remains forever associated with boatloads of immigrants sailing in past the Statue of Liberty and yearning to breathe free. Originally, Asian immigrants were processed at the Pacific Mail Steamship Company warehouse in San Francisco, but after 1910 they were quarantined on Angel Island in San Francisco Bay—sometimes for weeks or months—because of official fear of cholera and other epidemic diseases. Since 1920, despite a quota system, Canada, England, Germany, Southeast Asia, and especially Mexico and the Caribbean have helped keep the immigrant tradition alive. From 1981 to 1990, an average of 733,800 people have emigrated to America each year.

That, in brief, is the story of how and when most of our immigrant ancestors came to be Americans. If you want to learn more about your own ancestors' journey, I've listed some books in the bibliography. You can also learn more by checking with ethnic organizations, which you can find in many chapters in this book or through a directory of organizations at your library. In the following pages, however, I've listed in alphabetical order how the immigration tides ran for the principal ethnic groups in this country.

Africans

In the beginning, American colonists who depended on cheap labor relied mainly on European indentured servants, people who sold their labor for seven years in return for passage to America. Soon, however, the needs of southern planters outstripped the supply of these so-called bond servants, and black slaves were imported to take their place. The increase in the slave trade was so great, in fact, that by 1776 20 *percent* of the colonial population had African ancestors. Twenty-five percent of the blacks captured in Africa and sold to slavers came from Angola, another 25 percent from Biafra, and the rest from the Gold Coast, Senegambia, Sierra Leone, and other parts of West Africa.

An African's trip to America, described in Alex Haley's *Roots*, was almost unimaginable. Shackled hand and foot to a plank, with only eighteen inches of head room, he or she was forced to lie in body wastes for days, even weeks. If one could free himself, he often committed suicide. Many times half of those taken aboard did not survive the trip.

When the Civil War brought an end to the slave trade, there were approximately 4.5 million persons of African descent in America, 90 percent of them living in the South.

Canadians

Like the United States, Canada has been a mecca for European immigration and, in turn, has contributed an enormous number of emigrants across the border to the United States.

Among the first were the Acadians, 8,000 French Catholics who had settled in Nova Scotia and who were ordered out of the country by the British in 1755. They settled in Louisiana, where many of their descendants call themselves "cajuns."

Since 1862, 4 million other Canadians have emigrated to the United States, many of whom were Scottish Highlanders who went to Ontario Province in droves before 1850 and later crossed over into the United States.

By 1890, large numbers of French Canadians had moved into New England to work in the textile mills, and until the 1930s they proved to be one of the least assimilable groups of immigrants, fiercely maintaining their own French-speaking schools and churches, much like their counterparts in eastern Canada today.

Chinese

The Chinese began arriving on the West Coast during the 1850s and at first worked at resifting the dirt at worked-over gold-mining camps.

Later many moved on to jobs building the Central Pacific Railroad, helping to hack through mountains by hand. They were such valued and inexpensive workers (their wages were often two cents a day) that agents were sent to Canton to recruit thousands more to come work in the Golden Mountain.

After the railroads were built in the 1870s, trade unions and other labor groups protested the importation of such cheap labor. The result was the Chinese Exclusion Act of 1882, which stopped large-scale immigration, although thousands of Chinese able to pay their passage to Hawaii or California continued to come.

English

Most Americans—82 percent, in fact—can trace at least one genealogical line to English ancestors. The first of five million English immigrants to America arrived in Jamestown in 1607, adventurers and artisans sent by the London Company for the purpose of colonizing. They managed to gain a foothold on the swampy, fever-infested Virginia coast. Surviving starvation, disease, Indian troubles, and personal squabbles, they unknowingly set the stage for future disaster by buying the first black slaves, twenty persons from a Dutch trader in 1619.

In 1620 an even more famous band—the Pilgrims, who were separatists from the Church of England—landed to the north at Plymouth Rock. Barely half the company of 100 survived the rigorous first winter, but during the next thirty years about 20,000 English immigrants arrived at the Massachusetts Bay Colony, which gradually overflowed into what was to become Rhode Island, New Hampshire, and Connecticut.

If your forebears came from England in those early days as some of mine did, they underwent a terrible journey. The horribly overcrowded ships took six to twelve weeks to make the trip and often ran out of food, even though passengers were promised by the investors who financed such expeditions, "salt beefe, Porke, Salt Fish, Butter, Cheese, Pease Pottage, Water-grewell, and such kinds of victuals, with good Biskets and six-shilling Beere." One early immigrant ship lost

108 of its 156 passengers to starvation. These voyages were, despite their discomfort and possible death, very expensive. The average Puritan family of eight with a ton of freight spent thirty pounds on the trip (over a thousand dollars in our money today).

One group of English immigrants came involuntarily—in chains. From 1717 to 1775, 50,000 English convicts quite naturally chose deportation to the colonies for seven years rather than to hang. But one should not think too harshly of these convict ancestors, for in those days the penalties for crimes were unduly stiff—indeed, 150 crimes were capital offenses, including stealing a sheep, cutting down trees in avenues, sending threatening letters, or merely not answering one's "betters." The convicts were not unwelcome in America. Southern planters were eager to pay ten pounds to acquire their services, and many eventually achieved positions of responsibility. George Washington, for instance, was taught by a convict servant his father bought for a schoolmaster. For many, what was intended as punishment turned out to be their good fortune, and they became landowners. Some transported felons even became rich.

Another group of English people who arrived in this country before the Revolutionary War were indentured bond servants. Many respectable but destitute people actually sold themselves into temporary slavery to reach this country. In fact, half of all the English who emigrated came under a labor contract called an "indenture." This was an agreement, in exchange for passage to America, to work as a servant for a number of years (usually four, but in the case of children the term ran until they were twenty-one years old). Upon arrival in America, they were auctioned off by the ship's captain to the highest bidder.

Many captains engaging in this trade made enormous profits, so there were bound to be abuses. Starving families often sold one or two of their young children for a few coins. If a ship heading for the Colonies did not have its full complement of indentured men and women, a press gang would go out and shanghai the rest.

But the traffic was not entirely one way. In the 1780s one group of English emigrated from the newly created United States. Americans loyal to the English king fled in numbers estimated to be as high as

100,000. Since families were split, with son against father and brother against brother, many descendants of Loyalists, as they were called, still live in America. If it is possible that your ancestors were Loyalists, look for them in the records of England, Canada, and Nova Scotia (see chapter 9).

French

There have been French immigrants in America since the 1600s. They were planters in the South, fur traders in the Mississippi Valley, and merchants in Louisiana.

About 15,000 Huguenots—Protestants driven out of Catholic France in the 1700s—settled around Charleston, South Carolina. A few others went to New York and Rhode Island.

In the century between 1820 and 1920, about 1 million French-speaking immigrants came from France, Belgium, and Switzerland.

Germans

Before the Revolutionary War more than 200,000 Germans had congregated in New York and the Pennsylvania back country, where they became known as "Pennsylvania Dutch." Many of them emigrated from the German Rhineland, called the Palatinate, in order to practice a number of dissenting religions, including my Koon ancestors who were Anabaptists. Others were called Mennonites, Dunkards, Moravians, Schwenkfelders, or sometimes were all lumped together under the common title of the "Plain People." Later, Lutheran Germans came. Although they were industrious and sober settlers and usually welcomed, Thomas Jefferson, for one, was afraid of the influx of Germans and warned against foreigners deluded by "maxims of absolute monarchies." He needn't have worried about any such democratic backwardness. During the Revolutionary War, the Germans already in America so successfully propagandized the 30,000 Hessian mercenaries hired by the British that nearly half of them deserted and settled in New England and Pennsylvania.

After 1848—a time of destructive revolution, bad crops, and avaricious landlords in the German states—a new wave of 1.5 million German immigrants arrived to help develop the Middle West. They settled in Ohio, Wisconsin, Indiana, Michigan, and Iowa, traveling even as far as Texas, where one of their number is said to have originated a very un-German dish we know as chili con carne.

Middle Europeans—Including Czechs, Slovaks, Slovenes, Croats, Serbs

From 1880 to 1920, almost four million immigrants arrived from the old Austro-Hungarian empire. There were not many Austrians. Instead there was a mix of ethnically distinctive groups such as Hungarians, Czechs, Slovaks, Slovenes, Croats, and Serbs. In this country they became collectively known as Slavs.

Few of these southern and eastern Europeans were drawn to the land (most of the good homesteading land was gone by then anyway) but preferred the gregarious social life of their own urban ethnic neighborhoods.

Concentrating in Pennsylvania, and in the cities of Chicago, Akron, Toledo, Milwaukee, and Detroit, Slavic laborers provided much of the muscle needed for America's growing iron, steel, and coal industries.

Irish

St. Patrick's Day was celebrated with a grand feast by Boston Irish as early as 1737, but if you have Irish ancestry, the chances are they were immigrants after 1845. In that year a terrible potato blight in Ireland caused that food staple to rot in the ground, and thousands chose America over starvation. Many of those who left were so weak they did not survive the trip; in 1847 alone, 15,000 Irish died aboard ship. Nevertheless, over two million Irish, mostly Catholics from central and southern Ireland, came in thirty years. In all, nearly 4.4 million Irish have come (and are still coming) to this country as immigrants.

They clustered together in eastern cities and along the industrially developing shores of the Great Lakes. Although most had been farmers at one time, because the land had betrayed them they turned their backs on it, preferring to trust their stomachs to wages instead of crops. Many took tough construction jobs for thirty cents a day, and few early canals or railroads were built without their labor.

Italians

More than 5.3 million Italians have come to America since the first recorded one, Nicholas Biferi, arrived in Georgia in 1774 and billed himself as the "Musician of Naples."

Many of those who came in the late nineteenth century headed for California, where they worked in agriculture and developed the wine industry. Most came from northern Italy, but after 1900 it was the Italians from Mezzogiorno (the southern half of the peninsula and Sicily), fleeing poverty, overpopulation, and economic oppression. These former *contadini* (rural laborers) shunned the agricultural life, settling in cities north of the Ohio and east of the Mississippi.

Everywhere they replaced earlier immigrants (the Irish, in particular) in low-paying, pick-and-shovel jobs, building subways and railroads, and working in textile mills and the needle trades. Some became small merchants or opened restaurants. At one time in many eastern cities, barbering was virtually an Italian monopoly.

About 40 percent of Italian male immigrants eventually returned to Italy to see their families, to obtain brides, or to live out their lives on the luxuries made possible by American wages. The majority re-emigrated, but the back-and-forth travel continued until World War I.

Japanese

Until 1890, the emperor of Japan refused to allow emigration, and those who did emigrate to America were not allowed to return to their homeland. After the edict was rescinded, over 100,000 Japanese quickly boarded ships to escape poverty, ruling-class oppression, and military conscription. Most settled in Hawaii and on the West Coast and became small farmers, cannery workers, and the like. Altogether 400,000 Japanese immigrants have come to the United States since 1861.

Jewish

Between 1880 and World War I, 2 million Jews emigrated to America, one-fourth of the world's then Jewish population. They settled in ethnic neighborhoods in large cities—1.4 million in New York City alone, with additional large enclaves in San Francisco and Los Angeles.

Most of the immigrants were *Ashkenazim*, a Hebrew word meaning "German" but used to describe eastern European Jews as well. For the most part they were escapees from savage pogroms, forced conversion, army conscription, and laws denying them a livelihood.

They were not the first Jews to come to America fleeing persecution. In 1654, twenty-three Jewish *Sephardim* (Spanish or Portuguese in origin), escaping the Inquisition, landed in what was then New Amsterdam. Four years later, a small group arrived at Newport, Rhode Island. By the time of the Revolutionary War there were 300 Jews in New York, with smaller groups in Philadelphia and Charleston, South Carolina. Later, between 1820 and 1870, 400,000 German Jews became established along the Eastern Seaboard.

Today 6 million of the world's Jews are Americans.

Polish

The total number of Polish immigrants is buried in the statistics for Russia and Austria-Hungary, both of which dominated Poland at different times, but more than two million Poles flocked into America's expanding industrial cities after 1880.

The largest Polish communities grew up near the stockyards of Chicago, the steel mills of Pittsburgh, the auto plants of Detroit, and the metal industries of Buffalo. Many Poles also vied with incoming Italians, Irish, and French Canadians for jobs in the textile mills of New England.

Russians

The bulk of Russian immigrants were Jews from western Russia, but more than 1.2 million others were Russians, Lithuanians, and Ukrainians.

The largest immigration came between 1880 and 1920, much of it the result of an economic depression brought on by the disastrous Russo-Japanese war, forced military service, and the political unrest that resulted in the revolution of 1917.

Since the fall of Communism, Russian immigration has resumed, and several American cities—New York, Los Angeles, and Sacramento—have growing enclaves of new Russian immigrants.

Scandinavians

The Scandinavians—Norwegians, Swedes, Finns, and Danes—who came after 1840 went west and north to Minnesota, Wisconsin, and the Dakota territory, where the country more nearly replicated the climate of their homeland. Their glowing letters home emptied whole Scandinavian villages. "Anyone who wants to make good here has to work," one Swede wrote, "but here everything is better rewarded." Norwegian immigration was stirred by public readings in Norway of a book entitled *True Account of America for the Information and Help of the Peasant and Commoner.*

Immigrants were lured not only by a compatible climate but also by the promise of free land, the result of the 1862 Homestead Law, which promised every adult immigrant 160 acres of land if he lived on it and farmed any portion of it for five years. In all, 2.5 million Scandinavian immigrants helped fill up the Midwest, and they prospered perhaps more than any other ethnic group.

Scotch-Irish

Millions of Americans are descended from the 250,000 Scotch-Irish immigrants who came to America between 1717 and 1775. These people were actually transplanted lowland Scots who, in one of many English schemes to subdue the Irish, had been urged to emigrate to Ulster in Northern Ireland a century earlier by James I. It was thought that hard-nosed Presbyterian Scotsmen could better control the Irish than England's standing army, but by 1717 the Scotch-Irish were in trouble themselves. A depression in the flax industry, higher rents, severe frosts, a sheep disease, and a smallpox epidemic scourged Ulster.

They emigrated in waves to the Shenandoah Valley of Virginia, the Piedmont country of North Carolina, to New Jersey, Delaware, Maryland, New Hampshire, Maine, and Pennsylvania. By the time the Declaration of Independence was written, one out of every ten Americans was Scotch-Irish.

They brought an ethnic personality well fitted to westward-moving pioneers: they were religious, stubborn, and moral. After discovering that the prime land along the Eastern Seaboard had been taken by earlier arrivals, they quickly fanned out toward the Appalachians. Their sons and daughters were in the forefront of the western migrations in each succeeding generation.

Spanish Speaking

The Spanish and Mexicans had done some colonizing of southern Texas and New Mexico as early as the seventeenth century, and in the next century moved into California. But the biggest influx of Spanish-speaking people has been since 1920 with the arrival of roughly three million immigrants from Mexico, more than two million from the West Indies and Central and South America, almost a million from Cuba, and 250,000 from the Philippines.

More than 4.9 million Spanish-speaking Americans have been recent immigrants (540,000 in 1996 alone), and this figure excludes large numbers of Puerto Ricans—a group not counted as immigrants because they are American citizens. Adding these groups together, the total of Spanish-speaking mainland Americans probably is nearer seven million, the largest ethnic group in the country.

Other Immigrants

America, called "half brother to the world," has been more receptive to immigration than any other country. Almost every nation is represented in our ethnic makeup: Portugal has sent 850,000 immigrants, Greece 500,000, the Netherlands 350,000, Switzerland 350,000, Spain 250,000. From Turkey have come 380,000 people, primarily Armenians, Syrians, and Lebanese. From Australia have come 100,000, descendants of immigrants themselves. Finally, from Vietnam have come almost 200,000, most of them arriving since 1975.

If I have not mentioned your ancestral group—or even if I have— you will find a decade-by-decade description of the flow of your people to this country in a wonderful table in the 1995 *Annual Report*, published by the Immigration and Naturalization Service of the U.S. Department of Justice. Every library has it.

THE INNER MIGRATIONS: THE COMING OF ROADS

A great many, perhaps most, Americans no longer live near where their ancestors settled when they arrived in this country. If your forebears came after 1869, they may well have traveled by train from their arrival point, since by then the nation's rail system had developed. Or if they arrived more recently, of course, they may have migrated across the country by car or airplane. But in the early days of America, the inner migrations followed the coming of the roads.

"Westering," the lure of the western unsettled lands, took hold of early immigrants almost as soon as they arrived. They began by pushing out from Massachusetts to Connecticut. Axmen widened Indian trails to accommodate horses, then made them wider still for wagons loaded with household goods. Within fifty years after the *Mayflower* arrived, the King's Highway (later the Boston Post Road) carried mail—and migrants—from Boston to New York.

A stagecoach ride down the King's Highway was a rough experience. "You are fully exposed to inclement weather," one migrant wrote, "and soaked as if you were out of doors. You are crushed, shaken, thrown about, bumped . . . Every mile there is a new accident and you must get out into the mud while the damage is repaired. It is not unusual to see coaches shattered, the passengers crippled, and the horses downed."

After 1685, the King's Highway was extended from New York to Philadelphia, then on south to Norfolk, Virginia, and finally all the way to Charleston, South Carolina. And after 1744, another highway, the Great Road, funneled Scotch-Irish and German migrants from Philadelphia west and then southwest along the eastern edge of the Appalachians. Eventually the Great Road linked up with Daniel Boone's Wilderness Road, which passed through the Cumberland Gap and on to Louisville, Kentucky. By 1780, 12,000 settlers had crossed into Kentucky; by 1783, 22,000.

The Pittsburgh Pike, another early road in the original Thirteen Colonies, wound through the Pennsylvania forests from Harrisburg, taking migrating English, Scotch-Irish, and German settlers to the Ohio River, which by the early 1800s had become the quickest way to get to the newly opened western territories. A flatboat ride down the Ohio from Pittsburgh to Louisville, past sandbars, rocks, river pirates, and inhospitable Indians cost forty dollars, and migrants had to share accommodations with pigs and livestock. Later the Ohio became the tributary feeding boats into the Mississippi, the major river road to the South and to Texas.

Early roads began as blazed trails and became wagon tracks, but the federal government began to get into the road-building business in the 1800s with the National Road, a vast project that extended from Cumberland, Maryland, to the Indiana territory, which was built principally for military reasons because of American concern about the French presence in Louisiana. Once again, this extended the westward migration. A traveler on the National Road in 1817 wrote, "Old America seems to be breaking up and moving westward. We are seldom out of sight of family groups before and behind us."

To the south, the government built the Federal Road, which wound from Athens, Georgia, to just north of Mobile, Alabama. This became the jumping-off point for emigrants to New Orleans or Nashville. Far to the north, in upper New York State, the Erie Canal was opened in 1825 and was a big factor in the early settlement of the Northwest Territory. The canal was safer, cheaper, and shorter than the roads and rivers, and was a favorite mode of migration until the development of railroads.

One group of inner migrants, the American Indians, had little choice. By 1830 Congress had passed the Indian Removal Act, enabling the government to transfer the remaining eastern Indians west of the Mississippi River. In one of these removals, the trek of the Cherokees to Oklahoma, many died of hardship and disease on their trail of tears.

By 1850, the population of Ohio, Indiana, Illinois, and Michigan alone was 6,100,000, and the days of the canals and the old roads were over. Railroads were carrying migrants (in specially marked "immigrant cars") to where the "new West" began at the Mississippi River. With immigrants crowding eastern cities and farms, the West offered "elbow room" for which every pioneer yearned.

The first wagon train for Oregon started west in 1842; the first for California, in 1844. Riding in a covered wagon meant a bone-rattling trip, jammed into a ten-by-four-foot space with all the utensils, belongings, and other family members, across a 2,000-mile stretch of plains, alkali flats, rivers, deserts, and mountains. Most of the trains were made up in Independence, Missouri, headed along the south side of the Platte River to western Wyoming, then turned northwest on the Oregon Trail or went southwest through the High Sierras to the gold rush in California. The Santa Fe Trail took migrants south to New Mexico and then over the Old Spanish Trail through the desert to California.

Although we tend to think of the wagon train (and steamboat and railroad train) as the principal way our ancestors traveled West, many of them, believe it or not, actually walked—"shanks mare," it was called. If a migrant was a little better off than average, he could afford a horse to carry his wife and a handcart in which to push or pull some family belongings.

A lot of inner migrants never made it. There was no protection against sickness, and many of us have ancestors or their relatives who perished from cholera, childbed fever, or weariness. They left their names on markers such as this alongside the trail:

Jno. Hoover, died, June 1849
Aged 12 yrs. Rest in peace,
sweet boy, for thy travels are over.

By 1870, rails were carrying migrants west, and by 1890, the last wild frontier was conquered. Yet still the inner migrations continued—and are continuing—as wars, depressions, hard times, personal misfortunes, and also simply the promise of something better, have impelled people to pull loose from their roots and resettle elsewhere.

If some of your ancestors were in this centuries-long migration, and chances are they were, begin in the next chapter to search back along the trail they left to find your roots.

First Step Backward:
How to Take a Family History
and Gather Available Records

Now that you have some background—a sense of how names vary and perhaps some understanding of the immigration and migration patterns that might have affected your forebears, let us get down to the main task of actually finding your roots. While very few people can trace *every* branch on their family tree, there is hardly any family historian who cannot use the techniques I'm about to describe to trace his or her lineage to an early ancestor in *some* line of their family.

In this chapter, I'm going to show you how to start by interviewing your living older relatives in order to gather a recent history of the family. This might well be a kind of oral history—that is, spoken memories (which you will probably want to tape-record to transfer to your family history book later). Although oral history is a tradition older than writing, it has only recently become widely popular among students and scholars. For instance, the oral-history interviews of southern Appalachian mountaineers by high-school students resulted in the best-selling *Foxfire* books. Many colleges in the country are rapidly building oral-history libraries, recording the recollections of older local people. You can do the same with your own family. Or if you can't do it in person, you can probably get a family history by interviewing by mail or telephone.

Before we get to this, however, let me describe the equipment you need and the procedures to follow.

SETTING UP YOUR FAMILY HISTORY PROGRAM

Unlike photography, golf, and almost every other leisure-time pursuit, ancestor hunting requires very little equipment other than paper and pencil (or pen) to make a start. Here's what you need:

Two Loose-leaf Binders. Old ones recycled from school days are fine. One is for your notes and unfinished research. One is for your permanent Family History Book.

Pedigree Charts. See the examples in Figures 1 and 2. The Family History Book is really the culmination of your search. In it, in alphabetical order by surname, should go everything you acquire during your ancestor hunt—photographs, maps, letters, clippings, vital statistics, deeds, wills, and so on, including the Pedigree Charts and Family Group Sheets, described below.

You should give some thought to the paper you use inside. Ordinary bond paper will turn yellow and brittle in forty years or less even with maximum protection—which means storage in a cool, dark, temperature and moisture–consistent place. Both words and pictures should be recorded on acid-free permanent paper. Fifty percent cotton content or rag bond, Permalife document bond, or ledger-mounting stock will last 500 years or more. All city, county, and national records are recorded on permanent paper stock. So why not spend a few cents more at a stationery store and make your Family History Book also a lasting record? You can draw a copy similar to the one shown here onto 8½-by-11-inch white bond paper, and photocopy, say, twenty-five copies for starters. Or you can order a supply printed on special durable or acid-free paper from the nearest genealogy club, genealogy services store or library you'll find listed in Appendices in the back of this book.

I found the word *pedigree* awfully stuffy at first, since it reminded me of poodles and racehorses, but that's the term genealogists use. It doesn't mean these charts are only for people whose blood runs bluer than that of the French kings. They are for everybody.

Family Group Sheets. See the example in Figure 3. Like the Pedigree Chart, you can draw a copy similar to the one in this book and duplicate it, or you can order some sheets at the same time you order Pedigree Charts. If you use a computer, you can make both using your spreadsheet software.

Both the Pedigree Charts and the Family Group Sheets are your personal road maps to your family history, worksheets to show you how much information you have on your ancestors and how much more there is to discover. The reason for having both in standardized form is so that later you can exchange them with other members of your expanded family—and they'll be able to understand what you've done.

Family History Questionnaires. See the example in Figure 4. You'll need this when you go out to start gathering oral history from relatives, so that you won't forget the important questions to ask.

Tape Recorder and Cassettes. These are not mandatory, but they are helpful when you're talking with relatives—especially if you tend to be a slow note taker or become so fascinated you forget to take notes, as I do. More on this later.

How to Fill Out the Pedigree Charts

Pedigree Charts are really quite simple to fill out. Most family historians follow a few standard rules, which make charts consistent and thus easy to read and understand no matter who makes them. Starting off with a consistent form will save a lot of recopying later. Here's how you do it:

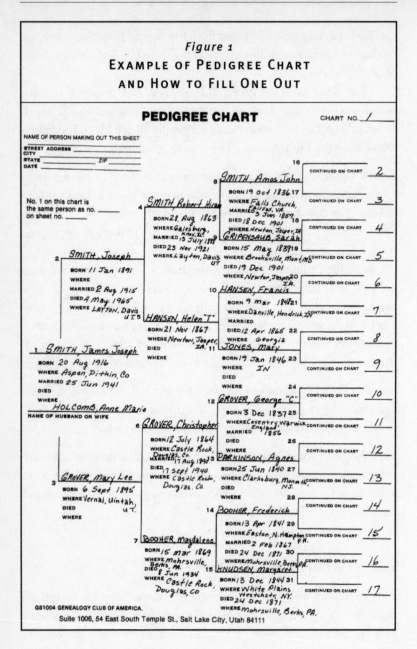

Figure 1
EXAMPLE OF PEDIGREE CHART
AND HOW TO FILL ONE OUT

PEDIGREE CHART

CHART NO. _1_

NAME OF PERSON MAKING OUT THIS SHEET

STREET ADDRESS _____
CITY _____
STATE _____ ZIP _____
DATE _____

No. 1 on this chart is
the same person as no. _____
on sheet no. _____

16
8 SMITH, Amos John   CONTINUED ON CHART _2_
  BORN 19 Oct 1836 17
  WHERE Falls Church,   CONTINUED ON CHART _3_
  MARRIED Tiffin, VA.
          3 Jun 1857
  DIED 18 Dec 1901   18   CONTINUED ON CHART _4_
  WHERE Newton, Jasper, IA
9 GRIPENSAUB, Sarah
  BORN 15 May 1839 19   CONTINUED ON CHART _5_
  WHERE Brooksville, Mont MO
  DIED 19 Dec 1901
  WHERE Newton, Jasper 20
                    IA.   CONTINUED ON CHART _6_
10 HANSEN, Francis
  BORN 9 Mar 1841 21   CONTINUED ON CHART _7_
  WHERE Danville, Hendrick IN
  MARRIED
  DIED 12 Apr 1865 22   CONTINUED ON CHART _8_
  WHERE Georgia
11 JONES, Mary
  BORN 19 Jan 1846 23   CONTINUED ON CHART _9_
  WHERE IN
  DIED
  WHERE
24   CONTINUED ON CHART _10_
12 GROVER, George "C"
  BORN 3 Dec 1837 25   CONTINUED ON CHART _11_
  WHERE Coventry, Warwick
        England
  MARRIED 1856
  DIED 26   CONTINUED ON CHART _12_
  WHERE
13 PARKINSON, Agnes
  BORN 25 Jun 1840 27   CONTINUED ON CHART _13_
  WHERE Clarksburg, Monm H
        N.J.
  DIED
  WHERE 28   CONTINUED ON CHART _14_
14 BOOHER, Frederick
  BORN 13 Apr 1841 29   CONTINUED ON CHART _15_
  WHERE Easton, N. Hampton
                     P.A.
  MARRIED 2 Feb 1867
  DIED 24 Dec 1871 30   CONTINUED ON CHART _16_
  WHERE Mohrsville, Berks PA.
15 KNUDSEN, Margaret
  BORN 13 Dec 1844 31   CONTINUED ON CHART _17_
  WHERE White Plains
        Westchstr, NY.
  DIED 24 Dec 1871
  WHERE Mohrsville, Berks, PA.

4 SMITH, Robert Hiram
  BORN 21 Aug 1863
  WHERE Galesburg,
        Knox, IL
  MARRIED 13 July 1888
  DIED 23 Nov 1921
  WHERE Layton, Davis
        UT

2 SMITH, Joseph
  BORN 11 Jan 1891
  WHERE
  MARRIED 2 Aug 1915
  DIED 4 May 1965
  WHERE LAYTON, Davis
        UT 5 HANSEN, Helen "T"
  BORN 21 Nov 1867
  WHERE Newton, Jasper
        IA.

1 SMITH, James Joseph
  BORN 20 Aug 1916
  WHERE Aspen, Pitkin, Co
  MARRIED 25 Jun 1941
  DIED
  WHERE HOLCOMB, Anne Marie
NAME OF HUSBAND OR WIFE

6 GROVER, Christopher
  BORN 12 July 1864
  WHERE Castle Rock,
        Douglas, Co.
  MARRIED 17 Aug 1893
  DIED 7 Sept 1940
  WHERE Castle Rock,
        Douglas, Co.

3 GROVER, Mary Lee
  BORN 6 Sept 1895
  WHERE Vernal, Uintah,
        UT.
  DIED
  WHERE

7 BOOHER, Magdalene
  BORN 15 Mar 1869
  WHERE Mohrsville,
        Berks, PA.
  DIED 8 Jun 1934
  WHERE Castle Rock,
        Douglas, Co

GS1004 GENEALOGY CLUB OF AMERICA.
Suite 1006, 54 East South Temple St., Salt Lake City, Utah 84111

44

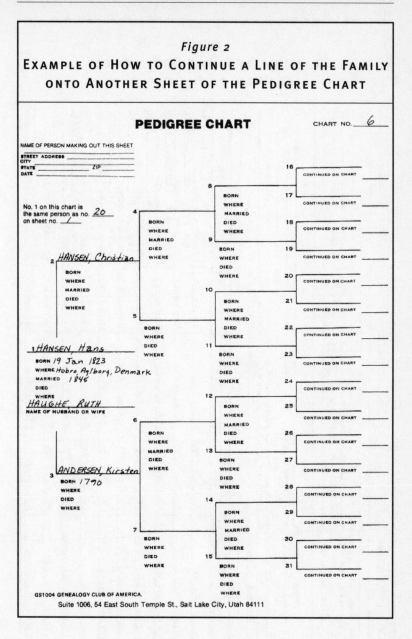

Figure 2

EXAMPLE OF HOW TO CONTINUE A LINE OF THE FAMILY ONTO ANOTHER SHEET OF THE PEDIGREE CHART

PEDIGREE CHART   CHART NO. _6_

NAME OF PERSON MAKING OUT THIS SHEET

STREET ADDRESS
CITY
STATE   ZIP
DATE

No. 1 on this chart is
the same person as no. _20_
on sheet no. _1_

2 _HANSEN, Christian_
BORN
WHERE
MARRIED
DIED
WHERE

1 _HANSEN, Hans_
BORN _19 Jan 1823_
WHERE _Hobro, Aglborg, Denmark_
MARRIED _1848_
DIED
WHERE
HAUGHE, RUTH
NAME OF HUSBAND OR WIFE

3 _ANDERSEN, Kirsten_
BORN _1790_
DIED
WHERE

4
BORN
WHERE
MARRIED
DIED
WHERE

5
BORN
WHERE
DIED
WHERE

6
BORN
WHERE
MARRIED
DIED
WHERE

7
BORN
WHERE
DIED
WHERE

8
BORN
WHERE
MARRIED
DIED
WHERE

9
BORN
WHERE
DIED
WHERE

10
BORN
WHERE
MARRIED
DIED
WHERE

11
BORN
WHERE
DIED
WHERE

12
BORN
WHERE
MARRIED
DIED
WHERE

13
BORN
WHERE
DIED
WHERE

14
BORN
WHERE
MARRIED
DIED
WHERE

15
BORN
WHERE
DIED
WHERE

16   CONTINUED ON CHART

17   CONTINUED ON CHART

18   CONTINUED ON CHART

19   CONTINUED ON CHART

20   CONTINUED ON CHART

21   CONTINUED ON CHART

22   CONTINUED ON CHART

23   CONTINUED ON CHART

24   CONTINUED ON CHART

25   CONTINUED ON CHART

26   CONTINUED ON CHART

27   CONTINUED ON CHART

28   CONTINUED ON CHART

29   CONTINUED ON CHART

30   CONTINUED ON CHART

31   CONTINUED ON CHART

GS1004 GENEALOGY CLUB OF AMERICA.
Suite 1006, 54 East South Temple St., Salt Lake City, Utah 84111

45

Figure 3
EXAMPLE OF FAMILY GROUP SHEET
AND HOW TO FILL ONE OUT

HUSBAND BIGLER, Jacob
Born 1752-53 — Place Bucks Co. PA
Chr. — Place
Mar. 29 Mar 1779 — Place Clarksburg, Harrison, WV
Died Will proved Sep 1829 — Place Enterprise Cemetery Harrison Co WV
Bur. BIGLER, mark (Immigrant) — Place
HUSBAND'S FATHER
HUSBAND'S MOTHER Catherine
HUSBANDS OTHER WIVES

WIFE BOOHER, Hannah
Born 1760 — Place Philadelphia, PA
Chr. — Place
Died 17 July 1853 — Place Shinnston, Harrison, PA
Bur. — Place Saltwell, Righter Cemetery, Harrison, WV
WIFE'S FATHER BOOHER, Henry
WIFE'S MOTHER KOON, Catherine
WIFE'S OTHER HUSBANDS

SEX M/F	CHILDREN GIVEN NAMES	WHEN BORN	WHERE BORN TOWN	COUNTY	STATE OR COUNTRY	DATE OF FIRST MARRIAGE TO WHOM	WHEN DIED
F	BIGLER, Sarah	30 Jan 1780		Bucks	PA	26 Apr 1795 Righter John	7 July 1880
F	BIGLER, Hannah	30 Jan 1783	Shinnston	Harrison	WV	18 Apr 1799 McCauly James	23 Sept 1834
M	BIGLER, Mark	19 May 1785	Shinnston	Harrison	WV	7 Nov 1805 Ogden Susannah	23 Sept 1839
F	BIGLER, Ruth	28 Apr 1788	Shinnston	Harrison	WV	4 Sept 1806 Whiteman Able	1830
F	BIGLER, Nancy	29 Apr 1790	Shinnston	Harrison	WV	1 Sept 1808 Whiteman Henry	1842
M	BIGLER, Jacob	9 Jun 1793	Shinnston	Harrison	WV	24 Mar 1814 Harvey Elizabeth	3 Sept 1859
M	BIGLER, Henry	24 Apr 1796	Shinnston	Harrison	WV	30 Oct 1822 Dickerson Hannah	8 Sept 1859
F	BIGLER, Bathsheba	29 Jun 1798	Shinnston	Harrison	WV	30 Sept 1821 Smith William	17 Nov 1826
F	BIGLER, Mariah	29 Jan 1801	Shinnston	Harrison	WV	Flowers William	1803
F	BIGLER, Rebecca	About 1803	Shinnston	Harrison	WV		About 1803

1. Study the five-generation Pedigree Chart in Figure 1. It will give you at a glance the names, births, marriages, and deaths of four generations of direct ancestors. The fifth generation is shown by name only, but each fifth-generation name is repeated as the first generation on the next consecutively numbered Pedigree Chart of that line (see Figure 2). In that way, you can extend any family surname back as far as you are able to and the numbering system will be simple to follow.

2. Record each person's full name, capitalizing the entire surname. For example, BARNES, John Joseph.

3. Record the day, then month, then year, like this: 16 Apr., 1853.

4. Always record the smallest geographical area first: Johnston City, Williamson County, Illinois, becomes Johnston City, Williamson, IL. Use standard Postal Service abbreviations for states, but do not abbreviate cities or counties.

5. Any information such as a birth date that is in doubt should be followed by a question mark in parentheses.

How to Fill Out the Family Group Sheets

A Family Group Sheet should be started for the marriage or marriages of every person shown on your Pedigree Chart. If your great-grandfather went to the altar five times, then he should have five separate sheets. (As you go back farther into your past, you'll find a number of men and women who were married more than once. One of my ancestors, Catherine Koon, outlived four husbands; another, Jonathan Nixon, married three times during his 103 years. In those days wives frequently faded after eleven children and husbands collapsed under backbreaking work. Often very little time elapsed between the funeral of one spouse and marriage to another. Pioneers of either sex did not do well alone on the frontier.

Here are a few guidelines I suggest to help you complete neat, consistent Family Group Sheets:

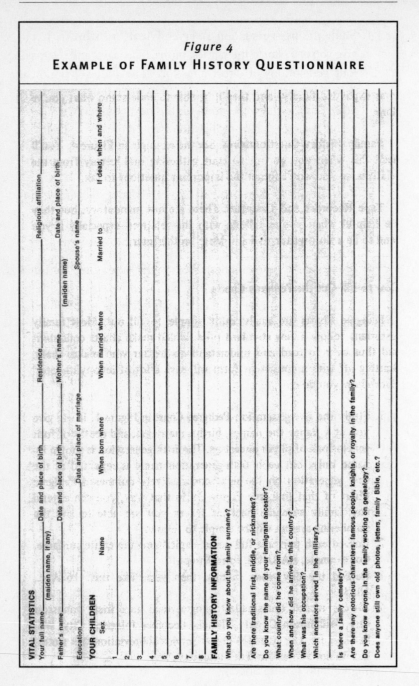

Figure 4

EXAMPLE OF FAMILY HISTORY QUESTIONNAIRE

VITAL STATISTICS

Your full name _____ (maiden name, if any) _____ Date and place of birth _____ Residence _____ Religious affiliation _____

Father's name _____ Date and place of birth _____ Mother's name _____ (maiden name) _____ Date and place of birth _____

Education _____ Date and place of marriage _____ Spouse's name _____

YOUR CHILDREN

Sex	Name	When born where	When married where	Married to	If dead, when and where
1					
2					
3					
4					
5					
6					
7					
8					

FAMILY HISTORY INFORMATION

What do you know about the family surname? _____

Are there traditional first, middle, or nicknames? _____

Do you know the name of your immigrant ancestor? _____

What country did he come from? _____

When and how did he arrive in this country? _____

What was his occupation? _____

Which ancestors served in the military? _____

Is there a family cemetery? _____

Are there any notorious characters, famous people, knights, or royalty in the family? _____

Do you know anyone in the family working on genealogy? _____

Does anyone still own old photos, letters, family Bible, etc.? _____

1. Record names, dates, and places in the same way you did on your Pedigree Chart.

2. Initials (if you do not know the full name) should be placed in quotation marks. For example, SMITH, John "P."

3. All uncommon first names—such as Evelyn for a boy or Georgie for a girl—should be underlined to show you know they are unusual and that they are not mistakes on your part.

4. If there were other marriages for either husband or wife, reference them by name so that they will be easy to find in your Family History Book.

5. In the upper right-hand corner mark the name and address of the Family Group Sheet preparer; also indicate your relationship to this family, such as great-great-granddaughter (or you can use "g-g-granddaughter").

6. Place an X next to the number of the child who is your direct ancestor.

7. If any children are twins, adopted, stepchildren, or stillborn, place the information in parentheses after the child's name.

That's all there is to it. After you get the Pedigree Charts and Family History Sheets drawn up, you can start getting the information you'll need to begin filling them in.

START WITH YOURSELF

You will probably be able to complete parts of these charts right now— perhaps back through your grandparents' generation. As soon as you collect more family history from interviews and the Family History Questionnaire I'll show you about, you should be able to fill in missing details and add another generation or two. Here's how to proceed.

Since chronologically you are the first person in your family history, you should start with yourself. Sit down with scratch pad, Pedigree Chart, and Family Group Sheet and spend some time searching your mind for family information. Who are your parents? Your aunts and uncles? Your grandparents? When and where were they born, married, and so on? Who are their children? You can use the Family History Questionnaire as your own guide. You'll be surprised at how many family facts you have tucked back in the corners of your memory. Enter names, places, and dates right on your charts. If you're not sure of some, put a question mark in parentheses after the entry. Then you'll know to check it later with some other family member.

After you've put down as much information as you can gather from your head or your own records (birth certificates, letters, old photographs, diaries, family Bibles, and so on), make out a list of older (and other) relatives you need to interview. You'll then be ready for the next step.

Interviewing Your Family Elders
and Other Relatives

The most critical thing you have to do as a family historian is to hurry to your oldest relatives before it is too late and get every scrap of information you can. This is the advice every professional genealogist gives all beginners. Few older relatives will refuse to cooperate. In fact, most will be flattered that they have information the younger generation wants and needs.

There are three ways to extract these family facts. Using the Family History Questionnaire (Figure 4) as a guide, you can:

1. talk to your elders face-to-face

2. interview them by mail, if they live some distance away

3. ask another relative or family friend to talk to them for you

The way to approach relatives is to inform the family in general that you're working on the family history—and to invite their comments and solicit their help. You can expect one of three answers when you tell members of your family that you're doing their genealogy: (1) "Wonderful, I was hoping someone would!" (2) "I knew there was a nut loose in this clan." (3) "Mind your own damn business and leave it alone." It may well be that the one who gives the third answer is the one you want to talk to first; you can bet that person hasn't forgotten any juicy particulars he or she ever heard. If any relatives balk, you can win them over easily with one statement: "Whatever I find out, I'm going to share with all of you."

A word of caution: Don't think just because you were particularly close to a certain older relative that you know all he or she has to tell. In researching my own Eddy line, I talked with many relatives, thinking I had heard all the family stories my grandmother knew. As I came to know more about my family, I realized that I had made a mistake by not going to her first. By then, however, Grandmother was in a convalescent home, senilely rocking away with her personalities, loves, tragedies, dates, names, and places of four generations locked in her mind—including the tragic fact of an illegitimate child that the rest of the family was still hiding a century later.

Now let me describe the three methods of interviewing relatives.

1. Face-to-Face Interviewing

The word *interview* sometimes sounds a bit too professional and off-putting to new family historians, but all it is, really, is just another term for a thorough conversation. You may be talking to family elders across a gap of several years, but you have a lot in common, for you're exploring important memories. Even a cranky aunt will be happier when she's recalling a time when she was happier. Of course, it can work the other way around, and you should be prepared for emotional moments when some long-gone loved one is remembered. My grandmother Anna Barnes, eighty-nine when I talked with her, cried for her baby, Robert, who had been dead for sixty-eight years.

Face-to-face interviewing is preferable to the other types of interviewing. As I mentioned, it is better to use a tape recorder (see the box on page 53), but it is not necessary. You can pick up nuances of feeling—sadness, joy, fear, evasiveness—that can quickly tip you off about whether you should pursue or drop a particular line of questioning. People also tend to go on longer when they're talking than when they're writing. When, during a face-to-face interview, you let an elder talk he or she will probably reveal many more insights and tidbits of family lore than you would have thought to ask about. Indeed, he or she might give you some information that leads you in an entirely new direction.

When I first started tracing my family history, I interviewed a great-great-uncle who was 104 years old. At the time I found it a terribly frustrating experience. He talked for hours as if he were still living on the Cherokee Strip in the Oklahoma Territory and reminisced about the prairie town that swelled to 5,000 people overnight, where drinking water cost fifty cents a dipper and raucous saloon girls mixed with desperate outlaws and even more lawless lawmen. While I tried to pin him down as far as dates and names were concerned, he meandered down verbal paths of his own choosing. Since then, however, I have learned to be less impatient with elders. Although statistics are significant to every family historian, it is obvious to me now that living details about the past flesh out these numbers and are every bit as important. In general, you can look forward to meeting your relatives on a genealogical level. Most interviews, in fact, serve to pull the family ties even tighter.

Interviewing an older relative requires thoughtfulness as well as tact. Here are a few courtesies you may want to observe to make the experience agreeable as well as informative:

1. Make the appointment no longer than an hour and a half. The idea is for the time to be pleasant, not exhausting. Make a second and a third appointment, if necessary.

2. Don't assume they can't hear well and shout at them. Just talk slowly, pronouncing words distinctly.

HOW TO RECORD YOUR INTERVIEWS WITH RELATIVES

There are two ways to record an interview: (1) using a tape recorder or (2) taking notes in your workbook.

The tape recorder (which is a relatively inexpensive investment for any family history maker or can be rented from a camera store) is by far the better technique. It frees you to listen more fully; you can be sure you are getting every word said; it allows you to be alert to every change of body language; and you won't have to decode your own handwriting days later, especially if you're like me and write sideways in margins with arrows everywhere. With tape you can record a real oral history of your family, one that you may want to save so that your children or theirs can hear them. Obviously, the sound of their voices and the accents or colloquial expressions they use will be extremely precious years later.

Recorders with built-in microphones are best, I've found. The interviewee usually forgets the recorder is there if he doesn't have a mike in his face. I use a voice-activated recorder so that I don't have to stop an interview to change tapes.

The tapes need not be high-fidelity. They can be cassette tapes of the least expensive variety unless you want high-quality recordings of some of the most important or colorful conversations. Be sure to mark the outside of the tape or cassette with the date, time, place, and name of the person interviewed.

If you rely on or prefer note taking, begin by identifying each interview by date, time, place, and person in your workbook. Then, as the interviewee talks, write like crazy. And try to remember that you will be the one to unscramble all those sentences that curve around the edge of the page. Obviously, it's a good idea to transcribe or type your notes as soon as possible after the interview.

3. The five Ws of reporting—who, what, where, when, why (and sometimes how)—are good guidelines for phrasing questions.

4. Interview the relative alone, if you can, to preclude any possible influence from others present. (Sometimes after individual interviews, a joint interview, with each person jogging the other's memory, will yield new information or correct and clarify the old.)

5. Ask important questions first. If you do, you'll have all the vital information in case your visit must be cut short for any reason.

6. Don't try to make them stick to your question if they don't want to. Let the conversation flow. Try to listen more than you talk. Later you can come back and say, "Now, what was Great-grandma's maiden name again?"

7. Send them a copy of the transcribed interview for their corrections. The value of this is great, for often they will add as much as they correct.

8. Don't overlook family friends and longtime neighbors when you interview. Even if they have no new facts, they may give a fresh perspective to the information you already have.

2. Interviewing by Mail

If you aren't in a position to take a vacation or business trip near the home of some relative whom you'd like to interview, you'll need to do it by mail. This is not unusual. Indeed, my own beginning family history research was accomplished at least 75 percent by mail. The way to do it is to mail out Family History Questionnaires. Here's how:

1. Write a cover letter explaining that you are compiling a family history and need their help (see sample in Figure 5).

2. Be sure to thank them in advance. They don't have to help, you know.

3. Assure all your relatives that you plan to share your mutual family's history with them.

4. Make one original and a copy to keep, so that you will not duplicate requests and will have a complete record of your family search right from the start.

5. Always include a self-addressed, stamped envelope with every request.

You should include a copy of your own Pedigree Chart to show them what you already know and a blank Pedigree Chart for their use. To make things even easier for them, send along a blank Family Group Sheet (see Figure 3) for them to complete about their own marriages—but be sure to explain how to fill it out, so it won't confuse them.

3. Interviewing a Family Friend or Another Relative

If you include the Family History Questionnaire as a basic guide, you may be able to interest a relative or trusted family friend in interviewing a distant relation for you. Usually several people in your family will be attracted to the family's history. They may not want to take on the job, but they usually don't mind helping out—especially when you promise to share your family-tree research results with them.

Be sure to tip off your friends to a common family problem: You know that Uncle Jack has been a font of information for years, but he's also been the family gossip. Unfortunately, Uncle Jack and your mother had a falling-out ages ago and he vowed never to speak to her again. Assuming the family feud extends to your generation, it is smarter (if a bit sneaky) to send Uncle Jack's favorite nephew, Norman, to do the interviewing.

Don't make the mistake of approaching the gentleman and being refused. This might just make him suspicious of anyone who comes around asking for family information, even Norman. It is also a good idea to remain in the background. Don't brag about fooling him—be-

---

Figure 5

COVER LETTER FOR INTERVIEWING RELATIVES
BY MAIL ABOUT YOUR ANCESTOR

Dear (name of relative):

I am trying to gather information on our family in hopes of putting together a history of it and making it available to other relatives.

I would be grateful if you could find the time to fill in the blank Pedigree Chart attached to this letter. Please fill it in as completely as you can and return it to me in the stamped, self-addressed envelope enclosed. I am also enclosing a copy of my own Pedigree Chart to show you how far I've been able to go with my side of the family.

It would also be very helpful if you could refer me to others in our family who might have information about our forebears. And, of course, I'd appreciate any information you could give me on family and related public documents (Bible records, certificates, photos, diaries) that I might copy and return. I sincerely want to record and preserve our family's heritage as accurately and completely as possible.

Thank you for your time and help.

Cordially,

---

cause Uncle Jack may also have other treasures, such as the family Bible or photos, and you'll want them later on.

Incidentally, be careful about probing emotional relationships too deeply. Some relatives may be ashamed of skeletons in their family's history. Of course, today's ancestor hunters live in a more relaxed moral climate, and most wouldn't be at all aghast at finding an illegitimacy, a prison sentence, insanity, a horse thief, or a pirate. Sometimes they actually add glamour to a modern family's history and make the people human. But respect the sensibilities of the people you are interviewing.

One final caveat: When Uncle Jack repeats the family story about G-G Grandfather Jones who rode with Stonewall Jackson and lost all in the Civil War, listen politely even though you've discovered that your ancestor was actually a deserter, who came home to bring in the harvest and then turned himself in to the nearest Union stockade. When he receives his copy of your Family History Book, he'll see the document from the National Archives that backs up your research. It will be easier on him than a confrontation, and better for your interview.

ATTIC ARCHAEOLOGY: FINDING FAMILY RECORDS

A family history contains more than vital statistics. Letters, diaries, wills, old photographs, memoirs, albums, clothing, and other family artifacts add flesh and blood to the ancestral bones and show your forebears' personalities. They also add a thrill of discovery, an awareness of the continuous line that stretches back to the past, of which you are a part.

Even with the mobility of the modern American family, a great mass of information about family heritage exists if you know where to look for it. When interviewing a relative, in person or by mail, always inquire if he or she has old Bibles, photos, scrapbooks, legal papers, or letters of your family ancestors that you can photocopy and return. It's amazing what you can find when you rummage through attics, basements, trunks, closets, and old shoe boxes.

Here is a checklist of items to look for that will add luster to your Family History Book:

1. *Personal records*—journals, diaries, letters, newspaper clippings, photos, baby books, wedding albums, funeral albums, employment and retirement papers. One of my prized possessions is a letter from my grandfather to my grandmother before they married, couched in formal but emotional language, begging her to set the date.

2. *Legal papers*—contracts, tax bills, wills, deeds, mortgages.

3. *School records*—diplomas, yearbooks, awards, alumni papers.

4. *Religious records*—marriage, baptism, christening, church membership, family Bible.

5. *Government records*—military discharge papers and awards, citizenship or naturalization papers, passports, business licenses, Social Security cards, income tax forms.

6. *Health records*—vaccination, hospital, insurance, doctor bills.

Unless you are interviewing or writing to your own parents, it is a good rule never to ask to borrow or keep personal treasures. Extract all the information you can from what you find and suggest that you might like to see the items again sometime. Often enough, on the second or third visit, I have received a spontaneous gift. A great-aunt gave me my great-great-grandfather's farm journal with a hand-drawn map of his orchard and several 125-year-old grocery shopping lists with prices. Another relative (this one a cousin I met only by questionnaire) sent me a perfectly preserved picture of my great-grandfather in his Union Army uniform and his yellowing discharge certificate, dated June 14, 1865.

Remember the serendipity factor and watch for every possible clue. One family archaeologist came to the razing of a family home expecting to make some kind of find and, sure enough, located a box of century-old love letters hidden between the walls in a bedroom.

Here are some things to watch for as you check family records.

1. *Family Bible.* You'll find that you can't always trust Bible data. One story I heard concerned a family Bible that had two complete lists of the same children, both written in the same handwriting but each list obviously written years apart. Since the first child entered had been born in 1899, the family detective checked the Bible's publication date, which was 1914. From that, she understood that the first list of entries had probably

been made from memory after 1914. The second complete list of children with their death dates was made years later, as indicated by the shaky handwriting and unfaded ink. Although the two lists contained good genealogical material, they also presented a problem. On the first list, a child was named Arthur Albert, on the second, Albert Arthur. Which was right? The searcher would have to go to vital records for a birth certificate.

2. *Letters.* In addition to what is revealed by their contents, make a note of their postmarks (postmarks started back in the sixteenth century), dates, and return addresses.

3. *Household effects.* Needlework keepsakes such as samplers and friendship quilts (each friend contributes a square) often give names, dates, and place clues. Spoons and teapots may also bear family names.

4. *Books.* Scrapbooks, photo albums, and other compilations of memorabilia are good sources for the ancestor hunter. And our ancestor's library shouldn't be overlooked. Not only will the choice of books give a valuable clue to his interests and character; there might also be solid gold hiding in the pages. In our grandparents' day, books were storage chests as well as reading matter. Flowers were pressed between their pages, calling cards and greetings were dropped in for safekeeping, and sometimes newspaper clippings, too. While leafing idly through a volume of my Great-uncle Righter's set of *Lee's Lieutenants*, a fifty-year-old newspaper article fell out in my lap. It was a full-page interview (dull to anyone but me) on the occasion of his father's investiture as commander of the local post of the Grand Army of the Republic. It gave Great-grandfather's version of the family history back to the Revolutionary War.

The important thing to remember is: Don't try to remember. Whenever you are checking through family records, have your looseleaf workbook handy for notes. Don't trust to memory. In genealogy, memory is never as good as documentation. If wills, deeds, or letters are too long, then have them photocopied or take extracts of the most important parts. Or, of course, you can use a tape recorder to tape your notes.

There you have it. Once you have drawn up or ordered the forms, you're ready to go.

NOW LET'S GET GOING

There is precious little time to waste in beginning to trace your family. A friend of mine tells how a month after his mother died he went through her personal things, with other members of the family, and found a photo album with some very old tintype pictures in it—judging by the clothing styles, probably dating back to the 1850s. No one could identify the pictures. It's sad to have photos of great-grandparents and others and not know who they are. That's something we should be trying to discover now, not after our grandparents and relatives are gone.

That's not the note I want to end the chapter on, however. I once asked a longtime professional genealogist what she advised beginners to do, expecting a very learned reply. Her answer: "Have fun!" So, start having fun with your own search for roots. You can, if you wish, carry your family search just to the extent I've described in this chapter—that is, interviewing relatives. That may well give you over a century of family history, compiled in charts and memorabilia, to place in your Family History Book. You'll treasure the results just as you treasure your school or wedding pictures.

But once you've gone that far, believe me, it's difficult to stop. You'll find yourself wanting to go beyond the memory of living relatives and family mementos to uncover more of your ancestral lines. In the next chapter, I'll show you a fast way to gather a great deal of already researched family history.

CHAPTER 5

Finding Your Roots with the Help of the World's Greatest Genealogy Collection

DEEP INSIDE MASSIVE vaults blasted out of the Rocky Mountains near Salt Lake City is the greatest treasure of genealogical information ever assembled. Here over 2 million microfilm rolls, equivalent to more than 2.3 billion book pages (with 5,000 rolls being added each month), line six rockbound chambers. Visitors are not allowed inside because dust particles on their shoes, hair, or clothing might contaminate the film. Filtered, humidified air circulates constantly in the artificial light, for these microfilms can never see the destructive light of day. This huge underground storehouse, constructed in 1965 at a cost of $2 million, is built to withstand any disaster, it is hoped—even a nuclear holocaust. More protected than the crown jewels of England, here are the records of 2.5 billion of our ancestors, gathered from 126 different countries, by over 200 microfilming crews filming religious, local, and national "people" records all over the world. The sponsor of this mammoth effort? The LDS (Mormon) Church.

Why does the LDS Church (short for The Church of Jesus Christ of Latter-Day Saints) have the largest collection of genealogical material in the world? For LDS Church members, genealogy is a vital activity and filled with religious significance. Simply stated, genealogy is the method by which the living Latter-Day Saints sanctify their dead.

In over forty world temples—closed to all but the faithful—members are married for "time and eternity," and the children are "sealed" to their parents so that the family will remain intact in the afterlife. This doctrine of the "exalted family" is also extended to ancestors who walked the earth long before the LDS Church was started by Joseph Smith in the 1830s.

And the reason for the huge genealogical collection is that ancestors, who have been identified through a genealogical search, are baptized by proxy—with the descendants standing in for their forebears. (Since 1842, more than 145 million ancestors have been baptized, 5 million in 1997 alone.) LDS members believe that their ancestors in the hereafter have the opportunity to accept or reject the baptism. If they accept, they will be reunited with all the baptized generations of their family after the resurrection.

If you're not an LDS member, you may wonder what use this genealogical collection is to you. The answer is that some of the 2.5 billion recorded ancestors the church has gone to so much trouble to find are probably yours. Whether or not you have ever had an LDS member in your ancestral family, there is a good chance that someone, as part of this religious belief, has compiled information on your forebears. Furthermore, this immense genealogical complex is open to everyone, not just LDS Church members. About 870,000 people a year come to the library, 40 percent of them nonmembers, and tens of thousands more visit the church's branch libraries throughout the world. As you can see, the implications for all family historians are simply enormous.

How You Can Use Those Buried Microfilms

If you are ever on a vacation or business trip near Salt Lake City, it would be well worth your time to stop, if only for a few hours, at the main LDS Family History Library at 35 North West Temple, an imposing granite structure in famed Temple Square where you can have access to the microfilms. Almost any family historian could probably add new branches to his family tree during such a visit, as I did. While at the library you'll want to consult the International Genealogical Index (IGI) where your ancestor's name (if you know it at this stage) might be listed; the Ancestral File, a computer database of family information; the millions of forms in the Family Group Records Collection; and, finally, the Family Registry where over 300,000 other family historians, willing to share their research, have registered.

But if getting to Salt Lake City is out of the question you can still take advantage of all these records, which have been incorporated into a computer disc called FamilySearch, by simply going to the LDS Family History Center near you. There are over 1,600 such facilities, with more being added each year. For the one nearest you write to the Family History Library at 35 North West Temple, Salt Lake City, Utah 84150 or call 800-346-6044. You can also access a listing of local Family History Center branches at *www.genhomepage.com/lds.html* (this is their address on the World Wide Web), a Web site that contains over 1,600 links to other genealogical information. If you don't have a computer, don't hesitate to telephone the main library. There is a thorough, but nonthreatening, voice-mail system that will connect you with a great deal of information, and I haven't encountered long waits.

Although LDS branch libraries are generally self-help, there are always volunteer genealogist-librarians who will assist you with just the source you need to carry on your ancestor search. And most centers conduct periodic classes and seminars that help you learn how best to use their collection and instruct you on the operation of the microfilm readers and their computer centers and FamilySearch software, which includes an ancestral file, Social Security death index, and much more.

LDS family history centers come in all sizes. Some are small with minimal microfilm and book collections of their own. Others hold large numbers of microfilmed census records, reference books, and issues of genealogical, historical, and family magazines. My own branch library has a copy of Harrison County, West Virginia, records going back to the 1700s, and my ancestors come popping out at me from almost every page. In one section, I found my g-g-g-grandfather Henry Amos suing several neighbors over disputed property lines, not once but several times. His granddaughter (my grandmother) inherited his sense of territorial rights and was notorious for elbowing people out of her kitchen.

These libraries can order rare microfilmed records for you from Salt Lake City for a small postage fee. Please contact a family history center in your area for more information and the cost involved. I recommend that you visit, not write, the nearest center, since they are not staffed to answer mail inquiries.

Sometimes when I've told beginning family historians about the LDS facilities, they've been concerned that they might be proselytized. In hundreds of trips to these libraries, I have never once had religion mentioned unless it was part of my research. Genealogy is what we're all after.

Using an LDS family history center in my hometown paid off for me. I was able to order records of my German immigrant g-g-g-grandfather, Jacob Bigler, which contained information on three older generations of Biglers, back to 1705. In another case I traced a female ancestor, Elizabeth Arnold, my fourth great-grandmother, and received information on her five children and whom they married; I also got her father's name, which took me back to 1733. Not everyone gets this kind of help from two microfilms, but you might get even more.

THE LDS SALT LAKE CITY FAMILY HISTORY LIBRARY

I once met a professional genealogy researcher who spends four months a year in Salt Lake City studying the LDS British materials. "For years I went to England to track down ancestors for my clients, going from parish to parish, shire to shire," he said. "Now I come to Salt Lake City because all those English records are here in one place."

The LDS library in Salt Lake City is an impressive place, covering five floors in a 142,000-square-foot building. Over 200 unfailingly courteous people, collectively fluent in thirty languages, work in the complex. In a year, well over 870,000 hungry ancestor hunters visit the library.

The first thing you notice is 500 microfilm readers whirring and flickering, singing of vital statistics, passenger lists, and war records. And the giant card catalog that used to occupy so much room when I started my family search is now completely computerized. In another section searchers squint at computer terminals using special software designed for the library, bringing the lives of their ancestors up on screen in a fraction of a second.

The library houses every kind of record. General reference works, LDS Church records, research materials for the United States and Canada, including North American Indians and black ancestral material and much more. As the church's membership expands around the world the records of many new countries are being added, but the library's collection of United States and Canada is the most complete. It is very strong on midwestern, southern, and New England material. For some states (Massachusetts, for example) they have just about every existing record.

The Correspondence Unit of the library receives many thousands of letters per month. Of course, they are not able to trace entire family trees, but they do try to answer specific questions and let people know how best to utilize their records. Sometimes they refer people to their nearest family history center; sometimes they suggest hiring an accredited professional genealogist who knows their main collection well.

A complete listing of the LDS library holdings at Salt Lake City would fill many catalogs, and new material is being added all the time. For a general overview, you can consult Mary L. Brown's *Handy Index to the Holdings of the Genealogical Society of Utah*, available at any

LDS family history center, but here is an abbreviated list of what you can expect to find:

- 200,000-plus volumes of genealogy and history
- 2-billion-name computerized index
- Genealogical periodicals from around the world
- U.S. census records up to 1920
- American Loyalists' claims with the British government
- Church registers (U.S. and foreign)
- Land grants and property deeds
- Marriage records
- Wills and other court records
- Tax and pension files
- Naturalization records
- Passenger ship lists
- Port of Hamburg passenger lists (surname index for years 1856–71), one of the two major European ports of embarkation.

Specific sections of the library are devoted to specific countries, nationalities, or ethnic groups, as follows:

Africa and Asia

This collection contains materials for all countries of the South Pacific, Asia, the Middle East, and Africa. The library has Taiwanese and Hong Kong records, and the People's Republic of China (mainland) has agreed recently to microfilm their records for the LDS library.

American Indian

If you have American Indian blood, you'll find helpful records on eastern as well as western tribes. Here's a partial listing which will give you a sense of the depth of the collection:

- Lives of famous chiefs
- History, biography, and genealogy of the Wampanoag tribe
- Handbook of American Indian languages
- Notes and monographs—Powhatan tribes of Virginia
- Early history and names of the Arapaho
- Report on Indians taxed and not taxed (1890)
- Abenakis of Vermont
- Census of the Bureau of Indian Affairs
- Census of Cherokee (1835)
- Iroquois anthropology at the midcentury (1850)
- Navajo
- Quinnipiock
- Ute tribal membership rolls and other tribe enrollments
- Sioux personal property claims
- Genealogy of Indian families of the Pima, Maricopa, and Papagos
- Indian deeds of Rhode Island (1638)
- Indian letters, talks, and treaties
- Shawnees in Kansas
- Confederate Indian soldiers

- Indian students (1826–35)

- Yakimas

African-Americans

The U.S. section contains African-American genealogical information, including special censuses taken by the southern states during the nineteenth century. The church has also begun to microfilm records in the French colonies of Haiti and Martinique.

Britain

The British section has extensive material from England, Wales, Scotland, the Channel Islands, and Australia. They also have large microfilm collections for Northern Ireland, Ireland, New Zealand, and the Republic of South Africa. The depth and breadth of this material is astounding.

Continental Europe

The Continental Europe collection contains records from both Europe and Asia. Some of the countries represented are: Poland, Germany, Romania, Slovenia and the Czech Republic, Bulgaria, the former Yugoslavia, Albania, Hungary, Austria, Switzerland, the Netherlands, Belgium, Luxembourg, France, Italy, Greece, Mediterranean islands, Spain, and Portugal. The LDS Church has been doing a great deal of microfilming in Bulgaria, Poland, and the former Yugoslavia and has a number of Polish records, some filmed before World War II. Until recently they had few records for many countries of the old Soviet Union, but that is rapidly changing. Unfortunately, four-fifths of the Soviet national records were destroyed by revolution and war. (You'll find more information about research in Russia and other eastern European countries in chapter 9, "Finding Your Roots Abroad.")

Latin America and the Iberian Peninsula

Records are sectionalized under South America, Central America (South and Central American Indians), and the Balearic Islands.

Other Collections

Smaller countries, islands, and groups of people are also indexed in the LDS library. For instance, if you needed information on an immigrant ancestor from Liechtenstein, the library has material on this tiny country. Add to this vast numbers of maps, books on heraldry, old newspapers, and gazetteers and you can see the mountain of information available to you — information that could take you back to your roots.

REACHING BACKWARD: USING LDS FAMILY HISTORY CENTERS

Many people don't know that the LDS Family History Library resources are open to everyone searching for their roots. Hardly a week goes by that I don't surprise someone with the news that the source he or she is so diligently looking for is probably located at the LDS family history center just across town, or can be easily ordered for a minimal amount from the main library in Salt Lake City.

There are so many ways that you can access the mountain of material, which is almost guaranteed to contain at least one of your ancestors and, if you're as lucky as I have been, dozens of forebears. Remember, you can visit the main family history library in Salt Lake City or access all its information through one of the many satellite centers nearest you. You can telephone or write, and you can expect a polite and usually helpful answer every time. Again, I urge you to visit one of these libraries if you possibly can. You will be amazed at how much easier it will make your ancestor search.

CHAPTER 6

Finding Your Roots with the Help of Public Libraries, Specialty Libraries, and Genealogical Societies

THE LAST CHAPTER established an important principle—namely, see if you can find out if other people have already researched your ancestors for you. Obviously, you would feel tremendously frustrated if you found out a few weeks or months down the road that you'd been blazing a trail that had already been traveled by someone else and you didn't know it.

For this reason, I feel you should definitely take advantage of the LDS library's immense stockpile of family history. However, despite the fantastic energy of LDS members, they haven't traced every ancestor or searched every record. There are a lot more family records out there. So, after you've checked the LDS library you should try looking for records of your ancestors in the following, which we will discuss in this chapter:

1. Public libraries

2. Genealogical-historical societies and their publications

3. Private libraries with special genealogical collections

4. State libraries or archives

Although you might not think so at first, these sources are useful even if you're a second- or third-generation American.

Before I explain libraries and archives, let me help you set up a simple system of record-keeping and research procedures.

YOUR RECORD-KEEPING SYSTEM

Even if you're using a fill-in-the-blanks computer genealogy program, you'll need to organize records. If you're not using a computer, your record keeping will be more extensive, but it need not be complicated. The following system will help you find a source or note when you need it. Here's how to do it:

1. You have some sort of workbook, which you call your Family History Book.

2. Into this Family History Book put—in alphabetical order by surname—all your records for each generation and each ancestor within that generation. You may want to label each surname with a colored plastic tab.

3. As you fill in Pedigree Charts and Family Group Sheets, place them in your Family History Book by family surname. I like to keep Family Group Sheets for a particular ancestor together with all his or her photos, copies of wills, deeds, biographical material, and maps.

4. Whenever you add any new family discoveries to your Family History Book, document your additions by naming the source (and date) of each find. (Label undocumented material "family tradition.")

5. As you write up family migrations and biographical stories from local histories, verify each one by listing the author, book, title, volume, publisher, date of publication, page, and library or genealogical society where you found it.

6. Keep a sheet in your workbook with the title "Negative Research." On it list all the sources you consulted that proved to be dead ends. By listing them, you won't be as apt to forget and look in these same sources again.

7. Write down *immediately* in your workbook anything you glean from a source, a relative, a librarian, or a microfilm. Several times, in a hurry, I have found a bit of information (such as an intriguing mention of an ancestor in a history book or a unique interpretation of one of my family surnames), neglected to jot it down, and later was unable to find it.

8. Keep a research reminder list in your workbook of sources you would like to check for a particular forebear. When you accumulate enough for a library visit or a research trip, you will be able to accomplish all you need to do from notes on this list.

9. Some genealogy software programs make keeping such records easy. *Family Tree Maker* has a "scrapbook" feature into which you can scan photos and records or even add sound. But you'll still want to keep your original records, and that means organizing paper in the method I've laid out here.

Procedures to Follow

The first decision you need to make is which line or surname of your family you want to trace first. The second is to determine what I call a "research locale."

After you have conducted your oral-history and mail interviews with relatives, you will probably have some information about a number of your family lines. LDS research may provide more. Now, instead of striking out in all directions at once, I recommend that you choose one line at a time and concentrate on it for as long as you can easily follow it. Most people, of course, want to trace their own surname first (women, their birth names), if you have too much trouble with *any* family line, drop it for a time and go on to another one. After all, the idea is to make your search fun, not drudgery. Next, determine your "research locale." A research locale is simply the place where you're likely to find the most records about the family line you've chosen to pursue. If you know that your Grandpa Henry was born in Lincoln, Nebraska, and you want to find out more about him and his forebears, then Lincoln (whether or not *you* live there) becomes your research locale, since it has all the vital records, such as birth certificates, that will likely give you the information you'll need to go back further.

Once you have determined the research locale, write to the research sources concerned with that locale—namely, as I said earlier, public libraries, genealogical-historical societies, private libraries with special genealogical collections, and state libraries or archives. The addresses for many of these sources are given in Appendix I, "State-by-State Family History Help List."

When you write to them, you'll get better results if you do the following:

1. Ask specific questions. For example: "Can you tell me if the name Alexander Luther Eddy, who resided in Dayton, Ohio, from 1850 to 1915, appears in any local histories or family genealogies in your collection?"

2. Ask the librarian to check for a family history if you think your ancestor may have lived in the area for any length of time. The chances may be slim, but who knows? Maybe a cousin has already written one and deposited it in the library. One of my Barnes relatives compiled such a history around 1930, had it printed, and deposited it in the local library. I was able to obtain this volume through an interlibrary loan and it proved to

be a bonanza—copies of wills, letters, stories, and even pictures of my ancestors from the 1850s, which I was later able to scan into my computer-generated Family History Book.

3. Ask if there is a local history or biographical book in which your ancestor might possibly be mentioned.

4. Ask if the librarian can suggest others to contact. Often he or she can direct you to people who are involved in local genealogical or historical research and might have unpublished information on your ancestor.

5. As a courtesy, enclose a stamped, self-addressed envelope. Offer to pay for any photocopying charges.

6. Don't mail librarians Pedigree Charts to complete or expect them to wade through page after page of family stories.

That's the basic program for extending your ancestor hunt to libraries and archives. The rest of this chapter describes the principal institutions to which to write. If you plan on visiting rather than writing to a library, see the box on page 76, which tells you about things to look for.

PUBLIC LIBRARIES

Almost every public library, no matter how small, has a genealogy and local-history section; some have quite large collections. Here are a few that are valuable not only to ancestor hunters living or searching in their own locales but also, because of the depth of their collections, to family historians all over the country.

Allen County (Fort Wayne, Indiana) Public Library

The Allen County library has an impressive holding of over 500,000 books, microfilms, and other genealogical records on midwestern forebears, including collections of records from England, Scotland, Ireland, and Canada. This is now the *second* largest collection in the country after the LDS library in Salt Lake City. They have a Research Center and for a fee will do either limited or more extensive searches for you. They publish the Pathfinder series of research brochures covering foreign countries and special categories of research. You can write to the Historical Genealogy Collection, Allen County Public Library, 900 Webster Street, Fort Wayne, IN 46801, or telephone 219-421-1225. To learn more about this major resource, go to their Web site at *www.acpl.lib.in.us.*

Free Library of Philadelphia

Philadelphia, which calls its library by its original eighteenth-century name, has records of immigration showing arrivals at the port of Philadelphia during the period of 1728 to 1808, lists of German immigrants, naturalization records for the years 1740 to 1773, early Pennsylvania land grants, vital statistics (births, marriages, and deaths) prior to 1885, census records, and 138 volumes of the Pennsylvania and Colonial archives. Write to the Free Library of Philadelphia, 1901 Vine Street, Philadelphia, PA 19103, or telephone 215-686-5322. You may access their extensive Web site at *www.library.phila.gov.*

Los Angeles Public Library

The Los Angeles City library system really caters to family historians in a big way. Over 45,000 genealogy books alone, 200,000 volumes in its history section, plus magazines, many microfilm rolls, and manuscripts deal with county, city, and family history, published vital records, military rosters, and books on surnames. They are particularly strong in biographies, travel, wars, the West, Native Americans, and, of course, Los Angeles history. According to their head genealogist, Michael Kirley, they have the largest historical map collection in American public libraries: over 80,000 dating back to 1849. If you visit this library, trained librarians will help you find and use the library's materials and suggest other sources when you run into dead ends. Contact the Los Angeles Public Library, 630 West Fifth Street, Los Angeles, CA 90017. Mail requests for name searches carry a fee payable in advance. For current fees, telephone 213-228-7400. To access the History and Genealogy Department's Web page, go to *www.lapl.org/central/hlhp/html.*

HOW TO USE LOCAL LIBRARIES

If you aren't as familiar with a library as you used to be, ask a librarian to give you a short tour, so that you'll be able to find things for yourself. He or she knows the collections and can unravel a research puzzle that has you up a tree (but not a family tree.)

Get acquainted with the computerized card catalog, which lists every book in the library alphabetically three ways—by author, title, and subject. You will find listings for all the books on genealogy in one place.

This index will list related subjects ("See Also") which will lead you to other sources the library has for you. If you're in the research locale in which the ancestor you're hunting for lived, check the listings for a book under your family name; it may even be a family history. Next try to find a book about the history of the locality or state. Look for a listing with the name of the state or county and the subheading "History" or "Genealogy." You just might find your ancestral name mentioned in such histories.

Go to the section of your library shelves numbered 929 (in the Dewey Decimal System) and browse; this is where you will find how-to books on genealogy and biography, surnames, nobility, and heraldry. (Also see the bibliography at the back of this book and suggested reading throughout the text.)

Nearby, in the 970 section, you will come across general United States history, as well as state, county, and local histories.

Ask your librarian if they have microfilmed census records. For example, the Atlanta Public Library has all Georgia census records on file, ➤

which could save having to write a letter to the National Archives in Washington, D.C. (see chapter 8).

If you need to search further or you haven't found what you are looking for to fill in the empty spaces of your research, be sure to ask the librarian whether there are photo or clipping files or other books you should consult in the library. Because of their value, many one-of-a-kind history books and rare reference works are not kept on the shelves or available for checkout, but will be made accessible to you if you ask.

New Orleans Public Library

This city library has developed an extensive collection full of fascinating local history—for example, 30,000 microfilmed photographs, Louisiana census schedules, naturalization records, passenger arrivals at the port of New Orleans, records of Mardi Gras memorabilia, and civil court records dating back to 1769. Although Collin Hamer, head of the collection, says the LDS Church has microfilmed extensively in the library, they did not microfilm court records. According to Hamer, some of these lawsuits going back to the early 1800s are fascinating material. The emphasis of the collections is on New Orleans, Louisiana, the southeastern United States, Nova Scotia, France, and Spain. You may address your questions to the Genealogy Section, New Orleans Public Library, 219 Loyola Avenue, New Orleans, LA 70112, or telephone 504-596-2610. There is a fee for research, so call ahead or access their extensive Web site, at *www.home.gnofn.org/~nopl*, for current fee schedules.

New York City Public Library

This library's Genealogy Division is one of the largest public library collections open to family historians in the country. Included here are many vital birth, marriage, and death records; city directories; bibliographies; indexes; genealogical reference works; and surname dictionaries. As you might suspect, this library is strong on New York sources.

Some specific items in the library that could be useful to you are:

- New York area newspapers and indexes on microfilm
- Genealogy and historical publications from the United States and Europe
- Local histories
- Scrapbooks and files of photographs of American towns during the past century
- International Index of scientists and aviators
- Index to New York probate and death notices
- Many maps of New York State, County, and City
- Passenger lists and indexes of vessels arriving in New York from 1820 on
- Naturalization petitions from 1792
- Military sources, including Revolutionary War pension files

A unique aid to genealogists provided by the library is the "let's exchange" file, which encourages an information swap between family researchers. (If you are searching for a New York City ancestor, you should check this file to see if any other genealogist is already working on your family tree.) This is another way to keep from duplicating research someone else has already accomplished.

The library also maintains a file in which all its uncataloged family material—such as letters and jottings not indexed elsewhere in the library—is arranged alphabetically by name.

For a small fee, librarians will answer brief, specific questions you may have about any New York ancestors whose names are on file with them. Address these questions to the Local History and Genealogy Division, New York City Public Library, Fifth Avenue and 42nd Street, New York, NY 10018, or telephone 212-930-0828. A comprehensive listing of the library's holdings can be accessed at *www.nypl.org*, with forty-one hotlinks to genealogical resources.

GENEALOGICAL-HISTORICAL SOCIETIES AND THEIR PUBLICATIONS

Family historians can reap several benefits by joining genealogical societies such as the National Genealogical Society (NGS), 4527 17th Street North, Arlington, VA 22207, telephone 703-841-9065, or access them at *www.genealogy.org*. And don't forget the group in your hometown or the one in your research locale. Membership in these societies includes a subscription to their publication, which is the best way I know to keep up with new sources for genealogical research. Addresses for many national and local groups can be found in the "State-by-State Family History Help List" at the back of this book. If you don't find the one you need listed, call the library in your locale. The librarian will know what genealogical groups exist.

Whether or not you decide to join a national or local genealogical-historical society, it can help you in your ancestor search. Many have established libraries that are absolute treasure troves, and some print well-documented family histories as well as local histories and genealogical research forms. The most prestigious and the oldest is the New England Historic Genealogical Society, founded in 1845. You can write to them at 101 Newbury Street, Boston, MA 02116, telephone 617-536-5740, or access their Web site at *www.nehgs.org/*. Specializing in New England families and history, its library, one of the largest of its kind in the world, holds 200,000 books and two million manuscripts. Members may borrow books by mail, a month at a time, for a nominal fee to cover mailing costs.

Even the smallest genealogical society seeks to collect as many books for its members as possible, and most have ongoing research projects, such as copying courthouse, cemetery, and church records.

And every genealogical society, no matter how small, generally publishes a magazine, if only a photocopied one. The style of publication is no reflection on its contents. One beginning Nevada genealogist, trying to trace a family pioneer, joined the Rapid City (South Dakota) Society for Genealogical Research just to get a subscription to its publication, *The Black Hills Nuggets*. The small investment paid off in a big dividend when she found her g-g-grandmother in the magazine's listing of gravestone inscriptions.

Genealogical publications can provide extremely useful information for the ancestor hunter. For instance, most run a "quest" column, which acts as a clearinghouse for people of the same surname who want to contact one another for help. *The New England Historic and Genealogical Register* has printed passenger lists and other records spanning oceans and covering literally thousands of subjects over the past 130 years. *The National Genealogical Society Quarterly* has reprinted family histories and an invaluable alphabetical "Index to Revolutionary War Pensioners," plus articles such as "Alaska's Native Population," "Finding Origins for Immigrant Females," and thousands more. The point is that such publications provide genealogical data that may save you from having to do the work yourself. To locate a genealogical library in your research locale, look in the "State-by-State Family History Help List" at the back of this book, or consult Mary Kay Meyer's *Directory of Genealogical Societies of the United States* in your library.

Often your genealogical search can be supplemented by work already published by one of the 4,300 local historical societies in the United States and Canada. In these printed local histories you may find a wealth of pure genealogical information as well as exciting stories and biographies of your forebears.

If you have been unable to find a local history by writing the public library in your research locale, look in the reference section of your local library for the *Directory of Historical Societies and Agencies in the United States and Canada*, published by the American Association for State and Local History. You'll find the address of the historical society that is nearest to your research locale. For example, if I wanted to see if my Barnes ancestors were mentioned in a local history (and the public library could not help me), I'd write to the Harrison County (West Virginia) Historical Society. The *Directory* will also give you the address of specialized historical societies for racial, religious, and ethnic groups—for instance, the American Jewish Historical Society, which publishes the *American Jewish Historical Quarterly* (now in its eighty-sixth year) and which has a large library containing almost everything that has appeared in print on local Jewish communities in the United States.

PRIVATE LIBRARIES WITH SPECIAL GENEALOGICAL COLLECTIONS

There are private libraries in every state that have special genealogical collections. Many are listed in Appendix I, the State-by-State Family History Help List. If one isn't listed for your research locale, check with the state library or archive for its location.

Of course, the largest private genealogical collection is the LDS library in Salt Lake City, but the second most important private resource is the Newberry in Chicago. Its outstanding holdings contain one million volumes and five million manuscripts, primarily concerning Western Europe and the Americas from the late Middle Ages to the present century. The Newberry's American records are strongest for the Midwest but contain some material on all regions of the United States and Canada as well. Here's a partial list of some of its genealogical treasures.

- 18,000 printed family histories

- Local county histories

- All major genealogical periodicals

- U.S. census records from 1790 to 1880

- Military records of the American Revolution, War of 1812, and Civil War

- Bohemian, French Canadian, Irish, Jewish, and Polish material

The Newberry also has some multivolume reference works usually found only in the largest public libraries, if at all, such as the *Dictionary of American Biography*, *Cyclopedia of American Biography*, and the *American Genealogical Index*. The library's own collection is a massive four-volume tome that was indexed in 1918, which, unfortunately, doesn't contain any item the library purchased after that year. Still it is worth consulting, according to curator David Thackery, particularly for nineteenth-century Chicago and Midwest records if you only have a surname with no dates to work with.

The Newberry Family History Room is staffed with people who are interested in helping you identify and locate materials that will help you find your ancestors, and they also will answer specific mail inquiries. Keep your questions brief and to the point, and expect to pay a service fee for material reproduced. Write to the Newberry Library, 60 West Walton Street, Chicago, IL 60610, or telephone 312-943-9090. For even faster service you can print out their search forms for an obituary, census, or city directory search from their Web site at *www.newberry.org*.

STATE LIBRARIES AND ARCHIVES

Another source to be aware of is the state library or archive in your research locale. (For addresses, again see Appendix I; the State-by-State Family History Help List.) Such libraries, which concentrate on state history, can be invaluable in tracking down an early forebear. For example, the Pacific Room of the state library of Hawaii in Honolulu has the only collection in the world on Hawaiian ancestry. The California Room of the California state library in Sacramento maintains a mountain of data on the early gold rush, on railroading, and on the Spanish colonial period. The Michigan state library has over 30,000 historical books and microfilms and, in addition, publishes *Family Trails*, a

Michigan family history magazine. The Texas state library at Austin has a vast amount of material with special emphasis on the South and Southwest. You can access all state libraries from one Web site at *www.state.wi.us/0/agencies/dpi/www/statelib.html*; or search the Web for any state library, and the state library Web site will be included.

The point of this chapter has been that someone may already have done a lot of your ancestor searching for you, and the best way to determine that is through libraries and genealogical-historical societies. In the next chapter, I'll show you how to go beyond such secondary research and get to the primary records themselves.

CHAPTER 7

Finding Your Roots Through Local Public Records

THERE ARE TWO TYPES of records useful to family historians—primary and secondary. In the last three chapters, I described how to use secondary sources—either secondhand personal information, such as oral history, or secondhand public information, such as written histories. Now let me tell you how to find primary sources, principally local public records—birth, marriage, and death certificates; wills, probate documents, and land deeds; and church and cemetery records.

Why should you be concerned with these? Three reasons:

First, you can use them to trace back another generation. Let's say you know your grandfather was born in Springfield, Missouri. By writing the courthouse there, you could obtain copies of his birth certificate. This might provide his father's name, thus giving you another generation. Then you can repeat the process, marching back through your family's history.

Second, you can use these records to authenticate information you aren't sure about—such as birth date, residence, or wife's name. (Some people have even found they were heirs to estates this way.)

Finally, such documents, often signed in your ancestor's own hand, are what make those long-dead forebears come alive for you. Imagine, for instance, coming across an old will in which a mother chastises her wayward son by leaving him twenty pounds, "to be paid him by my executors at such times as the overseers to this my will shal judge meet [that is to say] when he doth take good courses as to live orderly, & to follow the cordwainer's [shoemaker's] trade, & is clear of such debts as he now owes . . ."

Or, as in my own case, my g-g-great grandfather's will which left generous sums of money and property to most of his children but only one dollar to a daughter who had married a wagon maker against her father's wishes. In the same will, my ancestor directed that a "mulatto" slave named Martha be given her freedom when she reached the age of twenty-six years, leading me to suspect that this woman must have been a natural child of my forebear. Wills such as these give clues to character and personality, long-forgotten family conflict and drama, and will be among the most valuable parts of your Family History Book.

VITAL RECORDS

Vital records is the term used by historians to mean birth, marriage, and death certificates.

Birth certificates list the date, time, and place of birth, the sex of the baby, perhaps its name, and the names of the parents.

Marriage certificates list the woman's maiden name; residence; and the place, date and minister or official presiding.

Death certificates list name; age, date, place, and cause of death; and doctor's name.

The originals of all such vital records remain in the custody of town or county officials, but by law you are entitled to copies. Locating such certificates really isn't as difficult as it sounds.

Many such records have already been copied or extracted and published. Most libraries carry the Works Progress Administration

(WPA) *List of Vital Statistical Records* published by the federal government in 1943. This is a state-by-state compilation of the whereabouts of marriage, birth, and death records which was put together by unemployed writers indexing vital records for the WPA during the Depression of the 1930s. It is a good place to start unless you are looking for vital records in Alaska, Connecticut, Delaware, Hawaii, Maine, Maryland, Ohio, Pennsylvania, South Carolina, or Vermont; for those you'll have to go to your specific research locale, following the procedures below, which are also not difficult.

Birth and Death Records

You can get booklets from the federal government explaining how and where to find birth and death certificates. Write the U.S. Government Printing Office, Superintendent of Documents, Washington, DC 20402, and ask for the pamphlet "Where to Write for Birth and Death Certificates." (Or try your local library.) This lists the address, cost, and records available for each state and U.S. possession. With few exceptions, those records date from the late 1800s.

For earlier birth and death records you should write directly to your ancestor's town or county. In New England, births and deaths were kept by the town or village clerk. In the South and West they were usually kept by the county (or parish, in Louisiana) clerk.

For information on records of U.S. citizens who were born or died outside the United States, write to the Health Resources Administration, National Center for Health Statistics, Rockville, MD 20852.

Marriage Records

For marriage records filed since 1900, send for the pamphlet "Where to Write for Marriage Records" (there's also one called "Where to Write for Divorce Records"), U.S. Government Printing Office, Superintendent of Documents, Washington, DC 20402.

Before 1800, marriages were often recorded differently from the way they are today. In many places, legal documents called "marriage banns" or "bonds of intentions" were posted by the suitor, usually with a stiff financial penalty if he defaulted—an interesting way of making a suitor's word as good as his bond. Such fascinating old legal documents can be found among city and county records. In addition, since almost all marriages then were also religious ceremonies, they are also contained in church records, discussed below.

LOCAL PUBLIC RECORDS: WILLS, PROBATE DOCUMENTS, LAND DEEDS, AND OTHERS

There are a great many public records available in county courthouses that are prime sources of ancestral information: wills, probate documents, land deeds, tax and voting lists, and commissioners' records (showing locations of roads and mills).

Early land records with their grantor/grantee indexes and tract books showing time, place, length of residence are also real finds for the ancestor hunter. Often, these records in the hands of the county recorder also refer to a forebear's property ownership in other areas at an earlier time, or even to unknown relatives. Such information can mean extending your line back another generation or even two.

A photostat of such records costs very little and can be had by writing to the county clerk of the probate court—these offices are generally located in the county seat of your research locale. Or, if you can't get a copy of such a record in its entirety, you can get the essence of it through a technique called abstracting.

Here's the information you should be sure to abstract or ask for from your ancestor's last testament:

1. The name of the person making the will (or other document)

2. Any information about him or her, such as residence or health

3. All persons named in the document and their relationship to your ancestor

4. The essentials of bequests (if a will), including land and personal property descriptions

5. The names of executors and witnesses

6. A description of any signatures, marks, or seals (in the old days some people signed with special marks)

An in-depth lesson in researching probate and other court documents for genealogical information is given in Norman E. Wright's *Building an American Pedigree*.

STATE AND TERRITORIAL PUBLIC RECORDS

Most of the original states and states with former territorial governments have published a manual or index as to what material is in their archives. If you had an ancestor who helped open the Oklahoma Indian Territory, for instance, you would have to check with Oklahoma state archives, or the state census, which most state libraries keep on microfilm. The same holds true for all states, and the documents preserved constitute a prime source of genealogical information.

Besides the WPA *List of Vital Statistical Records*, another useful reference work is Jenkins and Hamick's *A Guide to Microfilm Collections of Early State Records*.

CHURCH RECORDS

When birth, marriage, and death certificates are not available to you from government records, you might find such information in church records, many of which have been published over the past century. For example, if you are researching an old American family, it is not unlikely that you have a Quaker ancestor on some branch of your family tree since it was a large sect 200 years ago—and the Quakers kept meticulous records. If you find—or just suspect—that you have a

Quaker forebear, you might check *The Encyclopedia of American Quaker Genealogy,* by William Wade Hinshaw, for your ancestor's surname. Many Quaker records have also been collected and indexed at the Friends Historical Library, Swarthmore College, Swarthmore, PA 19081, telephone 610-328-8496 or e-mail *friends@swarthmore.edu.* The library contains 13,000 Quaker family names, genealogical charts, 20,000 books, and 1,000 volumes of original Quaker meeting records.

During the nineteenth century, back-country, circuit-riding preachers often kept a journal of the services, marriages, funerals, and baptisms they performed. Thus, if you are having trouble finding vital documents for an ancestor, some of these journals can be found today in the historical archives of most churches. There are also some major church archives listed below, which contain valuable genealogical records.

American Church Archives

American Baptist Historical
    Society
1106 South Goodman Street
Rochester, NY 14620
Telephone/fax 716-473-1740
www.crds.edu/abhs.htm

American Catholic Historical
    Association
Catholic University of America
Washington, D.C. 20017
Telephone: 202-319-5065
*www.cus.edu/www/mullen/
archcoll.html*

Archives of the Greek Orthodox
    Archdiocese of North America
10 East 79th Street

New York, NY 10021
Telephone: 212-510-3565
www.goarch.org/goa

Archives of the Mother Church
The First Church of Christ
    Scientist
107 Falmouth Street
Boston, MA 02110
Telephone: 617-450-3793
www.tfccs.com

Church of Jesus Christ of Latter-
    Day Saints
Genealogical Association
Suite 1006, 54 East South
    Temple Street
Salt Lake City, UT 84111
Telephone: 800-346-6044

www.genhomepage.com/
LDS.html

Congregational Christian
   Historical Society
14 Beacon Street
Boston, MA 02108
Telephone: 617-523-0470
www.tsac.net/users

Lutheran Ministerium of
   Pennsylvania
Historical Archives
Lutheran Theological Seminary
7301 Germantown Avenue
Philadelphia, PA 19119
Telephone: 215-248-4616
www.elca.org

Mennonite Historical Library
Bluffton College

Bluffton, Ohio 45817
Telephone: 419-358-3000
www. bluffton.edu/acadaffairs/
bcintro.htm

Moravian Archives
North Main at Elizabeth
Bethlehem, PA 18015
Telephone: 610-861-1543
www.moravian.edu/dept/pub/
reeves/index.htm

Presbyterian & Reformed
   Church
L. Nelson Bell Library
310 Gaither Circle
Montreat, NC 28757
Telephone: 704-669-8012
www.montreat.edu/montreat/
facilities.htm

If you don't find your research church in this listing, try a search engine Web site that gives access to almost all the major religious denominations in the United States: *yahoo.com.Society_and_Cultural/ Religion/Christianity/Denominations_an.*

The best way to research church records for an ancestor is to study the membership rolls and records at the original church where your ancestors worshiped, either by going there in person or by writing them. Sometimes church records help to bring our ancestors and the times in which they lived into sharper focus. For instance, I researched the records from 1850 to 1900 for the St. Paul Baptist Church in Fairview, West Virginia, where my ancestor Michael Eddy was clerk for forty-nine years. One entry showed that Brother Eddy was paid the handsome amount of twenty bushels of corn for annually furnishing the meetinghouse with light and fuel. Another entry, written in his hand, reported that it was "moved and seconded that we as a church will exclude any member that will vend or retail ardent spirits." Unfortunately, not all my ancestors were so abstemious, certainly not Oral Barnes who operated a clandestine Appalachian still around 1900, although it must be added that he became a teetotaler and conservative Republican in later life.

SEARCHING CEMETERIES

Many people have a fascination with old graveyards, and in recent times the art of making rubbings of decorative gravestones (see the box on page 93) has become a popular pastime: one headstone in Old Deerfield, Massachusetts, for example, has had over 10,000 rubbings made of it. While such rubbings are too large to fit into your Family History Book, they can be framed and hung on a wall. Quite naturally you might not want to do this with a recent family monument, but the process of copying gravestones loses its morbid feeling when one is transcribing the sentiments of a tablet in an old western ghost town, a 200-year-old cemetery in New England, or a churchyard in Europe.

Most of the inscriptions on gravestones are straightforward or commonplace, but there are reports of discoveries like the following, which would do a Madison Avenue advertiser proud:

> *Here lies Jane Smith, wife of Thomas Smith,*
> *marble cutter. This monument was erected*
> *by her husband as a tribute to her memory*
> *and a specimen of his handiwork.*
> *Monuments of this style are fifty dollars.*

Or this reproof above the grave of an unforgiving woman:

> *I told you I was sick.*

More likely are inscriptions like the following found by a friend of mine of his ancestor in a Massachusetts cemetery:

Here lies interred ye Body of Deacon
Oliver Moor,
who deceased Dec. ye 23rd, A.D., 1774
Death is a Debt to Nature due,
Which I have paid & so must you.

Unless you know someone who lives in or is visiting the area of
your research locale, you'll probably have to visit the cemetery yourself, especially if you want to photograph the gravestones or make rubbings—although many of the oldest tombstone inscriptions have been
compiled and filed in nearby libraries. Some have even been published, such as *Gravestones of Early New England and the Men Who
Made Them*, by Harriette M. Forbes.

If you have the name of a cemetery but can't find the location (a
century ago there were many private cemeteries, and it was not unusual for people to be buried on their own land) try going to the area's
local library and asking for county maps and county atlases, which will
show the site of most graveyards. If those maps don't help you, try the
county surveyor's office, which will have aerial maps, county historians, or longtime residents.

Once you have found the cemetery where your ancestors rest, be
sure to go there with your workbook. Copy down the inscriptions *exactly* as you find them. (Don't correct any misspellings—they are part
of the charm and the record.) One person I know copied down a
gravestone inscription in German from a Vermont cemetery which,
when translated, gave him his ancestor's origins in Germany, the date
of his desertion as a Hessian mercenary soldier from the army of the
British redcoats in America, and other facts about his later life.

Many older private (or even public) cemeteries have been ill
cared for; and you may find stones fallen over or tall weeds obscuring
the epitaph. Having grass shears and a shovel in the trunk of the car
helps.

I visited two old family graveyards on former family property thousands of miles from my own home. In one I found the grave of
Jonathan Nixon, who bragged that he'd lived in three centuries from

PHOTOGRAPHING GRAVESTONES
OR MAKING GRAVESTONE RUBBINGS

Making the inscriptions stand out enough to be photographed often requires some work. Use wire and bristle brushes to scrape off lichen, dirt, and moss. Then rub soft, white chalk into the inscriptions to make them easier to read and photograph.

As for making gravestone rubbings, the process is simple. Take an ordinary wax marking crayon, masking tape, and a sheet of tough pliable paper (like a good-grade rice paper) to get started. Cut the paper to the size of the stone to be rubbed, stretch it flat, and tape it *securely* on all four sides (if the paper shifts, you will have a blurred inscription). Hold the wax crayon at a slight angle and rub gently, varying the pressure on the crayon, until the image or words appear. If you notice a part you would like to emphasize more, just go back over it with a firmer pressure on the crayon.

1699 to 1801. Looking at the worn headstone, I felt connected through him to most of the early history of this country. In another family resting place, an elderly cousin who had been tending the graveyard alone for thirty years walked with me down rows of tombstones with names on them as familiar as my own. Despite his efforts, it was overgrown and the once-ornate iron fence was falling down. I helped him clear weeds there that hot August afternoon, but I wondered who would care for the graves after he was gone. I photographed them all as a record because I knew that these old family cemeteries were fast disappearing.

SPECIAL PUBLIC RECORD SOURCES

The above are the general guidelines for searching for your ancestor in primary public records and cemeteries. If you are an adoptee of any race—yes, even some adopted persons can trace their natural parents and natural forebears—or if you are African American, Chinese American, Mexican American, or Native American, there are other public records you will want to know about. These are described below.

Adoptees

There are over 2.5 million adoptees in America who are excluded from the rewards of tracing their roots because many obviously do not know their own birth names. Some foreign countries (for example, England, Scotland, Israel, and Finland) open adoption records to adult adoptees. In the United States the system is more rigid. Although the laws governing adult adoptees are gradually changing, in most states adoption files are forever sealed, not to be opened unless an adult adoptee can show good cause and then only by court order—an order rarely given.

Still, during the past decades many adult adoptees have been increasingly successful at finding their natural parents, using the techniques of genealogical research. For example, one woman with only the surname Elliott and the information that her mother started college in 1940, wrote over 500 letters to New England colleges, inquiring about a young woman of that name who entered the freshman class of 1940. "I am searching the genealogy of the Elliott family," she wrote. Actually, this ruse masked her real purpose, which was to find out more about her natural mother's identity, information she could obtain in no other way. She was able to learn her mother's hometown and eventually trace her thirty years later to New York City.

Another adoptee, a college professor, found his mother after a ten-year search, which included many visits with child-welfare officials, from whom he demanded more information. The officials, somewhat intimidated, yielded one or two small scraps of information during each visit—information he eventually put together to find his mother.

Searching for natural parents has nothing to do with whether or not an adoptee loves his or her adopted parents. "A natural genealogical curiosity," says Los Angeles psychiatrist Arthur D. Sorosky, "is felt by even the most successful adopted." Everyone wants to know all there is to know about himself or herself. But adoption and government agencies have made finding natural parents difficult at best.

If you have any information *at all* about your birth identity, such as surname or birthplace or birth date, you can get some help from the following reference books found in most libraries, which tell you where such records are and how you can gain access to them: *Adoption Directory*, from Gale Research, Inc.; Jayne Askin's *Search: A Handbook for Adoptees and Birthparents*, from Oryx Press; and *You Can Find Anyone*, by Eugene Fararo. In addition, Val D. Greenwood's *The Researcher's Guide to American Genealogy* (see bibliography) may be helpful because it is one of the few genealogical research books that deals with *twentieth century* records, specifically vital statistics.

The principal agency helping adoptees in their search is ALMA (Adoptees' Liberty Movement Association), P.O. Box 727, Radio City Station, New York, NY 10101. You may telephone them at 212-581-1568 or find them on the Web at *www.almanet.com* for member and registry databank information. Founded by adoptee Florence Fisher after her successful twenty-year-long search for her mother, ALMA helps natural parents and adoptees find each other.

The registry databank is maintained for relatives who do not know each other's current names or addresses but who know the date of birth, sex, and place of birth of the adoptee. Because both natural parents and adoptees use the service, some matches and subsequent reunions have occurred, including Jeanie Jackson who runs the databank. She found her birth family shortly after registering.

ALMA also acts as a clearinghouse for research tips. Hundreds of adoptees have discovered research methods that work and have written to ALMA with their finds. These are disseminated to other ALMA members and passed along to members at Search Workshops in New York City.

Start your research at your own public library to see what resources they have to help you. Go into the automated catalog under the Subject option and type "adopt." To further refine your research check what is under subject headings "Adoption—Identification" and "Adoptees—United States—Identification."

Also, there is a world of help for the adoptee on the World Wide Web. I entered "adoptees search" and scrolled through dozens of sites such as the Adoptees Resources Home Page (*http://psy.ucsd.edu/~jhartang/adoptees.html*), which has dozens of links to other helpful sites, and is especially strong on adoption laws. I used my search engine "Excite," although any search engine will give you similar results.

Another site adoptees won't want to miss is BirthQuest (*www.access.digex.net/-vqi/top.html*). You're free to search the site by birth date, but there is a charge to post your own information. Twenty-two-year-old Michigan resident Carolyn McKee found her birth mother at BirthQuest the first time she searched the site. Reu-Net (*www.reunion.com*) also matches people by their postings for a fee. There will be much more about searching the Web in chapter 10.

If you have some basic personal information, such as name and birthplace, you can continue your search by using good genealogical records search techniques (outlined in this book) to find your natural parents, and from them go on to your ancestors. If you have been denied even the knowledge of your own name, you should contact ALMA for help.

As this book is being written, ALMA is readying a lawsuit to challenge constitutionally the sealed record laws that keep adoptees from their birth families. You can learn the progress of this suit at their Web site.

Native American

Many tribal councils formed since 1934 have detailed enrollment records. These rolls usually give the Indian name, "English" name, age, and family relationship.

If your ancestor was a member of the Choctaw, Chickasaw, Creek, Seminole, or Cherokee tribes, you can check with the Indian Archives of the Oklahoma Historical Society. They have the book

Final Rolls of the Citizens and Freedmen of the Five Civilized Tribes of Indian Territory, which lists tribal members by name, age, sex, degree of blood, and census card number. Another good reference is Emmet Starr's *Old Cherokee Families,* which is indexed alphabetically by surname.

Numerous other Native-American records are at the LDS library, and still others are at the National Archives, especially their Fort Worth, Texas, branch.

Church records are especially important if you have Indian ancestors because more often than not missionaries kept records of Indians they converted. Some church records, particularly the Spanish Catholic records, date from the early 1500s and detail christenings and births, marriages, deaths, and burials. Beyond the essential vital statistics, these records often list clues to occupations and places of residence.

C. A. Weslager, professor of history at Brandywine College and an authority on the Delaware tribe, suggests that, in addition to knowing special records sources, it is advisable to become familiar with the native customs of your ancestral tribe. However, even at that, he feels it is virtually impossible to trace lineage beyond the time when English surnames were adopted—at least if you are looking in the 1700s beyond the reach of oral family-history traditions. But tracing beyond 1700 is not easy for any genealogist and shouldn't discourage you. Three hundred years of personal history is still a major achievement.

Dr. Weslager identifies naming practices as one of the two major problems in tracing Native American ancestors. The other is kinship systems. A family historian with such a line should determine tribal kinship terminology before attempting a records search. In some tribes, the words for "brother" or "sister" could also mean "cousin"; the words for "father" or "mother" also meant "uncle" or "aunt."

A good guide to repositories of Indian records is *Reference Encyclopedia of the American Indian,* by A. Klein, but the California Indian Library Collections and the Native American Research collections from the Library of Michigan are also helpful.

A major source today for Native-American genealogists, as it is for all family historians, is cyberspace. Two sites, in particular, are crammed with amazing resources. One is Cyndi's List for Native Americans, at *www.oz.net/~cyndihow/native.htm*. Besides links to general resource sites, you'll find mailing lists, professional researchers, publications, some extracts from actual vital-statistics records, and a long list of tribal and nation resources. You should also try *www.mcn.net/~aminlnks.html* for a link to the American Indian Tribal Directory and Indian Country Today Online. One final site I'll mention here, but certainly not the last one you could search, is America Online's *www.members.aol.com/bbbenge/front.html*. This site contains a link to Native American bookstores, maps, and tribal home pages, plus help for American-Indian adoptees.

African-Americans

Although Alex Haley, with his monumental work *Roots*, brought African-American genealogy into sharp focus, he is not the first to be highly conscious of his family's past. For example, in his autobiography, *Dusk of Dawn*, W. E. B. DuBois, founder of the National Association for the Advancement of Colored People (NAACP), traced his genealogy back to the seventeenth century. The poet James Weldon Johnson, in his book, *Along This Way*, traced his ancestors back to uprisings in the West Indies in the late 1700s. Robert Russa Moton, former president of Tuskegee Institute, in his autobiography, *Finding a Way Out*, writes with deep sensitivity of his grandfather, a proud African chieftain engaged in slaving, who fell victim to the trade himself.

Although more and more libraries are collecting works on the 15 million black Africans brought to America, the major library for black family historians (outside of the National Archives—discussed in the next chapter) is the Schomburg Center for Research in Black Culture, 515 Malcolm X Blvd., New York, NY 10037, telephone 212-491-2203, or go to their Web site at *www. nypl.org/research/sc/sc.html* and click on their Online Multimedia Samplers or Selected Internet Sources on Africa and the African Diaspora. The center itself has a number of useful tools, including a complete set of the federal population censuses from 1790 to 1890, which, most importantly, includes the slave schedules. It also has valuable papers, pictures, and other memorabilia of prominent black families; the ten-volume encyclopedia, *The Negro Heritage Library*; and extensive church and military records valuable to African-American ancestor hunters. In addition, its collection contains specialized histories such as *The Negroes of South Carolina*, a half century of African-American periodicals, and the Harry A. Williamson collection of *Negro Masonry*.

The Schomburg Center will act as a repository for any family histories that African-American ancestor hunters compile. If you decide to deposit a copy of your research with the center, you will know that your work has helped to illuminate what historian Wyatt Tee Walker has called the "cultural blackout" for the African American in America.

In the South, state archives, probate court records (which house wills), and county records are good places to look for the "owner" of slave ancestors. Plantation owners' wills, especially, listed slaves by specific names (something the federal census did not do until 1870) and often contained bits of narrative about slaves' personalities. A deed to the slave (who was considered property) was filed by the owner at the county courthouse.

Because many slaves were not able to read and write (indeed, were forbidden to learn), most slave records in the South are owners' property records. A great collection of these plantation daybooks, auctioneers' sales charts, slave registrations, and even insurance policies on slaves—can be found in the state archives of many southern states, and at Louisiana State University, Department of Archives, Baton Rouge, LA 70803, telephone 504-388-2217, or *www.lib.lsu.edu/index.html*.

As a general rule African-American family historians with northern ancestors will find a number of published records, particularly in Philadelphia, the city that had the highest concentration of black population prior to 1900. Early Philadelphia newspapers published marriage, birth, and death notices of "free people of colour." The obituaries are, as usual, the best source for mining family genealogical detail.

Other Philadelphia records are listed in Jane Aitken's *Census Directory for 1811*, the first census to enumerate African-Americans; Lebanon Cemetery records for the earliest chartered African-American cemetery; and voting lists prior to the disfranchisement of free African-Americans by the Pennsylvania legislature in 1838. A final separate Philadelphia census was taken in 1838 by Benjamin Bacon and Charles Gardner and included intriguing material on occupations, religious affiliations, and even family life.

The Historical Society of Pennsylvania, 1300 Locust Street, Philadelphia, PA 19107, telephone 215-732-6201, *www.libertynet.org / ~pahist/*, has early material considered by many to be among the most important sources for the African-American family historian. A full list is available in its printed catalog, *Afro-Americana, 1553–1906*, and some information can be accessed at their Web site. The rare records include:

- An extensive collection of manumissions (freedom papers) and indentures (extremely valuable because they contain information on African background)

- Papers of the Pennsylvania Abolition Society

- Collection of the American Negro Historical Society

- Letters, pamphlets, and books by African-Americans and abolitionists from 1500s to the Civil War

- Records of the first (founded in Philadelphia) Bethel African Methodist-Episcopal Church.

In addition, you should be aware of the African American Genealogy Group, P.O. Box 1798, Philadelphia, PA 19105, telephone 215-572-6063, *www.libertynet.org/aagg/*. They have an on-line surname list and other aids.

While you're on the Web, check out the Afrigeneas site at *www.msstate.edu/archives/history/afrigen/*. They have a surnames home page, archival postings, a bibliography, and links to African-

American genealogy resources. For other African-American genealogy home pages try *www.mindspring.com/~sapart/links.html* and Cyndi's List of Genealogy Sites on the Internet (African American), *www.oz.net/ ~cyndihow/african.htm.*

Chinese-Americans

For Chinese ancestors who landed in California during the last century, the best information is contained in Thomas W. Chinn's *Genealogical Sources of Chinese Immigrants.* This paper can be found in the LDS library in Salt Lake City or one of its many branches.

For other records (and even complete family genealogies), you should contact the Columbia University Starr East Asian Library, 300 Kent Hall, 2960 Broadway, New York, NY 10027, telephone 212-854-4318, *www.columbia.edu/cu/libraries/indiv/eastasian/staff/*; and Harvard University's Yenching Institute, the largest East Asian research center in the Western world, at 2 Divinity Avenue, Cambridge, MA 02138, telephone 617-495-3327, or access their home page at *www-hcl.harvard.edu/hyl/hylhome.html.*

The Chinese in Hawaii have an active genealogical organization in the Hawaii Chinese History Center, 111 North King Street, Room 410, Honolulu, HI 96817, telephone 808-521-5948. This group has put together a number of locally published booklets, which are invaluable guides for the Chinese-American family historian. The best one is Jean Bergen Ohai's *Chinese Genealogy and Family Book Guide.*

A special record source for Hawaiians of Chinese and Polynesian ancestry is the Aloha Chapter Memorial Library (Daughters of the American Revolution), 1914 Makiki Heights Drive, Honolulu, HI 96822, telephone 808-949-7256. Many Hawaiians have New England bloodlines reaching back to the *Mayflower,* owing to the presence on the islands of early whalers and missionaries.

The Chinese Culture Center, 750 Kearny Street, 3rd Floor, San Francisco, CA 94108, telephone 415-986-1822, has a special two-part program for young people searching for their roots: a year-long research project followed by a trip to China to the villages from which their ancestors emigrated. For more information, access *www.c-c-c.org/act/events98.html*. For a strictly cultural site, try *www.channela.com*.

Mexican-Americans

Consult the following extra sources for early Mexican ancestors.

1. Special state censuses for Arizona (1864, 1866, 1867, 1869) and for New Mexico and Colorado (1885), at the Arizona State Department Archives, 17 West Washington, Phoenix, AZ 85007, telephone 602-549-4159, or *www.dlapr.lib.az.us/archives/ardiv.html*. You can e-mail a research request from this site.

2. Three population censuses for New Mexico, now in the custody of the Historical Services Division, State Records Center and Archives, 404 Montezuma Street, Santa Fe, NM 87503, telephone 505-827-7331, or *www.nmculture.org/*.
   a. Spanish Colonial Census of 1790
   b. Mexican Colonial Census of 1823
   c. Mexican Colonial Census of 1845

3. Texas census schedules for 1829–36. The originals are in the Lorenzo De Zavala State Archives and Library Building, 1201 Brazos Street, Austin, TX 78701, telephone 512-463-5463, or *www.tsl.state.tx.us/lobby/genealogy.htm*. You can e-mail research requests from this helpful site, which has many links to other genealogical resources.

4. Printed work entitled *Origins of New Mexico Families in the Spanish Colonial Period*, by Angelico Chavez, a Catholic priest.

5. Roman Catholic church records in the Southwest, primarily registers of baptisms, marriages, and deaths.

6. The California State Library, 1020 "O" Street, Sacramento, CA 95814, telephone 916-653-7363, or *www.ss.gov/archives/*

archives_home.htm for data on early Spanish-Mexican colonial families.

For other on-line state library and archival information, you can access *www.yahoo.com/Government/States/.*

For a list of Hispanic/Latin American resources, go to *www.futureone.com/~jazz/genealogy/hispanic.htm.* This interesting Web site contains a link to Spanish Coats of Arms and the Judeo-Spanish home pages.

I've explained in this chapter how to search public records at the local, regional and state levels. In the next chapter I'll show you how to find your forebears in federal records.

CHAPTER 8

Finding Your Roots
Through Federal Records

THE HERITAGE of the Past is the seed that brings forth the Harvest of the Future." That is the inscription on the Pennsylvania Avenue side of the National Archives and Records Administration (NARA) in Washington, DC. And indeed it is true for the family historian; the incredibly rich store of data stowed by the federal government can give you a harvest of information about who you are and where you come from.

Here in the nation's capital is a wealth of census records, military records, veterans' pensions and bounty land grants, ships' passenger lists, naturalization records, and other materials. These are available not only through the NARA but also from the Immigration and Naturalization Service, the Veterans Administration, the Library of Congress, and the Smithsonian, all of which are headquartered in Washington.

Thus, if you want to find out about an ancestor and everyone who was living in his household, whether he homesteaded, what his military record was, and when he immigrated to America and from where, Washington is a great place to look. Let's start by showing you what's in the National Archives—the central depository for U.S. records.

THE NATIONAL ARCHIVES AND
RECORDS ADMINISTRATION

The National Archives is a colonnaded Greco-Roman building not far from the Capitol. Here, under a seventy-five-foot-high dome and enclosed in helium-filled brass cases are housed the Declaration of Independence along with the Constitution and the Bill of Rights, the Louisiana Purchase, the Homestead Act, the Monroe Doctrine and similar historical documents. Here also are field dispatches from General George Washington, written as hundreds of Revolutionary War soldiers, among them my g-g-great-grandfather, Corporal Peter Righter, were dying of battle wounds. Here also are the surrender papers from Appomattox, signed while my Confederate great-grandfather, Henry Jones, according to family legend, was escaping from the Yankees into the West Virginia mountains. (But documents retrieved from NARA told me that Henry Jones had deserted and turned himself in to a Union stockade; obviously not a story he wanted to pass on to his descendants.)

As you view the priceless records in this building you clearly see that the history of this country is really the history of countless average families, and that we are, all of us, part of it.

After looking over the original documents in the National Archives building that recorded the founding of this country, you will be ready to go ahead with the search for your own history.

Enter the Pennsylvania Avenue side of the National Archives, sign in with the guard, and go to room 200-B, where you will be asked to complete an application and are given a researcher's identification card (good for two years) and a kit of pamphlets about the archives' genealogical records and their uses. An experienced staff member will direct you to proper sources in the reading rooms.

If you can't travel to Washington, that doesn't lock you out of these records. You can write to the National Archives and Records Administration at Seventh St. and Pennsylvania Ave., N.W., Washington, DC 20408 or telephone 1-800-234-8861 for their free genealogy packet. Visit their extensive Web site at *www.nara.gov*, where you'll find a detailed listing of their thirteen regional branches, including their holdings and how to gain access to them.

National Archives—New
  England Region
380 Trapelo Road
Waltham, MA 02154
617-647-8100; e-mail
archives@waltham.nara.gov
*Records for Maine, New
Hampshire, Vermont, Massachu-
setts Rhode Island, and
Connecticut*

National Archives—Pittsfield
  Region
100 Dan Fox Drive
Pittsfield, MA 02101
413-445-6885; e-mail
archives@pittsfield.nara.gov
*Census, military, bounty land
warrants, naturalization,
passenger arrival, and court
records for New England area*

National Archives—Northeast
  Region
201 Varick Street
New York, NY 10014
212-337-1300; e-mail
archives@newyork.nara.gov.
*Records for New York, New Jersey,
Puerto Rico, and the U.S. Virgin
Islands*

National Archives—Mid
  Atlantic Region
Ninth and Market Streets
Philadelphia, PA 19107
215-597-3000; e-mail
archives@philarch.nara.gov
*Records for Pennsylvania,
Delaware, Maryland, Virginia,
and West Virginia*

National Archives—Great Lakes
  Region
7358 South Pulaski Road
Chicago, IL 60629-5898
773-581-7816; e-mail
archives@chicago.nara.gov
*Records for Illinois, Indiana,
Michigan, Minnesota, Ohio, and
Wisconsin*

National Archives—Central
  Plains Region
2312 East Bannister Road
Kansas City, MO 64131
816-926-6272; e-mail
archives@kansascity.nara.gov.
*Records for Iowa, Kansas,
Minnesota, Missouri, Nebraska,
North Dakota, and South
Dakota*

National Archives—Southwest
  Region
501 West Felix Street, Building 1
Fort Worth, TX 76115
817-334-5525; e-mail
archives@ftworth.nara.gov
*Records for Texas, Arkansas,
Oklahoma, and Indian Territory
documents*

National Archives—Rocky
  Mountain Region
Denver Federal Center,
Building 48
Denver, CO 80225
303-236-0817; e-mail
archives@denver.nara.gov
*Records for Colorado, Montana,
New Mexico, North Dakota,
South Dakota, Utah, and
Wyoming with special collections
of homesteading and mining
documents*

National Archives—Southeast
  Region
1557 St. Joseph Avenue
East Point, GA 30344
404-763-7477; e-mail
archives@atlanta.nara.gov

National Archives—Pacific
  Southwest Region
24000 Avila Road

Laguna Niguel, CA 92677
714-360-2641; e-mail
archives@laguna.nara.gov
*Records for Arizona, southern
California, and Clark County,
Nevada*

National Archives—Pacific
  Sierra Region
1000 Commodore Drive
San Bruno, CA 94066
650-876-9009; e-mail
archives@sanbruno.nara.gov.
*Records for northern California,
Guam, Hawaii, Nevada (except
Clark County), American
Samoa, and the Trust Territory of
the Pacific Islands*

National Archives—Pacific
  Northwest Region
6125 Sand Point Way N.E.
Seattle, WA 98115
206-526-6507; e-mail
archives@seattle.nara.gov

National Archives—Alaska
  Region
654 West Third Avenue
Anchorage, AL 99501
907-271-2441; e-mail
archives@alaska.nara.gov.
Records for Alaska

Each branch has a library of National Archives microfilm rolls, and all have the federal population census schedules, a basic reference library, computers, microfilm readers, and document reproducing machines. Material common to most of the branches are records of U.S. district courts and courts of appeals, and records of the Bureau of Customs and the Office of Engineers for their districts. Each branch also contains specialized collections for its region; for example, Al Capone in Chicago and Bonnie and Clyde in Fort Worth.

Each branch will answer mail and on-line inquiries about the documents in their control if given specific information to help with their records search. Luckily for ancestor hunters, research can be initiated by telephone, mail, or electronic mail (e-mail).

For more detailed information about branch holdings access the NARA Web site, or write Washington, DC, for the free pamphlet "Regional Branches of the National Archives."

What can you expect to find in the National Archives in Washington? As a brand-new researcher, you are entitled to a consultation with a staff research aide (the three I talked with had a cumulative experience of over 100 years at the Archives), who will direct you to the proper sources in the reading rooms.

You will be in good company. Barbara Tuchman worked there on her biography of General Stilwell, the late Senator Sam Ervin loved looking through Revolutionary War records, film star Robert Redford boned up on the Old West there, and author Bruce Catton often researched Civil War material in the reading rooms.

Alex Haley also first conceived the idea for *Roots* there. He visited the archives out of curiosity about the names of some slaves his grandmother had mentioned. Too embarrassed to ask about them, however, he just took a cursory look through the census records and, finding nothing, decided to leave. On his way out, he passed through the main reading room. "I was struck by all those people intently scrutinizing old documents," he wrote. "It occurred to me that they were really trying to find out *who* they were." He went back to the microfilms and, after hours of searching, finally found the entry for his great-grandfather, "Tom Murray—black."

Someday, you may be able to access most records right from your personal computer, but that day is not here yet. NARA says it will be many years before electronic access to a significant portion of their genealogical records is possible. In the meantime, they've made it much easier to find our ancestors than it has ever been before.

MAKING SENSE OUT OF THE CENSUS

Haley's breakthrough came while searching census schedules—something nearly every ancestor hunter can find gold in. The census, which first began in 1790 and for which records are available to you up to 1920 (the ones after that are kept confidential by the restrictions of the 1974 Privacy Act), can give you a great deal of information, such as the following:

1. You ancestors' occupations

2. Their immigration or migratory patterns—something you can put on a map and place in your Family History Book

3. The property—land and farms they owned, and their whereabouts

4. The increase or decrease in your family from decade to decade

5. Which people died and at what ages

6. Whether someone remarried and had two distinct families in one household

You might even be able to trace your family back one more generation if you have not been able to do so from local and family records. For instance, say you know an ancestor was forty years old in 1880 and lived in a particular county, but you don't know his parents' names. By looking for his surname in the 1850 census (when he would have been ten years old), you might then be able to find the names of the people heading the household he lived in—his parents. With such information you can flesh out the bones of information you have acquired elsewhere.

If you know the county and state in which an ancestor was living during the year a census was taken, you can obtain census information about him (up to 1920) in several ways:

1. Through the LDS library and its branches, which give you access to most census rolls up to 1920.

2. Through regional branches of the National Archives, which have all census microfilm rolls. They can give you the number of the microfilm roll containing information about your forebear, and you can arrange to borrow that roll from the National Archives branch.

3. Through state libraries, which often have copies of the federal census for their states.

4. By buying the exact census microfilm roll you want and finding a local library with a microfilm reader (which should not be too difficult). The way you do this is first to determine the roll number of the census you want by checking the National Archives booklet "Federal Population Censuses, 1790–1920" (a catalog of microfilm copies of the schedules). You will find order blanks in the back of this booklet.

A good reference on the early federal census is Caroll D. Wright's *The History and Growth of the United States Census, 1790–1890.* (Write to the National Archives and Records Service, Publications Distribution, Room G9, Dept. P, Washington, DC 20408 for a copy or call their toll-free telephone number, 1-800-234-8861, for their price list for other publications valuable to ancestor hunters.)

Here is one good way to search through census records:

1. Start with the most recent census—in this case, the one for 1920—and follow your family back through the earlier censuses as far as you can.

2. For every census available, there are genealogical census work sheets, which will make it easier for you to take information off the microfilms. (Most genealogy clubs or bookstores will have them available or you can easily make your own.) I often copy the information onto a Family Group Sheet and place it directly into my Family History Book. Why do double work?

3. To get an idea of the changes in your family line's structure during the censuses from 1790 to 1920—assuming you are tracing a family line that extends back into this early period in America—use a United States Census Summary Chart like the one shown in Figure 6, p. 114.

4. Take down *all* census data listed about your ancestral family whether you can use it now or not. Later some stray fact could prove important.

5. Watch for different surname spellings. A name could change every ten years, since early census takers weren't always careful about spelling.

6. Since prior to 1920 America was full of small towns where people of the same surname might well be related to one another, when searching census rolls you should extract all information for different families with your surname. It's not unusual to find a family connection later.

7. Do not assume that all children listed in one household in the censuses of 1850, 1860, and 1870 were necessarily members of the same family. They might have been nephews, cousins, even servants. It was not until 1880 that census takers listed all members by their relationship to the head of the household.

8. Finally, allow for some errors. In the early days, heads of households thought census takers were tax collectors in disguise. The census takers may thus have written down erroneous information from neighbors, failed to count people too difficult to reach, and even invented people—a practice that was especially prevalent when census takers were paid by the number of families they canvassed. In short, census information is not necessarily conclusive.

Mortality schedules—which are a census extract—taken from the 1850 through the 1880 censuses are particularly valuable aids to the family historian because they answer the question of who died within the twelve months preceding the taking of the census. This helps you pinpoint a death date, which can lead you to other records, such as the cemetery or the records of the probate court, discussed in chapter 7. You can discover just how these mortality schedules were taken for your research locale in "The Mortality Schedules," *National Genealogical Society Quarterly*, June 1943, a publication found in libraries with genealogical collections. See Figure 7, page 115, for information contained on all these federal census schedules.

The Bureau of the Census does not provide general genealogical information as such, relying on the National Archives as its depository except for the brief search mentioned below. For more information about the bureau you may access their Web site at *www.census.gov*.

The Censuses from 1790 to the Present—in Reverse Order

The Present. The federal Privacy Act of 1974 forbids the release of federal records if they are less than seventy-two years old. Thus, if your parents or grandparents immigrated to the United States after 1920, you should write for a census search to the Personal Census Search Unit, Bureau of the Census, P.O. Box 1545, Jeffersonville, IN 47131, telephone 812-285-5314. You will be sent a form to complete (the government doesn't do anything without a form, of course) and asked for an advance fee. For this fee, the bureau staff will copy the personal information—such as age, place of birth, and citizenship—from your ancestor's census records.

1920 and 1910. These latest census releases give the family historian valuable information, which includes the birthplace of the parents of each person. For a list of the thirty-two questions asked in 1910, go to *www.firstct.com/fv/1910.html* and for the twenty-eight questions in 1920, *www.firstct.com/fv/1920.html*. See Figure 7, page 115, for the first time the census asked for specific information.

1900. The 1900 census, released in 1976 from most of the restrictions imposed under the Privacy Act, was a source most genealogists had been waiting for, since it was the first census to give *exact month and year of birth* of every person in the United States. You will find this census, a project of the WPA from the 1930s, completely indexed by state and surname.

1890. This census was almost completely destroyed in 1921 by a fire in the basement of the Commerce Department building. An index at the National Archives and major genealogical libraries lists the names of householders in the few surviving schedules. Also escaping the fire was a portion of the 1890 census dealing with Union Civil War veterans and their widows. This special census answers such questions as veteran's rank, company, regiment or vessel, dates of enlistment and discharge, length of service, disability and assumed name if the veteran enlisted under one.

1880. This census was the first to give the relationship of family member to the head of the household, as well as the birthplace of the parents of each person listed. Such information can often push one's family history back another generation, to his immigrant ancestor's foreign birthplace. The 1880 census (and all subsequent surviving census records) is also indexed alphabetically by family name under the Soundex or Miracode system, methods of indexing that use the sound

Figure 6
EXAMPLE OF UNITED STATES
CENSUS SUMMARY CHART

Name of Family:	1790	1800	1810	1820	1830	1840	1850	1860	1870	1880	1900	1910	1920
Husband's Name:													
Wife's Name:													
Children's names:													

Summary of Where Family Resided When Census Taken

Where Taken

Date Census	
1790	
1800	
1810	
1820	
1830	
1840	
1850	
1860	
1870	
1880	
1890*	
1900	
1910	
1920	

*1890 Census destroyed by fire

Figure 7
INFORMATION CONTAINED ON
FEDERAL POPULATION CENSUS SCHEDULES

QUESTION	1790	1800	1810	1820	1830	1840	1850	1860	1870	1880	1890*	1900	1910	1920
1. Name of head of family	X	X	X	X	X	X	X	X	X	X	X			
2. Number of free white males	X	X	X	X	X	X								
3. Number of free white females	X	X	X	X	X	X								
4. Place of residence	X	X	X	X	X	X	X	X	X	X	X			
5. Number of foreigners, not naturalized				X	X									
6. Name of each family member							X	X	X	X	X			
7. Age of each family member							X	X	X	X	X			
8. Month and year of birth											X			
9. Sex of each family member							X	X	X	X	X			
10. Value of real estate								X	X					
11. Whether married within the year							X	X	X	X				
12. Whether deaf, dumb, blind, insane					X	X	X	X	X	X				
13. Whether a pauper or convict							X	X						
14. Whether attended school							X	X	X	X	X			
15. Whether read or write						X	X	X	X	X	X			
16. Whether father or mother of foreign birth									X	X				
17. Month of birth, if born within year									X	X				
18. Relationship to head of family										X	X			
19. Marital status										X	X			
20. Birthplace of mother and father										X	X			
21. Number of months unemployed in year										X	X			
22. Occupation							X	X	X	X	X			
23. Whether sick or temporarily disabled										X				
24. Whether permanently disabled										X				
25. Color of each family member							X	X	X	X	X			
26. Number of years married											X			
27. Mother of how many children											X			
28. How many children living											X			
29. Year of immigration to U.S.											X			
30. Whether speak English											X	X	X	X
31. Ownership of home											X			
32. Civil War veteran												X		
33. Family Identification Number												X	X	
34. County of residence												X	X	

* The 1890 census was destroyed by fire.

of the surname as well as the first letter. Vowels have been dropped and replaced with a number code. It makes perfect sense after you're used to it, but in the beginning ask your librarian for help.

1870. This was the first federal decennial census to list African- Chinese- and Native Americans by name. This census also shows the month of birth of all citizens born within the year and month of marriage, if married within the year.

1860 and 1850. The information on the 1860 census was much the same as in 1850, which was considerably broadened in scope over prior censuses. Here for each *free* person in a household—not just the head of the house, as in earlier censuses—there was the name, postal address, age, sex, color (white, black, or mulatto), occupation (if the person was over fifteen years of age), value of real estate owned, place of birth, and whether or not the person was married within the year. For each slave an entry gave the name of the owner, the age, sex, and color (but not the name) of the slave, and whether or not he was a fugitive. There was also information on the number of slaves freed by each owner. The 1850 census has been computerized by the LDS genealogical library and is available through LDS branches in book form, indexed by name—a tremendously important tool, making the work of family historians much easier.

1840. In 1840 questions about military pensioners (especially of the Revolutionary War) were added to the census and printed separately by the Department of State in *A Census of Pensioners for Revolutionary or Military Services.* This is available through the LDS library and its branches.

1830. The 1830 census shows family members broken down by five-year age groups for those under twenty years old, and ten-year age groups for those over twenty.

1820. In 1820, in addition to name of head of family, and number of free white males and females, householders were asked about aliens in the family unit.

1810, 1800, 1790. The 1790 census was the first census, and the next two censuses were much the same. If you have traced any line back to before 1800, you have a good chance of finding your ancestor among the four million people counted in the 1790 census. It is indexed by surname and state and published in book form, and is available at the National Archives and in most libraries with genealogical collections. Only the heads of families are actually named, but all other free white males and females and slaves are counted. Unfortunately, the schedules for much of Virginia, Delaware, Georgia, Kentucky, New Jersey, and Tennessee were lost when the British burned Washington, DC, during the War of 1812. Parts of these schedules were later reconstructed from state tax lists.

An invaluable aid in researching 1790 census records is E. Kay Kirkham's *Research in American Genealogy*, which reproduces Bureau of the Census maps for that period. Kirkham also computed the frequency with which your family name appears in the 1790 census, so you can tell at a glance how many families in what states comprised your 1790 family surname tree.

MILITARY RECORDS, VETERANS' PENSIONS, AND BOUNTY LAND GRANTS

Finding your ancestor's military record will add to your family history in two ways. First, it is often a good way to locate male ancestors if you cannot find deeds, wills, or census records. (This is especially true if they were of military age during a major war.) Second, military records can include accounts of your forebear's military exploits, which help make your Family History Book more colorful and valuable to you.

If you want a copy of your ancestor's military service record for your Family History Book or to fulfill requirements for joining a patriotic organization, this is what you should do:

1. Telephone the National Archives at their toll-free number, 800-234-8861, and ask for a copy of NATF Form 80. If you are

in a hurry, ask them to fax the form to you, fill it out, and fax it back to fax number 202-501-7170.

2. Complete the form with the name of the veteran, war in which he fought (if Civil War, whether Union or Confederate), and state from which he enlisted. (Don't despair if you have few facts to go on. The National Archives audiovisual specialists have been able to compare the uniform in the photo of a Civil War veteran with others on file and come up with the exact military unit and the veteran's complete service record.)

3. Add any other information that will help the National Archives locate your ancestor's file—for example, his unit (regiment, company, ship); birth date; date and place of death; and whether he claimed bounty land or a military pension.

National Archives staff members will make a search of their files, notify you if they have photocopies of your ancestor's records, and bill you ten dollars. (Or you may use your credit card when filing the form. If they find nothing, there is no charge for the search.)

For more facts on the military records in the National Archives, write for their free pamphlet, GIL 7, "Military Service Records in the National Archives of the United States." For records of military service and pensions after 1914 ask the National Archives, using their toll-free telephone number, for Standard Form 180. (You must, however, be the veteran or next of kin.)

Although the archives' military records contain everything from Mathew Brady's Civil War photos to Admiral Perry's reports on the opening of Japan for trade to George Washington's Revolutionary War expense accounts, chances are you will have to dig deep for records of older military ancestors, since fires in Washington destroyed many Revolutionary War records. But the archives has some remaining military records dating from 1775 to 1800, with the majority dating from 1800 to 1912. Many Union and Confederate veterans also have their service records in the National Archives, which list rank, age, place of enlistment, and often complete service. Other files on veterans of the Confederacy can be located in state archives and southern historical societies. Don't overlook the records of old soldiers' homes, where I found the military history of one of my Confederate ancestors written in his own hand to prove his eligibility to enter the home.

A partial list of National Archives military records is given in the box on page 120.

If you have traced a military veteran ancestor, a pension or land-grant file could very well offer the high point of your whole search. Many of these records are literally crammed with affidavits from relatives, old comrades-in-arms, and even whole pages torn from family Bibles—all material needed to justify the veteran's claims. The birth dates, marriage dates, birthplaces, lists of children, and other scraps of family history buried in those files can even provide you with a nearly complete genealogy of two or three key generations.

Pensions and land-grant applications after military service in the early days of the country contain the most genealogical information of all military records in the National Archives. The National Archives has millions of pension records for the period from the Revolutionary War through the Indian wars of the late 1880s.

Bounty land claims were based on military service between 1776 and 1855. Originally these land grants were made by land-rich but money-poor state governments as a way of paying off their militia after the Revolutionary War. Colonels got up to 500 acres and privates 100 acres of prime western wilderness (my ancestor Corporal William Barnes got 160 acres in 1781, of which I still own 12.7 acres), a method of payment that quickly filled the back country of Virginia, North Carolina, Pennsylvania, and New York.

Both pension and bounty land-warrant application files usually show name, rank, and military unit of the veteran, plus his place of residence and often a detailed description of his battlefield service.

To obtain a copy of your ancestor's pension or bounty land-grant files (or to see if your ancestor, his widow, or dependents filed any such claims) check the appropriate box at the top of Form NATF 80. One family historian discovered he had a Revolutionary War hero for an ancestor with a file thick with valuable family documents, which had been gathering dust in Washington, D.C., for more than 150 years.

Many of these Revolutionary War pension records have been microfilmed by the LDS library and are available through its branches. You may be able to view the file before ordering it from the National Archives.

A full listing of pension, bounty-land, and homestead (land grants after 1862) records can be found in the National Archives publication "Guide to Genealogical Records in the National Archives," available for a small charge.

PARTIAL LIST OF MILITARY RECORDS AT THE NATIONAL ARCHIVES

- Regular Army service records, 1800–1912

- Commissioned Army officer records, 1805–1917

- Commissioned Navy officer records, 1794–1930

- Marine officer records, 1798–1941

- Army officer correspondence to the Adjutant General's office, 1805–1917

- Army muster rolls, 1784–1912

- Register of Army commissions, 1792–1899

- Civil War staff officers

- Military histories of officers, 1789–1903

- United States Military Academy records, 1805–1917

- Records of Annapolis appointees, 1862–1922 ➤

- Army enlistment papers for enlisted men, 1800

- Marine enlisted service records, 1798–1895

- Navy service record for enlisted men, 1798–1919

- Books, manuscripts, and photostats relating to soldiers, wagon masters, and others, 1775–98

- Pay records

- Payrolls of vessels, 1798–1844

- Military service records of volunteers

- Records of the War of 1812

- Records of the Indian wars, 1817–58

- Records of the Mexican War, 1846–48

- Records of naval apprentices, boys aged thirteen to eighteen, 1837–89

- Records of the Civil War, 1861–65

- Records of the Spanish-American War, 1899–1901

- Records of the Philippine Insurrection, 1899–1903

- Prisoner of war records

- Civil War draft records

- Burial records of soldiers, 1862–1939

- Service files for Revenue Cutter and Life-Saving Services and the Bureau of Lighthouses (which became the Coast Guard in 1915), 1791–1929

SHIPS' PASSENGER LISTS
AND NATURALIZATION RECORDS

Passenger lists are a means of determining when your ancestors came to this country and, in some cases, include their native countries. As you can imagine for a nation with the massive, long-term flow of immigration of the United States, these lists are far from complete.

The National Archives has passenger-arrival lists for ninety-five Atlantic and Gulf of Mexico ports. Some of the lists date back to 1798, but most of them are for the years 1820 to 1945. There are many gaps, indeed whole decades are missing from some of these lists. And many lists do not have complete information concerning passengers— names are illegible, occupations are omitted, and so on—but they remain a major source for family historians to check when looking for immigrant ancestors.

The original lists were prepared on board ship by the captain of the vessel and filed later with the collector of customs when the ship reached port. You will find the following information in them: names of vessel and master, and port of embarkation; date and port of arrival; name of passenger, age, sex, and occupation; name of country or countries from which he came, and country to which he was going. If he died en route, the date and circumstances of his death were recorded.

Fewer than 1 percent of passenger records from 1790 to 1820 survive. For a bibliography of early passenger lists you should look at A. Harold T. Lancour's *Passenger Lists of Ships Coming to North America, 1538–1825*, which can be consulted at the New York City Public Library. (A few of the most easily accessible lists for early immigrants can be found at the end of this book.) From 1820 to 1919, the National Archives has many, if incomplete, ships' passenger lists. Most passenger records dating after 1919 are located in the Department of Immigration and Naturalization, 425 "I" Street N.W., Washington, DC 20536, telephone 202-514-2000 or *www.ins.usdoj.gov/*.

The National Archives will search their passenger list indexes for you if you can give them the passenger's full name, port of arrival, approximate date of arrival, and name of the vessel (helpful but not necessary if you have the other three facts).

For detailed information about East Coast and Gulf ports lists, consult the National Archives publication "Guide to Genealogical Records in the National Archives." (Some of the major ports of entry for immigrants and the extant passenger lists are given at the end of this book.)

The ships arriving in San Francisco during gold rush days came from the East Coast, from Panama, and directly from European and Chinese ports. Although these San Francisco passenger lists were destroyed by fire, San Francisco historian Louis J. Rasmussen has undertaken the monumental task of re-creating them from old San Francisco newspapers and other sources. Expected to be fifteen volumes when it's finished, the records have so far been published by San Francisco Historic Records under the title *San Francisco Passenger Lists*. The entire work covers the period 1850 to 1975 and lists both passengers and cargoes. The big help for family historians here is that Rasmussen has fully indexed the volumes by subject and surname, making it relatively easy to locate your ancestor. Rasmussen is also publishing an eighteen-volume work of passenger lists entitled *Railway Passenger Lists of Overland Trains to San Francisco and the West*, covering the period 1870 to 1890; it is indexed by train passengers' names.

If you are able to obtain ships' passenger information from the National Archives or any other source, you will have sufficient data to write to the Immigration and Naturalization Service and request a copy of your immigrant ancestor's naturalization petition. It will contain a wealth of family information such as birthplace and parents' names (be sure to ask for the entire file), and should lead you directly back to the ancestral homeland.

For more information about how naturalization records can help you in your ancestor search, see *Locating Your Immigrant Ancestor: A Guide to Naturalization Records*, by James C. Neagles and Lila Lee. If it's not in your nearest genealogical library, try to obtain it through interlibrary loan.

For a fascinating look at emigration and ship lists, you should access *www.geocities.com/Heartland/5978/Emigration.html*. It contains a treasure trove of information from 1635 to the twentieth century.

OTHER GOVERNMENT AIDS:
THE LIBRARY OF CONGRESS, SMITHSONIAN,
AND SERVICES FOR ETHNIC GROUPS

The National Archives hosts an annual genealogical seminar for advanced family historians with specialized classes taught by authorities in such fields as census records, legal records, military service, colonial handwriting, cartography, migration patterns, oral genealogy, and Spanish and French colonists. As is true of everything else it does, its archive classes are well worth the trouble of attending. (Branch libraries also hold regular genealogical workshops and classes.)

But the National Archives is not the only source of information. Within walking distance of its Washington headquarters are the Library of Congress and the Smithsonian Institution.

The Library of Congress, 101 Independence Avenue S.E., Washington, DC 20540-4660, researchers' telephone 202-707-5537, Web site at *http://lcweb.loc.gov/rr/genealogy/*, has a Local History and Genealogy Reading Room in the Thomas Jefferson Building which has 50,000 published family histories, one of the largest collections in the country. In addition, it has over 100,000 works on local American history, which give a great deal of information on early settlers, churches, and communities.

The Library of Congress is not a lending library and requires you to be at least eighteen and have a photo ID before you are allowed to search. Although the library cannot undertake involved searches for family or heraldic reformation, consultants are happy to point you in the right direction when you visit.

The LOC also has various name and place catalogs, including a coat-of-arms index plus a wealth of map, newspaper, and rare-book collections.

If you are unable to visit the Library of Congress in person, their Web site offers a short tutorial on what they have and how you can use it. You can also search on-line (*http://lcweb.loc.gov/catalog*) to discover if they have your family history in their collection. Then, by writing the LOC Photo Duplication Service, Washington, DC 20540-5230, you can obtain a photocopy. It may be the only one of its kind. While some family histories run to fewer than 200 pages, which would cost about fifty dollars (that's fifty cents for a double page) others run a great deal more. (My own "Eddy Family in America" contains over 1,000 pages plus supplements.) If this service would be too expensive, you may want to consider hiring a certified professional genealogist, who could go to the library and extract just the information you need for your ancestral line. (Or try an antiquarian bookseller to see if he or she can locate your family history at a reasonable price. Write the Antiquarian Booksellers Association of America, 50 Rockefeller Plaza, New York, NY 10020, telephone 212-757-9395, or for an on-line list of antiquarian dealers near you, go to *www.clark.net/pub/rmharris/ booknet1.html.*)

The Library of Congress has many reference guides to help you in your ancestor hunting, including guides to genealogical research, reference services, and facilities of the Local History and Genealogical Reading Room; and the best of these guides is accessible from the reading room's home page (see above).

Don't think the LOC is limited to United States research. They are particularly proud of their international collection, which can help most family historians no matter what their country of origin. The LOC serves a diversity of ancestor hunters—young, old, and of every ethnic and racial background. Its local history and genealogy reading room is one of the busiest of the twenty-one reading rooms in the library and can provide a number of family histories—British, Irish, German, and many others.

If you can't check on-line, the bibliography *Genealogies in the Library of Congress*, by Marion J. Kaminkow, is worth looking at to see if your family history has been placed in this library. For a listing of local directories, James C. Neagle's *Library of Congress: A Guide to Genealogical and Historical Research* is particularly recommended.

The Smithsonian Institution, really a complex of seven museums, does not contain genealogical information so much as samples of the

WHEN AND HOW TO HIRE A PRO

There are four occasions when you may want to consider hiring a professional genealogist:

1. When you seek research from a distant public institution or library and need an expert in the area.

2. When you wish to join a lineage society.

3. When you are ready to publish your family history and want to fill in some obscure or difficult lines.

4. When you don't have time to or don't wish to do your own research.

You can hire a professional genealogist by writing to the following: (a) the Board for Certification of Genealogists, P.O. Box 14291, Washington, DC 20044, (b) The Genealogical Society of the Church of Jesus Christ of Latter Day Saints, 54 East South Temple St., Salt Lake City, UT 84111, (c) libraries or genealogical societies in your research locale for a list of people familiar with their collection. The Board for Certification of Genealogists licenses American professional researchers for a five-year period. Applicants take an exhaustive examination. You can get an idea of its scope by checking their Web site at *www.genealogy. org/~beg/educ.html*. The LDS Genealogical Society certifies professional genealogists after equally comprehensive examinations for specific areas of the United States and for foreign countries in which they have a proven language ability. When you contact the accrediting agencies, they will send you (for a small fee) a list of names, addresses, and the specialties of all the professional genealogists currently on their rolls. Costs of professional genealogical services vary widely, generally starting at $10 per hour on up.

Choose a researcher in your research locale. If you are searching for early Virginians, for example, one with a specialty in records of the South will be the best selection. In your initial letter or telephone call, tell him or her what work you want done and ask these questions: ➤

1. Can you handle this assignment?

2. When can you begin work?

3. How often will you make reports?

4. What are your fees?

5. Are there ever extra charges? For what?

6. Do you require a deposit?

Most professional genealogists complain that queries are too vague. Here is what you should give them:

1. A precise statement of your objective. (For example, "I want to find the parents of Elizabeth Booher.") Or, if you have a general objective, such as tracing one line back as far as possible, be sure to send Pedigree Charts and Family Group Sheets. Send every known fact you can, including a record of any negative research so you won't have to pay twice for it.

2. Immediately reply to all correspondence from him or her. (Keep a copy so that you will have a record of your part of the transaction.)

3. Prompt payment of fees.

As the client, here is what you should expect:

1. A full, written report, citing sources of all new information.

2. Photostats or photocopies of marriage records, wills, birth certificates, and deeds.

3. An accounting of how your money was spent.

4. Report of any additional records found and an estimate of the cost of searching for them or obtaining copies.

Most professionals are honest and will usually give more than a fair return for their wages, but if you believe you have been the victim of ➤

WHEN AND HOW TO HIRE A PRO

(continued from page 127)

shoddy practice, you should report the incident to the source from which you received the referral.

In the wake of the astounding popularity of Alex Haley's *Roots*, persons and agencies involved in other lines of work—finding missing persons, people who skip out on their bills, and the like—tried to cash in on the genealogy boom. Most family historians are more savvy these days, but *caveat emptor* is still the watchword.

No professional can *guarantee* positive results, and in rare cases, you may end up paying to find out that there is nothing to find out. However, at least this will release your energies to search in some fascinating new directions.

actual tools, clothing, and weapons your ancestors may have used. When you look at a wooden plow covered with straps of iron, or a rigid pair of shoes (each shoe made to fit either foot), a lovingly carved bride's chest, ungainly long rifles, and delicate silver spoons, they give your vision of your forebears' lives more reality. If you can't get to Washington, the book A *Nation of Nations* is a Smithsonian catalog that will give you the feel of the everyday objects immigrant ancestors brought with them to America and the ones they found when they arrived. The Smithsonian has many publications regarding its collections, containing family traditions, anecdotes, old sayings, and biographical sketches. For a list write or call the Smithsonian Information, SI Building, Room 153, MRC 010, Washington, DC 20560, 202-357-2700, or access their informative Web site at *www.si.edu.organza.musovrvw/start.htm.*

SOME OTHER SPECIAL GOVERNMENT SOURCES

African-Americans, Chinese-Americans, Japanese-Americans, Mexican-Americans, and American Indians should take note of the following specific kinds of information:

Native Americans

Because of their special status as wards of the federal government, Native Americans have available to them a great many government records with which to trace their forebears.

Indeed, this kind of ancestor hunting might even provide a financial return. A $29.1 million government settlement went to satisfy the claims of the Yurok, Wintu, and other northern California tribes, and the Mesquakie tribe in the Midwest was awarded $6.6 million.

The National Archives is particularly strong on records of Native Americans who kept their tribal affiliations. Here is a general (but by no means complete) listing of tribal records in the Washington archives:

- Removal records, 1815–1850 (mostly of the Five Civilized Tribes—Cherokee, Chickasaw, Choctaw, Creek, and Seminole)

- Tribal enrollment records, 1827–present; annuity rolls, 1841–1959

- Land allotment records, 1856–1935

- Census rolls, 1884–1940 (arranged alphabetically by Indian agency, tribe, year, and name)

- Probate records (heirship papers, 1907–present, end wills, 1906–21)

- Carlisle Indian School reports, 1879–1918

- School census records, 1912–39

Most of the records are full of family history details such as both Native American and "English" name, sex, degree of Native American blood, names of family or guardian, tribal and "band" affiliation, residence, and occupation.

Any Native American who fought with federal troops may also have a record of veteran's benefits. The National Archives has in its military records section a separate alphabetical file for each Native American veteran who served prior to 1870.

One of the largest single collections of Native American genealogical material is located in the National Archival branch at 501 West Felix Street, Building 1, Fort Worth, Texas 76115. (A full list of their holdings can be obtained by writing Chief, Archives Branch, Federal Archives and Records Center at that branch or accessing their Web site [see earlier in this chapter].) Some of their material is microfilmed and available through interlibrary loan. In other words, the film could be borrowed by your local library for examination by you. A few of the documents valuable to Native American family historians at this branch are the following:

- Records of the Bureau of Indian Affairs, 1856–1952

- Kiowa Agency records, 1881–1952 (on Kiowa, Comanche, Wichita, Apache, Delaware, and Caddo Indians)

- Chilocco Indian School, 1890–1952

- Concho Agency, 1891–1952 (contains records for Cheyenne and Arapaho)

- Miami Agency, 1870–1952 (contains records for Seneca, Eastern Shawnee, Quapaw, Ottawa, Peoria, and Miami Wyandot; also for Captain Jack's band after the Modoc war and Chief Joseph's band of Nez Percé)

- Osage Agency, 1858–1952

- Pawnee Agency, 1870–1952 (contains records for Pawnee, Otoe, Kansa, Ponca, Kaw, and Tonkawa)

- Shawnee Agency, 1870–1952 (contains records for the Sac and Fox Indians)

Other published material the Native American family biographer will want to read are "American Indian Genealogical Research," by

Jimmy B. Parker in the *National Genealogical Society* quarterly, March 1975; "American Indian Records in the National Archives," by Edward E. Hill, a long paper presented at the 1969 World Conference on Records and available in most genealogical collections and at the LDS library or its branches. This booklet will also give you a good, basic understanding of the major changes in federal policies toward Native Americans over the years.

Every Native American family historian will want to access the special internet site called Cyndi's List of Genealogy Sites on the Internet (Native American) at *www.cyndislist.com/native.htm*, which lists dozens of resource sites, each of them having dozens more, a true bonanza for the Native American genealogist. Other rich sites can be accessed from A Barrel of Genealogy Links at *http://cpcug.org/user/jlacombe/mark.html*.

African-Americans

The National Archives has published "A Guide to Documents in the National Archives for African-American Studies," which encompasses black history in the United States, the West Indies, and Latin America.

There are also a number of plantation and slave sale records, a list of free heads of families mentioned in the 1790 census, and the federal census schedules for 1870 and after. If you are searching for slave ancestors, the 1880 census may lead you to owners' locations through parents' birthplaces and thus to even earlier generations.

You should also visit Cyndi's List of Genealogy Sites on the Internet (African-American) at *www.cyndislist.com/african.htm* for a large number of resources and hotlinks to African-American genealogical and historical societies, archives, libraries, bookstores, and slave records.

An additional Web site of interest is *www.mindspring.com/~sapart/links.html*, which will also take you to the Afrigeneas homepage, or you can go straight to *www.msstate.edu/Archives/History/afrigen/*. For general information, African-American ancestor hunters will find a great deal of help at the AlGenWeb site at *http://members.aol.com/blountal/Gen.html*. There are links to many other sites, each with more links, one with a searchable database of over 230,000 names of men who served in the United States Colored Troops.

Don't forget the African American Genealogy Group mentioned earlier at P.O. Box 1798, Philadelphia, PA 19105, telephone 215-572-6063, and its Web page(*www.libertynet.org/aagg/*), which has a sur-name list link.

Chinese-Americans

Chinese ancestry can be traced back to the 1870 census, when Chinese-Americans were listed for the first time.

Japanese-Americans

With the opening of the 1900 census, Japanese-Americans gained useful genealogical information, including place of birth in Japan if this is unknown to you.

Mexican-Americans

Of special value are the census schedules for Arizona, California, Colorado, New Mexico, and Texas, beginning with the 1850 census.

THE PATRIOTIC LINEAGE ORGANIZATIONS

If you have military forebears, membership records of patriotic heritage societies are sometimes an excellent source of genealogical information.

Most of these organizations keep files and pedigree information on members by surname and can add to your family history. In order to join these societies, whose aims are primarily educational and heritage preservation, an applicant must submit documented proof of descendance. To join the Daughters of the American Revolution, for instance, one must provide evidence that a forebear was a Revolutionary War soldier, sailor, or prominent patriot (man or woman).

Today the DAR and other lineage societies demand good genealogical proof before admitting applicants to membership, but such was not always the case. In earlier days, slipshod research got into DAR lineage books, and this earlier research is of little value to conscientious family historians today. For instance, Gilbert Doane, author of the respected *Searching for Your Ancestors*, tells the amusing story of a certain woman, prominent in her own city, who became a member of the DAR based on papers showing the service of one Hezekiah Royce. "Now it happened," Doane says, "that there were two Hezekiah Royces, one of whom was a notorious Tory and the other a brave young man who marched to the defense of Bennington in 1777. The lady's ancestor was actually the Tory Hezekiah."

It is doubtful that such a mistake could slip past the scrutiny of experienced genealogists who pass on DAR pedigrees today. Application papers must be accompanied by certified Bible or civil records and detailed data for each generation leading back to the Revolutionary War participant. Indeed, the DAR and other patriotic societies have done much in recent years to raise the standard of genealogical research to its present height.

The DAR and SAR (Sons of the American Revolution) maintain genealogical reference libraries and will answer mail queries, especially if you express an interest in membership.

Some patriotic and lineage societies you could consider as sources for your family tree research are as follows:

Colonial Dames
1300 New Hampshire Avenue, N.W.
Washington, DC 20036
202-293-1700
For female descendants of an ancestor who lived in one of the original colonies prior to 1701

Ladies of the Grand Army of the Republic
c/o Mrs. Elizabeth Koch,
National Secretary,
119 North Swarthmore Ave., Apt. 1H,
Ridley Park, PA 18078;
(*http://suvcw.org/lgar.htm*)

For female descendants of Union soldiers

National Society, Daughters of the American Revolution
1776 D Street, N.W.
Washington, DC 20006
202-628-1776; (*www.dar.org*)

For female descendants of Revolutionary War patriots

National Society, Sons of the American Revolution
c/o Executive Director Dr. Arthur E. Chapman
1000 South Fourth Street
Louisville, KY 40203
502-589-1776; (*www.sar.org*)

For male descendants of Revolutionary War patriots

National Society United States Daughters of 1812
1461 Rhode Island Avenue N.W.
Washington, DC 20005
202-745-1812;
(*www.execpc.com/~drg/wid1812. html*)

For female descendants of ancestors who rendered civil, military, or naval service from 1784 through 1815

The Society of the Cincinnati
2118 Massachusetts Avenue N.W.
Washington, DC 20008
202-785-2046

For male descendants of officers in the Revolutionary War

Sons of Confederate Veterans
P.O. Box 59
Columbia, Tennessee 38402
1-800-MY-DIXIE;
(*http://scv.org/scvinfo.htm*)

For male descendants of Confederate soldiers

United Daughters of the Confederacy
328 North Boulevard
Richmond, VA 23220
804-355-1636

For female descendants of Confederate soldiers

By now you have a good working knowledge of all the family history resources you can search in this country. To what has it all been leading? The mother country, of course: tracing your ancestors back to their native land, where your family forebears lived for centuries, if not from the beginning of time. In the next chapter, I'll show you how you can extend your search beyond the borders of the United States and make a unique connection to the roots of your family tree.

CHAPTER 9

Finding Your Roots Abroad: Sources in Your Ancestral Homeland

IT IS NEARLY impossible to describe the emotions you have when you return to the land of your ancestors. It does not matter what country or which generation of your forebears left it—the feeling is the same.

"When I first arrived in that tiny town, I was seized with a peculiar elemental feeling," said one friend of mine who returned to her ancestral home on a vacation visit. "It was as though I were coming back to my own personal cradle of civilization. I thought if nothing else happens beyond this, the feeling alone is worth the trip."

Something else could well happen. You could turn up relatives to visit and to correspond with for a lifetime. After another friend of mine searched out his cousins and uncle in Budapest, he went on to Rotterdam and stayed with second cousins there. "Even though there were language problems," he said, "there was a natural kind of communication, because we were all family. It's hard to describe how that trip made me feel—like I belonged to more of the world than just the United States."

Still another family historian I know, a thirteenth-generation descendant of an English rector, wrote to me about visiting her ancestral town. "Today Mr. Luckett, the present vicar, showed me the old church registry. All the entries from that time had been written in William's own hand in a parchment book; it's a beautiful work and has artistic decorations. I saw the baptismal entries for his children, and I discovered to my surprise that he had a daughter with the very same name as mine."

To find a sample of your ancestor's own handwriting and get to know the place where he lived is to truly find your own roots. And it is why so many Americans today find genealogy far more than just another hobby.

FINDING THE HOMES OF YOUR FOREBEARS

Before you go beyond the U.S. borders, you should make every effort to gather all the facts you can collect about your immigrant forebears. Whether your heritage is European, Asian, Latin American, or any other, the procedure is very much the same: you will need (1) your ancestor's name, (2) the locality in the old country from which he or she originally came, and (3) the date (at least approximate) of his or her migration. Your ancestor's occupation is also helpful, especially if his name was William Smith or John Jones. Without this minimal amount of information, you will probably not find your family beginnings—at least for this one line. (But remember, if you have trouble locating one immigrant ancestor, you can always try tracing another branch of your family tree. You have dozens—all of them unique.)

After getting all the facts you can about your progenitor on your own, make sure to search through the LDS foreign records in Salt Lake City—or through one of their branch libraries—before you undertake further research that involves an overseas trip or even extensive correspondence with officials of a foreign country. In some cases—in England, Germany, and Denmark, for example—LDS genealogists have microfilmed many of the available civil and church records. And they have quantities of filmed records available to the public on most other countries that have supplied America with immigrants. The

LDS Family History Library has also published inexpensive research outlines on most countries that includes maps, language tips, and an overview of the country's history. Check with the publications office in Salt Lake City (see chapter 5) or your local branch to obtain a copy for your country of origin.

Foreign research can be undertaken by mail and, even with a language barrier, can be just as fruitful as doing research in person. The general procedures are the same as doing research in the United States. You will find many similarities among the records of every country in the world. Nearly all governments have found it necessary to gather census data; keep military records; certify births, deaths, and marriages; and tax their citizens. These activities have formed a body of records that vary little from country to country. Of course, some countries (England, for example) have much more information for family historians than do others, particularly totalitarian countries that do not encourage genealogy, although recently eastern European countries and countries formed from the old Soviet Union have begun to assist genealogists. Even the People's Republic of China welcomes Chinese-Americans searching for their families' history.

It is a good idea for any ancestor hunter to study the history of the country and locality of his ancestral home. Knowledge of the general history of your country of origin may give you clues to what records were kept in the past, where they may be found now, what language they were written in, and what authority (civil, military, or church) initiated them. For instance, if your ancestors emigrated from Alsace-Lorraine, a territory that was alternately governed by Germany and France for centuries, you will be able to chart a much better search campaign with a general knowledge of the area's history.

It is always a good idea to write for advice to the genealogical society nearest your foreign research locale. And, by all means, drop in when you get there. Societies' members are people with your same interests, plus a knowledge of their country's or region's records. They may even be able to put you on to a local family historian working on your line. And, of course, if you run into language barriers (as you may, especially if your search takes you to small towns away from the metropolitan areas), a local genealogical society can help you hire a native genealogist who speaks English. Many such societies are listed in this chapter.

There are two courtesies to observe when writing to foreign countries:

1. Send international Postal Reply Coupons (you can purchase them at any post office) when you expect an answer to your questions. All letters come airmail, and one coupon will cover the cost of one-half ounce. For a package of information, you'll need to know its weight so that you can send enough coupons to avoid surface mail, which can take weeks.

2. When paying fees or sending search deposits, send American Express money orders or go to your bank and get a draft in the money of the country.

A word about maps, which can be an important part of your search: A map of the locale of your ancestral home could be helpful when you return to the area, and it would make a delightful addition to your Family History Book. The Heritage Map Museum, P.O. Box 412, Lititz, PA 17543, telephone 800-432-8183, is a good resource. Try their Web site (*www.carto.com/intro.html*) to determine if one of their 20,000 maps is one you might want. Old maps are often so detailed that they show individual farmhouses and thus could pinpoint the exact site of an ancestral cottage. You should have two pieces of information before you can successfully search for a map.

1. The village, town, or nearest city to your ancestor's home. (Although some villages have disappeared in the wars that have swept back and forth over Europe, the number is surprisingly small. In most cases, villages have been absorbed into expanding neighboring urban areas.)

2. The name of the state, shire, province, or county of the particular country in which your town is located. (There are dozens

of towns named Neudorf and Holzhausen in Germany, for instance.)

In this chapter I have tried to include the mother countries of
most of our immigrant ancestors, but it is impossible to cover the entire world's records, especially when boundaries have shifted so radi-
cally since our forefathers lived there. If you don't find your ancestor's
country of origin listed here, the best and easiest way to find out where
to write is to contact the LDS library in Salt Lake City. On the rare occasions when they can't help you, write to that country's Washington,
DC, embassy. (A reference librarian can give you the address.)

There are times when embassies write back saying they know of
no genealogical interest in their country. Don't believe it. Cultural at-
tachés don't know everything. In that case, simply get the address (from
a library) of the American embassy in your ancestor's country and write
to them about your problem. If it's a record of birth, death, or marriage,
often they can get it for you or tell you how to proceed. If it's a question
abut genealogical research in that country, they may be able to direct
you to the national archives or some native family history expert.

As you will learn in the upcoming chapter on cyberspace genealogy, the World Wide Web is full of information for family historians,
including many sites that deal with foreign research. If your ancestor's
country of origin is not included in this chapter, simply go to your Internet service provider's search area and type "Hungarian Genealogy"
or "Bohemian Genealogy," for example, then click on search.

The countries and origins discussed in this chapter are as follows:

Africa (including The Gambia,
Ghana, Guinea, Ivory Coast,
Liberia, Senegal, Sierra Leone,
and Togo)
Australia
British Isles (including England
and Wales, Northern Ireland,
and Scotland)

Canada
China, People's Republic of
Czech Republic
Denmark
France
Germany
Greece
Ireland, Republic of

Italy   Poland
Japan   Russia
Jewish Ancestors   Spain
Mexico   Sweden
Norway   Switzerland
Philippines, Republic of the

Africa

So far, only about a dozen Americans descended from African slaves
have been able to trace their ancestors back across the sea. Author Alex
Haley, of course, is one; the late tennis champion Arthur Ashe, a member of the Blackwell family on his maternal side, is another. But in the
years to come, many more African Americans will gain this prize. Due
to growing interest, new resources are being developed literally every
day.

The key to unlocking the puzzle is often a family oral-history tradition of Africanisms—words or place names that can be traced to
present-day African countries. Haley, for instance, was able to track ancestor Kunta Kinte to the Mandingo people of The Gambia because
his family had a tradition of using African expressions containing "k"
sounds, which he discovered to be common in the Mandinka language of the present-day Mandingos. There is often a lack of paper
documentation, for Africans have been a people whose history has
been transmitted from generation to generation by word of mouth. As
a result, it is said in Africa, "Every elderly person who dies is a book
that disappears forever."

Below is a list of West African embassies and other information
about these countries, from whose territory most slaves originally came.

The Gambia. Write to the embassy, 1155 15th Street N.W., Suite
1000, Washington, DC 20005, telephone 202-785-1399. To access
more information on The Gambia, go to *www.sas.upenn.edu/African_
Studies/Country_Specific/Gambia.html.*

Ghana Write to the embassy, 3512 International Drive, N.W., Washington, DC 20008, telephone 202-686-4520. For addresses in Ghana; access *www.wtgonline.com/country/gh/add.html* or write to the Embassy of the United States of America, P.O. Box 194, Ring Road East, Accra, Ghana, (21)775-347.

You may also contact the following sources if you think you may have been of Ghanaian descent:

1. President, African Descendants' Association Foundation, P.O. Box 2024, Accra, Ghana

2. Institute of African Studies, University of Ghana, Legon, Ghana

3. The Bureau Director, Bureau of Ghana Languages, P.O. Box 1851, Accra, Ghana.

In addition, historians at the University of Ghana History Department in Legon may be able to give help and advice.

Republic of Guinea Write to the embassy, 2112 Leroy Place, Washington, DC 20008, telephone 202-483-9420 (*www.sas.upenn.edu/African_Studies/Country_Specific/Eq_Guinea.html*).

Ivory Coast Write to the embassy, 2424 Massachusetts Avenue, Washington, DC 20008, telephone 202-797-0300, or access a Web site with historical and cultural information (*www.traveldocs.com/ei/index.htm*).

You may also want to contact an expert on the African oral tradition, Professor Georges Bouah Niangoran, Université Nationale d'Abidjan, Abidjan, République de Côte d'Ivoire.

Liberia Write to the embassy, 5201 16th Street, Washington, DC 20011, telephone 202-723-0437.

Senegal Write to the embassy, 2121 Wyoming Avenue, Washington, DC 20008, telephone 202-234-0540, or for cultural and historical information access *www.wtgonline.com/country/sn/add.html*. The Embassy of the United States of America's address is BP49, avenue Jean XXIII, Dakar, Senegal, telephone 234-296.

Sierra Leone Write to the Embassy, 1701 19th Street, Washington, DC 10009, telephone 202-939-9261, access their Web site at *www.wtgonline.com:8080/Country/sl/add.html,* or write the Embassy of the United States of America, corner of Walpole and Siaka Stevens Streets, Freetown, Sierra Leone.

Togo Write to the embassy, 2208 Massachusetts Avenue, Washington, DC 20008, telephone 202-234-4212.

For listings of other African embassies (or any foreign embassy) in the United States, access *www.embassy.org/embassies/eep-1100.html.*

Australia

Early emigrants to America, Canada, and Australia from Britain tend to be from the same stock, and so all have many ancestors in common. Therefore, contacts with Australian records and genealogists could prove useful to you.

Each of the six states of Australia has its own registration authority. In addition, there is the Australian Capital Territory and the Northern Territory. Thus there are eight separate authorities to be considered when undertaking family research.

Birth, Marriage, and Death Records. Applications for copies of birth, marriage, and death certificates should be addressed to the following:

1. *Australian Capital Territory. Archives Officer, ACT Administration, PO Box 148,* Canberra, ACT, 2601, telephone 06-207-5921, or access their home page from *http://www.tased.edu.au/archives/contact.htm.*

2. *New South Wales.* The Archives Authority of New South Wales, Level 3, 66 Harrington Street, Sydney, NSW, 2000. To

access an inventory of their records go to *http://www.records.nsw.gov.au/index.html.*

3. *Northern Territory.* The Archivist, GPO Box 874, Darwin, NT, 0801, telephone 08-8924-7677, or access their home page from *http:www.tased.edu.au/archives/contact.htm.*

4. *Queensland.* The State Archivist, 435 Compton Road, Runcorn QLD 4113, telephone 07-3875-8755, or go to their Web site at *http://www.archives.qld.gov.au/about_us.html* for a breakdown of their organizational chart.

5. *South Australia.* The State Archivist, 282 Richmond Road, Netley, or P.O. Box 1056, Blair Athol West, South Australia 5084, telephone 08-226-8000, or access their home page from *http://www.tased.edu.au/archives/contact.htm* for a list of publications, including *Ancestors in the Archives.*

6. *Tasmania.* The Archives office of Tasmania, 77 Murray Street, Hobart, Tasmania, 7000, international telephone 61-3-6233-7488, or check their Web site at *http://www.tased.edu.au/archives/contact.htm* to click on their e-mail for instant queries.

7. *Victoria.* The Archivist, Level 2, Casselden Place, 2 Lonsdale, Melbourne, Victoria, 3000, telephone 03-9285-7930, or access their search rooms at *http://home.vicnet.net.au/~provic/1-1.htm.*

8. *Western Australia.* The Archivist, LISWA, Alexander Library Building, Perth Cultural Centre, Perth, WA, 6000, telephone 08-9427-3151, or access their Web site at *http://.liswa.wa.gov.au/currbuy.html.*

Immigration Records. At some time in your Australian research, it will become necessary to check to see when the emigrant you are looking for arrived in the country. Some of the lists refer to the parish in Britain from which the ancestor originated. You can check shipping lists at the following libraries, or for more information you can access the Australian Archives Library Web site at *www.aa.gov.au/AA_WWW/AA_Sect_Serv/AA_Library/AA_Library.html*. Each of these libraries contains published information about Australian history and genealogy.

1. *New South Wales.* Public Search Room, State Library of NSW, Level 17, Sydney Central 477 Pitt Street, Sydney NSW, 2000, telephone +61-2-9201-3100, e-mail *refnsw@aa.gov.au*.

2. *Queensland.* Public Search Room, State Library of QLD, 996 Wynnum Road, Cannon Hill, QLD, 4170, telephone the office at +61-7-3249-4222, e-mail *refqld@aa.gov.au*.

3. *South Australia.* Public Search Room, State Library of SA, 11-13 Derlanger Avenue, Collinswood, SA, 5081, office telephone +61-8-269-0100, e-mail *refsa@aa.gov.au*.

4. *Tasmania.* The office of the State Library of Tasmania, 4 Rosny Hill Road, Rosny Park, TAS, 7018, telephone +61-3-6244-0111, e-mail *reftas@aa.gov.au*.

5. *Victoria.* Public Search Room, 2nd Floor Casselden Place, 2 Lonsdale Street, Melbourne, Victoria, 3000, office telephone +61-3-9285-7979, e-mail *refvic@aa.gov.au*.

6. *Western Australia.* Public Search Room, 384 Berwick Street, East Victoria Park WA 6101, office telephone +61-9-470-7500, e-mail *refwa@aa.gov.au*.

Other Australian Resources on the Internet: Australian genealogists have set up several World Wide Web sites crammed with information. The Australian Family History Compendium at *www.cohsoft.com.au/afhc/* contains a tutorial on how to use the site along with a listing of Australian genealogical records on the Internet, and a number of in-country archives, libraries, LDS Family History Centers, maps, Aboriginal materials, and genealogical societies, including the quaintly named Dead Persons' Society of Canberra. Other sites you should visit are *www.nla.gov.au/oz/genelist.html*, which has links to genealogical societies and associations, and *http://genealogy.org/~gwsc/gwscintl.htm*, which lists genealogical societies for Australia and dozens of other countries.

BRITAIN

England and Wales

As always, you should begin your quest by determining if any other family historian has worked on your line. You can do this by visiting or writing the following organizations in England (remember to enclose International Reply Coupons and a long envelope):

1. Society of Genealogists, 14 Charterhouse Buildings, Goswell Road, London EC1M 7BA, telephone 0171-251-8799

2. The Institute of Heraldic and Genealogical Studies, 79-82 Northgate, Canterbury, Kent CTI IBA, telephone 01227-768-664

3. Federation of Family History Societies, 2 Killer Street, Bury BO 9B2

4. Federation of Family History Societies, Birmingham & Midland Institute, Margaret Street, Birmingham B3 3BS

5. Guild of One-Name Studies, Box G 14 Charterhouse Buildings, Goswell Road, London EC1M 7BA

6. Association of Family History Societies of Wales, c/o Mrs. J. Istance, 13 Harold Street, Hereford HR1 2QU

If your research objective is well defined, the staff of these organizations can advise you on how best to proceed and give you an estimate of costs, if any.

Another amazing resource is the annually published *Genealogical Research Directory*, which is a source of names being researched worldwide, and available in the U.S. from Mrs. J. Jennings, 3324 Crail Way, Glendale, CA 91206.

To hire an experienced researcher, contact the Association of Genealogists and Record Agents, 29 Badgers Close, Horsham, West Sussex RH12 5RU, and send five International Reply Coupons for a complete list of accredited members, one of which will surely be expert in the area of your search.

If you want to track down your ancestor on your own while in England or by mail, here are some useful addresses.

Birth, Marriage, and Death Records. On orders of Queen Victoria, all civil registration in England and Wales began in 1837, and these certificates formerly kept at St. Catherine's House are now available from the Family Records Center, Myddleton Street, London EC1R 1UW. In person, you may have access to the indexes but not to the certificate records themselves. Copies are made for a fee and usually require about twenty-four hours to prepare. You may request copies by mail from the General Register Office, P.O. Box 2, Southport, Merseyside PR8 2HH. Telephone 151-471-4524 for credit card orders.

Probate Records. Copies of wills filed since 1958 can be obtained from the Principal Probate Registry, Somerset House, Strand, London WC2. Earlier wills can be located in the regional courts. Some of the records go far back to medieval times (for example, the probate records for York commence in 1389).

Census Records. The 1841-through-1891 census records are kept at the Public Record Office, Somerset House. (The 1841-through-1861 censuses are on microfilm at the LDS library in Salt Lake City and are available through its branches.) The 1851 census is the first to give the birthplace (parish and county) of each member of the household, a fact that could lead you to earlier church records (see below). Census returns after 1901 are considered confidential, but some information will be provided. Some local genealogical societies have indexed by surname some censuses for their region.

Church Records. The most valuable genealogical information for the years before 1837 can be found in the 14,000 parish church registers throughout England and Wales. Many go back as far as 1538 and have been copied for the library of the Society of Genealogists in London, where you should check first (if you have already checked the LDS Family History Center). For a small fee, you can search the society's general index of more than 4,000 registers containing three million names. If you do not have the time to search, professional genealogists on duty at the library will search for you for a fee.

For American genealogists, the chance that their ancestors were outside the established Church of England is rather high. If you have Quaker ancestry, their records begin in the 1650s and can be found in the Public Record Office, Chancery Lane, London WC2A 1LR (which houses most pre-1700 records); if Catholic, check the Catholic Record Society, c/o 114 Mount Street, London W2Y 6AH; if Huguenot, the Huguenot Society (three out of four Britons have Huguenot ancestry, including Winston Churchill), c/o University College, Gower Street, London, W2Y 6AH; if Methodist, contact the Methodist Archives, University Library, Deansgate, Manchester M3 3EH; or if Baptist, write the Baptist Historical Society, 15 Fenshurst Gardens, Long Ashton, Bristol BS18 9AU.

Miscellaneous Sources. It is also quite possible that you had an immigrant ancestor who was transported as punishment for one of hundreds of crimes that carried a sentence of death. Over 50,000 English men, women, and children were exiled to the Colonies before 1750, so don't overlook court records in your area of research.

The College of Arms on Queen Victoria Street, London EC4V 4BT (discussed at length in chapter 11) has more than the records of English heraldry. It is possible to find an authenticated family tree deposited there by a distant relative who was once looking for his coat of arms. The college has a vast number of unpublished pedigrees, stretching back centuries. Searches can be made (although usually these take more time than you may have on a vacation).

Wills probated prior to 1858 are available for a small fee from the Public Record Office (address above); after that date they can be found by writing the Chief Clerk, Probate Registry Search Queries, Duncombe Place, York YO1 2EA.

If you are unable to find what you are looking for in London, you may want to go directly to a local record office in your search area. A full list of *Record Repositories in Great Britain* has been prepared by the British Records Association and the Historical Manuscripts Commission, The Charterhouse, London EC1M 7BA.

Before starting your research in England and Wales, it is a good idea to consult *Genealogical Research in England and Wales,* by Frank Smith and David Gardner, a four-volume work that covers the records of England in great genealogical detail. Volume I details vital records, the census, and church records. Volume II offers research planning advice plus military record information. Volume III is helpful to anyone planning a great deal of research in parish registers, where he or she will encounter Latin abbreviations and Old English handwriting. Volume IV describes apprentice and school records and township and country records. You can find these reference volumes in most genealogical libraries.

Other books you may wish to consult are *Tracing Your English Ancestors,* by Colin D. Rogers, and *Town Records* and *Village Records,* both by John West.

For a quick and quite thorough tutorial on hunting your ancestors in the UK, visit the British Tourist Authority's Web site at *www.visitbritain. com/activities/wtd%2D9.htm.* Another Web site where you could find your English ancestors is *http://148.100.56.24/bis/fsheets/3.htm,* which contains information about military records.

Although Welsh records have been administered by England for centuries and can be found in all the above repositories, if you have a Welsh Jones in your background as I do, you won't want to overlook the National Library of Wales, Penglais, Aberystwyth, Ceredigion

SY23 3BU, telephone 01970-623816. For more specific Welsh genealogical sources access *http://midas.ac.uk/genuki/big/wal.* You'll find a link to the National Library of Wales's home page, which features online information about their collections. To find out about the Welsh-American Genealogical Society, send a self-addressed, stamped envelope to WAGS c/o RR2, Box 576, Lewis Road, Poultney, Vermont 05764, telephone 802-287-9149. The Welsh genealogical society Mentro-Cymru can be accessed via *www.data-wales.co.uk/mentro.htm.*

Northern Ireland

There is some crossover of record keeping between Northern Ireland and the Republic of Ireland. You should try both authorities if the first does not yield a record. (See also the Republic of Ireland, below.)

Birth, Marriage, and Death Records. In Northern Ireland, Protestant marriages have been recorded since 1845; births, deaths, and Catholic marriages, since 1864. The original certificates are in the custody of the registrar of each district in which the event took place. Since 1922, central record keeping has been under the Jurisdiction of the Public Record Office, 66 Balmoral Avenue, Belfast BT9 6NY, telephone 1232-661621, or access their Web site at *www.nics.gov.uk/ proni_old/exhibition/index.htm.* This office also maintains an index.

Probate Records. Many old wills were destroyed by fire in Dublin during 1922, but copies and extracts from thousands of Ulster wills are preserved in the Principal Probate Registry, Royal Courts of Justice, Chichester Street, Belfast BT1 3JF.

Church Records. Parish records for Northern Ireland were also largely destroyed by fire in 1922, but some do remain in the custody of individual parish clergymen. Most of them do not go back beyond the 1700s.

Miscellaneous Sources. There are two aids Americans with Northern Irish ancestry should not overlook:

1. Information about Ulster forebears can be obtained by contacting the Ulster Historical Foundation, 12 College Square East, Belfast BT1 6DD.

2. For a brief tutorial and other invaluable information you should access the North of Ireland Family History Society Web site at *www.os.qub.ac.uk/nifhs/*; also general Irish links at *www.lib.siu.edu/projects/irish/irelinks.htm*. For a look inside recreated Irish cottages where our ancestors lived, access The Northern Ireland Tourist Board's Ancestral Heritage site at *www.interknowledge.com/northern-ireland/ukiher01.htm*.

Scotland

Do you have a colorful tartan-wearing Scottish ancestor in your background? Many Americans can claim Scottish ancestry and easily find him or her. Unlike England and Ireland, the Scots have gathered together all their parish registers in one place, New Register House (see below)—a great help to ancestor hunters.

Birth, Marriage, and Death Records. Compulsory registration of vital statistics began in 1855 and contains such complete family information that genealogists consider it superior to almost any other country's system. You can have these records searched by accredited genealogists, a list of which can be obtained from the Scottish Genealogy Society, 15 Victoria Terrace, Edinburgh EH1 2JL, or you can go in person or write to New Register House, the Registrar General, Princes Street, Edinburgh E1H1 3YT, international telephone +44-131-334-0380. If the search is not a long one, they will undertake it for a small fee. (The LDS genealogical library in Salt Lake City has microfilm copies of certificates from 1855 through 1875 and 1881 through 1891.)

Church Records. The Registrar General also has 4,000 old parish registers (few of them indexed), some dating from the 1500s. The established church in Scotland is the Church of Scotland, or the

Presbyterian Church. Baptismal records are unusually (and, for the family historian, beautifully) complete.

Most registers for nonconformist denominations, Catholics, and Jews are in the custody of the local minister, although some are on microfilm at the Salt Lake City LDS library.

Probate Records. Leave the New Registry Office and step next door to the Scottish Record Office, Princes Street, Edinburgh EH1 3YJ, which contains indexes of wills, deeds, and other legal documents as well as court records that may be extracted for a fee. Before 1850, the Scots called wills *testaments.*

Census Records. Census returns for the years 1841, 1851, 1861, 1871, 1881, and 1891 are available for genealogical researchers. Application forms can be obtained from New Register House (see address above).

Miscellaneous Sources. For further aids in hunting your Scottish forebears you should contact the Scottish Genealogy Society (Ceud Mile Failte), 15 Victoria Terrace, Edinburgh EH1 2JL. You can telephone or fax their library and family history center at +44-0131-220-3677 or e-mail them at *scotgensoc@sol.co.uk.* They have the facilities to microfilm or microfiche material you might want. The society (membership is twenty-eight dollars for U.S. members) also publishes a quarterly, *The Scottish Genealogist,* and maintains a list of knowledgeable genealogists who will research your family in Scotland for a fee. The society has over 300 published titles. If you wish to write to them, send a self-addressed, stamped envelope with two International Reply Coupons. You may join by credit card via their Web site (*www.taynet.co.uk/users/scotgensoc/*). This site also includes a list of regional Scottish genealogy societies and their addresses.

If you can trace your ancestry back to a Highland clan, you may wish to contact the Highland Family History Society, the Honorable Secretary, c/o Reference Room, Public Library, Farraline Park, Inverness IV1 INH, to learn more about the tartan identified with your family. Also check with the society to see when your clan will gather next.

You would certainly want to plan your visit to Scotland to coincide with such a once-in-a-lifetime event.

It is particularly important to get Scottish place names right when attempting research in Scotland by mail. The *Genealogical Gazetteer of Scotland* from the Everton Publishers, Logan, UT 84323-0368, telephone 800-443-6325, Web address *www.everton.com*, contains locations of places, with a map of each Scottish county to facilitate area searches.

You'll want to see what's on the Internet about Scottish genealogy. Try the GENUKI (short for genealogy, UK and Ireland) pages first at *www-theory.dcs.st-andrews.ac.uk/%7Emnd/genuki/* and *www.oz.net/~cyndihow/scotland.htm*, both with many links to other sites you'll want to explore.

When you go back to Scotland (at least some of your genes have been there before), you'll want to immerse yourself in Scottish traditional dancing, piping, and heavy athletics. There's no better place for this than the Scottish Games at Braemar, said to have been started by the Malcolm who defeated Macbeth. The clan chiefs used the games to determine the strongest warriors. My nephew Norman Dawson, a braw lad indeed, went back to Scotland to find his roots and entered the Braemar games in the "all comers" class. During the one-day event he tossed an eighteen-foot caber (it looks like a telephone pole), competed in putting the stone, a twenty-eight-pounder, and throwing the twenty-two-pound hammer, while wearing his Davidson kilt. He says, "I had the pleasure of being badly beaten by the best in the world. Believe me, it was a thrill!" Highland games are also held in the U.S. by the Scottish American Athletic Association. For more information, write to the SAAA, 1028 2nd Street, Sacramento, CA 95814, or access them at *www.highlandnet.com/info/ath/heavyath.html*.

And finally, consult *Scottish Family History: A Handbook,* by Rosemary A. Bigwood, a comprehensive guide with strong emphasis on nineteenth-century sources.

CANADA

There was a great deal of traveling back and forth between the United States and Canada in the early days of the republic. There were no border guards, no formalities to observe, so it is highly possible that many ancestors of today's Americans simply got on their horses and rode from Canada to their new home. The migration went the other way as well. Thousands of Americans loyal to the British king emigrated to Canada during and after the Revolutionary War (1775–83). The National Archives of Canada (see address below) contains a great many sources relating to what they call United Empire Loyalists.

Research in Canada is not difficult. The National Archives, Genealogy Unit, Researcher Services Division, 393 Wellington Street, Ottawa, Ontario K1A, telephone reference service at 613-996-7458, corresponds to the National Archives in Washington. The services offered are similar in nature to those of the National Archives in that they will do a limited amount of research on request and make copies (photocopy or microfilm) for a small fee. They also have a list of capable professional genealogists who will undertake research too extensive for the archives' staff.

Census Records. Census returns from 1851 through 1901 list each person individually with his or her country or province of birth—very helpful information for any family historian. The archives has published checklists of census records. These lists are set up geographically. The archives also has on microfilm some early census rolls dating from 1666.

Birth, Marriage, and Death Records. The following provincial archives are in charge of civil registration (vital records):

1. *Newfoundland.* Colonial Building, Military Road, St. John's, Newfoundland A1C 2C9, 709-729-3065.

2. *Nova Scotia.* Public Archives of Nova Scotia, 6016 University Avenue, Halifax, Nova Scotia B3H 1W4, 902-424-6060.

3. *Prince Edward Island.* Public Archives and Records Office, Box 1000, Charlottetown, Prince Edward Island C1A 7M4, 902-368-4290.

4. *New Brunswick.* Provincial Archives of New Brunswick, P.O. Box 6000, Fredericton, New Brunswick E3B 5H1, 506-453-2122.

5. *Québec.* Archives nationales du Québec, 1012, avenue du Séminaire, C.P. 10450, Sainte-Foy, Québec G1V 4N1, 418-643-8904.

6. *Ontario.* Archives of Ontario, 77 Grenville Street West, Toronto, Ontario M7A 2R9, 416-327-1600.

7. *Manitoba.* Provincial Archives of Manitoba, 200 Vaughan Street, Winnipeg, Manitoba R3C 1T5, 204-945-3971.

8. *Saskatchewan.* Saskatchewan Archives Board, Regina Office, University of Regina, Regina, Saskatchewan S4S 0A2, 306-787-4068; Saskatchewan Archives Board, Murray Building University of Saskatchewan, 3 Campus Drive, Saskatoon, Saskatchewan S7N 5A4, 306-933-5832.

9. *Alberta.* Provincial Archives of Alberta, 12845-102 Avenue, Edmonton, Alberta T5N 0M6, 403-427-1750.

10. *British Columbia.* British Columbia Archives, 655 Belleville Street, Victoria, British Columbia V8V 1X4, 250-387-1952.

11. *Yukon.* Yukon Archives, P.O. Box 2703, Whitehorse, Yukon Territory Y1A 2C6, 403-667-5321.

12. *Northwest Territories.* Archives of the Northwest Territories, c/o Prince of Wales Northern Heritage Centre, Yellowknife, Northwest Territories X1A 2L9, 403-873-7698.

Family historians with Acadian or French-Canadian lines have some of the best-documented ancestors in the world. Pedigrees based on marriage records can be extended back ten to fifteen generations. One source for Acadian genealogy, called "Gaudet's Notes," is at the National Archives of Canada. These give birth, marriage, and death dates of early Acadian citizens. Another comprehensive holding of Acadian sources is at Le Centre d'études acadiennes, Université de Moncton, Moncton, New Brunswick E1A 3E9. Family historians should also consult Donald J. Hebert's *Acadians in Exile*, which includes the censuses of 1671, 1686, and 1714, plus an inventory of resources.

Church Records. The National Archives has some original parish registers but not a comprehensive number. They have prepared A *Check-List of Parish Registers*, listing the churches for which they have material on file.

Property Records. The National Archives has records relating to land titles of crown lands dating back to 1764, plus a list of holdings in each province.

Military Records. According to archival sources, except for the South African War, detailed personnel records for Canadian soldiers were not kept until after 1900. Records of some British regular units and Canadian militia (including some Loyalist units from the Revolutionary War) exist, but most of them date from 1812.

Immigration Records. Canada does not have extensive passenger-list records. Those they do have date from 1865 for the port cities of Québec and Halifax. For access to these records or for copies of naturalization and citizenship records, write to the Department of Citizenship and Immigration, Public Rights Administration, 300 Slater Street, 3rd Floor, Section D, Ottawa, Ontario K1A 1L1.

Miscellaneous Sources. The Public Archives has on file valuable genealogical information relating to United Empire Loyalists, including detailed claims for losses sustained during the Revolution and requests for land grants.

For additional information on the holdings of the National

Archives of Canada, write and ask for a free copy of the pamphlet "Tracing Your Ancestors in Canada." You may also access more information at *www.archives.ca/www/memories.html* and *www.archives.ca/ www/Genealogic]Services.html*.

If you have many Canadian lines, you may want to study the specifics of Canadian genealogy in more detail. A good place to start is Eunice Ruiter Baker's paperback book, *Searching for Your Ancestors in Canada.*

Two Canadian genealogical societies are particularly recommended to ancestor-hunting Americans. One is the Ontario Genealogical Society, 40 Orchard View Boulevard, Suite 102, Toronto, Ontario M4R 1B9. The other is the Alberta Genealogical Society, 116, 10440-108 Avenue, Edmonton, Alberta T5H 3Z9. The addresses of all major genealogical societies in Canada can be accessed from *www.archives, ca/www/OtherSources.html.*

PEOPLE'S REPUBLIC OF CHINA

The People's Republic of China, unlike the eastern European communist countries in the past, encourages visits to ancestral villages and contacts with relatives and clanspeople in mainland China.

If you plan a trip to China, you are advised by Chinese genealogists to write to relatives well in advance of your trip, outlining your desire to learn more about your family history.

There will be several possibilities for advancing your personal genealogy in China. Although conditions vary from one district to another, it is possible to locate cemeteries and ancestral tablets in your clan temple or ancestral hall. Each of these tablets contains from three to five generations of male lineage.

Thus far, Chinese-American genealogists attempting to gain access to written records under the jurisdiction of the People's Republic of China have not been too successful. Perhaps with increased interest and further cultural exchange, this situation will change for the better.

Although a great deal of early Chinese genealogical material remains in libraries and genealogical collections, many priceless manuscripts and ancient genealogies were burned between 1950 and 1955 during an effort to eradicate "publications characteristic of reactionary thought of bourgeois society and feudal ideology."

Nevertheless, there is a continuing publication of clan and family genealogies in Taiwan. For information about these works (and for inquiries about family histories that were removed from the mainland in 1949) contact the chief librarian of the National Central Library in Taipei, Taiwan.

The definitive work on the current status of Chinese genealogy was written by Professor Hsiang-lin Lo, entitled "The Extent and Preservation of Genealogical Records in China." This pamphlet was published by the World Conference on Records in 1969 and can be located in any LDS branch library or ordered from the main library in Salt Lake City. The monograph contains an extensive bibliography of published material.

Another and more up-to-date book by Jeanie W. Low is *China Connections: Finding Ancestral Roots for Chinese in America*, which you can order on-line at *www.books.com/scripts/view.exe?isbn~0963883518*. Other Internet sites of interest to the Chinese-American genealogist are: *www.geocities.com/Tokyo/3919/*, which has a link to the Hundred Families Surnames site, and *www.oznet/~cyndihow/asia.htm*. An interesting site to explore for members of the Chou clan (and others) is *www.idis.com/ChouOnline/genregis.html*. Their records in Chinese go back to 2205 B.C., and they have genealogical records for other clans: Chang, Ching, Lum, Ing, Goo, Choy, Chiang, Ho, Kee, Mau, Sun, Yap, Wong, Lai, Woo, Loui, Lau, Kwock, Dang, and Young. You can write to the Chou Clansman Association, P.O. Box 4004, Honolulu, HI 96812, and they request that you send them your E-mail address for an immediate reply. A cultural site you may want to explore is *www.zhongwen.com/f2box/htm*, with a clickable Chinese character dictionary.

Other research papers that can be ordered from the main LDS library which might help Chinese-American family historians are *The Content and Use of Chinese Local History,* by Tsun Leng, and *History and Arrangement of Chinese Clan Genealogies,* by Hsiang-lin Lo.

A helpful list of Chinese organizations in the U.S. can be accessed at *www.idid.com/ChouOnline/CHIorg. html.*

CZECH REPUBLIC

Although church registers go back as far as the 1600s, civil registration of births, marriages, and deaths did not begin until 1918, when Czechoslovakia (Bohemia, Moravia, and Slovakia) was created as a nation. Parish registers (almost 7,000 of them) for both Catholic and Protestant churches remain in the local parish jurisdiction.

For information regarding research of Czech or Bohemian ancestors of German origin (Sudeten Germans) you should write to the German-Bohemian Heritage Society, P.O. Box 822, New Ulm, MN 56073 and access their home page on the Internet (*www.rootsweb. com/~gbhs/US*). For other Sudeten German societies, go to *www. genealogy.com/gene/reg/SUD/sudet_en.html.* Another resource for Czech ancestor-hunters is the California Czech and Slovak Club, P.O. Box 20542, Castro Valley, CA 94546, telephone 510-581-9986.

Source for Vital Records. The Central States Archive is located at Státní ústřední archiv v Praze, Karmelitská 2, CZ-118 01 Praha (Prague) 1—Malá Strana, Czech Republic, telephone +420-2-245 102 10.

Zdenka Kucera, a Czech genealogist, reports that genealogical records inside the country are quite good, and that a well-stated and precise letter should bring positive results.

For an extensive list of state and city archives within the Czech Republic, you should access their very thorough Web site at *www. genealogy.com/gene/reg/SUD/crarch-list.html.*

Another Internet site you'll need to search is *http://genealogy. org/~czech/index.html.* It contains links to other Czech research sites and an ancestor locator file.

DENMARK

Before working with Danish records in Denmark or at the LDS library in Salt Lake City or through one of the LDS branches, it is a good idea to learn a bit about Danish history. Off and on throughout its history, parts of Denmark were governed by Germany and Norway, which makes a difference in the kinds of records you will find and where you might find them. Fortunately for ancestor hunters, the LDS church has done a great deal of microfilming (over 90,000 rolls) and has published a very helpful and inexpensive research outline.

Birth, Marriage, and Death Records. Many parish registers were ill kept before 1814, when each parish was issued a printed book so that all information included would be uniform from parish to parish. The Danish provincial archives (Landsarkivet) are the most important sources for parish registers belonging to the Lutheran National Church and all other denominations. Some parish registers go back to 1660. Following is a list of regional archives:

1. Landsarkivet for Sjaelland m.m., Jagtvej 10, DK 2200, Copenhagen N.

2. Landsarkivet for Fyn, Jernbanegade 36, DK 5000, Odense.

3. Landsarkivet for Norrejylland, Ll. Sct. Hansgade 5, DK 8800, Viborg.

4. Landsarkivet for de Soenderjyske Landsdele, Haderlevvej 45, EK 6200, Aabenraa.

Census Records. The Danish National Archives (Rigsarkivet), Rigsdagsgården 9, DK 1218, Copenhagen K, are the genealogical source for census forms dating from 1787. From 1845 onward these rolls contain information about birthplaces. The archives also contain some immigration records. Many of these records are at the LDS library.

Military Records. The draft register located at the National Archives (see above for address) goes back to 1788, when all peasants' sons were registered for the draft from birth. Regimental records can be found at the Military Archive, Haerens Arkiv, Slotsholmgade 4, DK 1216, Copenhagen K.

Property Records. The Landsarkivets, or regional archives, also contain land registers that can yield information about land tenants back as far as the early 1700s. The regional archives also have the burgess rolls of towns in their area. These rolls contain professional information and descending genealogy of citizens.

Immigration Records. The Danes Worldwide Archives, Udvandrerarkivet, Arkivstrade 1, DK 9100 Alborg, telephone +45-99 31 42 20, e-mail *emiarch@vip.cybercity.dk,* has copies of the original immigrant lists compiled by the commissioner of the Copenhagen police. These archives will also advise on genealogical problems if you can furnish enough detail.

Miscellaneous Resources. The Danish Immigrant Museum, 2212 Washington Street, P.O. Box 178, Elk Horn, IA, near Des Moines, is worth a stop when you're in the area. You can write the Danish Genealogy Group, c/o Minnesota Genealogy Society, P.O. Box 16069, Saint Paul, MN 55116. Internet sites of interest are *www.rootsweb. com/~iashelby/danish.htm,* with links to other sites, including the always helpful Cyndi's List, and *www.denmarkemb.org/tracing.htm,* the Danish government site with a complete tutorial on tracing your Danish ancestors.

FRANCE

In France, there is a vast storehouse of genealogical information in some of the earliest records of Europe, dating back to the eleventh century. The key to successful family historical research in France, just as in every European country, is to know where (village or city) your ancestor was born. In this way you will be able to find the right *département*, since each French "state" has kept its own records separate from the national government's. A directory of French departmental archive addresses was published in 1992 and can be found in large genealogical libraries. These archives are generally located in the largest city in the *département*. For a current map and a French research outline, contact the LDS Family History Library or your nearest branch.

Birth, Marriage, and Death Records. From 1539 to 1792 and during the French Revolution, vital records were kept in registers by the parish priest. After that time, these became civil records kept by the state. The older registers are now in the regional (*département*) archives.

Census Records. Some early census records go back as far as 1590, but modern census rolls begin in 1836. They have been taken every five years (with time out for major wars) to the present time. You can find them in the regional archives for your ancestral home.

Immigration Records. Passenger lists from 1686 to the present are located at the National Archives or Archives Nationales de France, 11 rue des Quatre-Fils, 75141 Paris 3e. They will answer questions about services. A French genealogical society has found a century-old card file of passengers from 1780 through 1840 leaving from Le Havre and will search for a specific name if you send a self-addressed envelope with three International Reply Coupons. Write to: Liste de passagers, Groupement Généalogique du Havre et de Seine-Maritime, B.P. 80, 76050 Le Havre Cedex.

Military Records. Army and navy personnel files (mostly of officers), with name, birth date, place of birth, address, and physical description, are preserved from about 1600 to the present. Most of these records can be found at the Military Archives in Vincennes, and are not on microfilm.

Church Records. You can locate some Protestant registers by contacting Bibliothèque de la Société d'histoire du Protestantisme Français, 54 rue des Saint-Pierres, 75007 Paris. There is a charge for searching.

Probate and Property Records. Land and property records and wills from 1300 to today can be researched at the office of local notaries for more recent records, and at the National Archives, see above address, for ancient ones.

Miscellaneous Sources. Feudal and allegiance records from 1050 to 1700, containing names of lords, serfs, taxpayers, lists of men owing allegiance to lords, and dates of feudal contracts, can be seen at the National Archives.

The National Archives of France will undertake to answer a specific question by mail, such as "What was the birthplace of Jean Favier who emigrated to the United States in 1896 from Le Havre?" They will not, however, do any pedigree or genealogical work beyond that. For professional help, access the Web site of the Center for Genealogical Research (in France) at *www.astarte.ch/cgr/cgre.htm.* You can click on the site for their free brochure in English. In the U.S. you should contact the American-French Genealogical Society, P.O. Box 2112, Pawtucket, RI 02861.

The Internet provides a bonanza for Americans searching for their French forefathers. Minitel is a twenty-four-hour computer service, using phone lines, which includes databases of French telephone directories, lists of genealogical societies, indexes, advice, and other services. Minitel's address in the United States is Minitel Services Company, 888 7th Avenue, 28th Floor, New York, NY 10106, telephone 212-399-0080, fax 212-399-0129. Another Web site you'll want to access is *www.cam.org/~beaur/gen/france-e.html,* with both historical and genealogical information.

GERMANY

One out of every six Americans today is of German descent. Aside from the British Commonwealth, most Americans heading for overseas reunions with their ancestral beginnings travel to Germany. And since the reunification of Germany in 1989, genealogical searches are easier than when the country was split with East Germany closed to family record-searchers.

German genealogical research is a special science in itself. According to Dr. Heinz F. Friederichs, an expert on German ancestor hunting, the best way to find your ancestors in Germany is to get in touch with the genealogical society in your research area and get some help from them.

The biggest problem you will have with German research is German history. During the last century, when most civil record keeping started, Germany had thirty different independent states, all with their own record systems. Today, for instance, some church parish registers are collected into state archives (*Staatsarchiv*), some remain in the original parish, and still others (in former French communities on the west side of the Rhine) are located in the mayor's office.

It would be impossible to list here the variations of record keeping for Germany. Your best bet (if you want to do your own searching) is to locate the regional archives, since the federal archives have few genealogical records, from the following list and write to them, asking for the whereabouts of the information you need. They will refer you to a town archive or town genealogical society. (You can also find them in the LDS library or one of its branches.)

State Archives

Baden-Württemberg:

1. Generallandesarchiv Karlsruhe, Nördliche Hildapromenade 2, 76133 Karlsruhe

2. Staatsarchiv, Freiburg, Colombistr. 4, 79098 Freiburg im Breisgau

Bayern (Bavaria):

1. Generaldirektion der Staatlichen Archive Bayers, Schönfeldstr. 5-11, 80539 München

2. Staatsarchiv für Coburg, Rosengasse 1, 96450 Coburg

3. Staatsarchiv Bamberg, Hainstr. 39, 96947 Bamberg

4. Staatsarchiv Würzburg D 8700 Würzburg, Rresidenz-Nordflügel, 97070 Würzburg

Berlin:

1. Staatsarchiv, Archivstr. 12-14, 14195 Berlin

2. Landesarchiv, Kalckreuthstr. 1-2, 10777 Berlin

Brandenburg:

Staatsarchiv, An der Orangerie 3, 14469 Potsdam

Bremen:

Staatsarchiv, Am Staatsarchiv 1, 282203, Bremen

Hamburg:

Staatsarchiv Hamburg, ABC-Str. 19A, 20354 Hamburg

Hessen:

1. Hessisches Hauptstaatsarchiv, Mosbacherstr. 55, 65187 Wiesbaden

2. Hessisches Staatsarchiv Darmstadt, Schloss, 64283 Darmstadt

Mecklenburg-Vorpommern:

Mecklenburgisches Landeshauptarchiv, Graf-Schack-Allee 2, 19053 Schwerin

Vorpommersches Landesarchiv, Martin-Andersen-Nexö-Platz 1, 17849 Greifswald

Niedersachsen (Lower Saxony):

1. Niedersächsisches Hauptstaatsarchiv, Am Archiv 1, 30169 Hannover

2. Niedersächsisches Staatsarchiv Wolfenbüttel, Forstweg 2, 38302 Wolfenbüttel

3. Niedersächsisches Staatsarchiv für Bückeburg: Schloss, 31675 Bückeburg

4. Niedersächsisches Staatsarchiv für Stade, Am Stade 4c, 21682 Stade

5. Niedersächsisches Staatsarchiv für Oldenburg, Damm 43, 26135 Oldenburg

6. Niedersächsisches Staatsarchiv für Osnabrück, Schlossstr. 29, 49074 Osnabrück

Nordrhein-Westfalen

Nordrhein-Westfälisches Personenstandsarchiv Rheinland, Schlossstr. 12, 50321 Brühl/Rheinland

Pfalz (Palatinate):

Staatsarchiv Speyer, Postfach 1608, 67326, Speyer

Rheinland (Rhenania)

Staatsarchiv Koblenz, Postfach 1320, 56013 Koblenz

Saarland:

Landesarchiv Saarbrücken, Scheidter Str. 114, 66123 Saarbrücken

Sachsen (Saxony):

1. Sächsisches Haupstaatsarchiv Dresden, Archivstr. 14, 01097, Dresden

2. Sächsisches Staatsarchiv Leipzig, Schongauerstr. 1, 04329 Leipzig

Sachsen-Anhalt:

1. Landeshauptarchiv Sachsen-Anhalt Magdeburg, Hegelstr. 25, 39104 Magedeburg

2. Landeshauptarchiv Sachsen-Anhalt, Aussenstelle Wernigerode, Orangerie Lustgarten 21, 38855 Wernigerode

Schleswig-Holstein:

> Landesarchiv Schleswig-Holstein, Schloss Gottdorf (Prinzenpalais), 24837 Schleswig

Thüringen (Thuringia):

1. Thüringisches Hauptstaatsarchiv Gotha, Schloss Friedenstein, 99867 Gotha

2. Thüringisches Staatsarchiv Meiningen, Schloss Bibrabau, 98617 Meiningen

3. Thüringisches Staatsarchiv Rudolstadt, Schloss Heidecksburg, 07407 Rudolstadt

4. Thüringisches Hauptstaatsarchiv Weimar, Marstallstr. 2, 99423 Weimar

For a more complete listing of state and city archives running to many pages, you should access *www.bawue.de/~hanacek/info/darchi01.htm.*

National Genealogical Society: The Deutsche Zentralstelle für Genealogie, Postfach 04002, 04109 Leipzig, has collected German church records and is the center for genealogical research in Germany. For a fee they will do a limited search for materials. Check with this organization for a list of regional genealogical societies in your area of research. When making inquiry, be sure to give complete details of the research you need and the research already done. Do not forget to include International Postal Reply Coupons. If you do not speak German, you may want to obtain the LDS publication "German Letter-Writing Guide."

Miscellaneous Sources. There are a number of German genealogical societies in the U.S. Be sure to send an SASE for information:

1. German Genealogical Society of America, P.O. Box 291818, Los Angeles, CA 90029

2. German Genealogical Society, P.O. Box 16312, St. Paul, MN 55116

3. German Research Association, Inc., P.O. Box 711600, San Diego, CA 92171

4. Palatines to America, Capital University, Box 101, Columbus, Ohio 43209.

5. German Interest Group, P.O. Box 2185, Janesville, WI 53547. Are you descended from one of the many Germans who migrated to Russia during the years 1763 to 1862 and thence to the United States? If so, you should contact the Germans from Russia Heritage Society, 1008 E. Central Avenue, Bismarck, ND 58501.

An extraordinary source book on the subject of German family trees is the *Encyclopedia of German-American Genealogical Research*, by Clifford Neal Smith and Anna Piszczan-Czaja Smith, published by R. R. Bowker Company, 121 Chanlon Road, New Providence, NJ 07974, telephone 908-464-6800. Sections include information on church records, vital records, census and military records, along with passenger lists of emigrants and muster rolls of German mercenaries (Hessians) in the American Revolution.

For help from the Internet go to *www.genealogy.com/gene/faws/sgg.html*. This site contains a thirty-one-item table of contents with many links, including a surname register so you can discover other family historians looking for your German ancestor. Other genealogy sites for German research you'll want to explore are *www.rootsweb.com/~wggerman/*, *members.aol.com/KarenBeid/germany.html*, and *www.execpc.com/~kap/gene-de.html*.

GREECE

If you know the name and birthplace of your Greek ancestor, you should have no trouble locating him or her. In each Greek community the birth records of males and females have been kept since 1833 in a town archive. The registrar is usually the mayor.

Church Records. Church registers have been kept traditionally in all parishes, usually in three separate books, one each for marriages, births and baptisms, and deaths.

Probate Records. In Greece there are three kinds of wills: handwritten, secret, and public. These are held by the notary public drawing up the will until the death of the testator.

Miscellaneous Sources. There are several Internet sites that should give you additional information. For heritage queries from other Greek and Cypriot ancestor hunters, go to *www.dsenter.com/worldgenweb/Europe/Greece/queries.htm.* For the Greek Genealogy Web page, which includes cultural and tourist information as well as genealogical data, go to *www.dsenter.com/worldgenweb/Europe/Greece/index.html.*

REPUBLIC OF IRELAND (EIRE)

Written records in Ireland have suffered much from the unsettled history of that country. You will find that most of the remaining record sources of genealogical information are maintained in Dublin. As with any genealogical research, you are best advised to start with the LDS records. Write or call (see chapter 5 for access information) and order their inexpensive *Research Outline for Ireland,* which includes good search strategies peculiar to this country. In addition, the Family History Library has extensively microfilmed Irish records, and these are available through their branches. Remember that England ruled Ireland for many centuries and many Irish records can be found in English repositories (see British Isles).

Birth, Marriage, and Death Records. These vital records are written in Latin and go back to January 1864. They are kept at the public records office in Northern Ireland (see Northern Ireland) or at the

General Register Office of Ireland, Joyce House, 8/11 Lombard Street East, Dublin 2.

Census Records. These records are kept at the National Archives, Bishop Street, Dublin 2, telephone +353-1-4783711. Most of the early census records of Ireland were destroyed and are incomplete until 1901. There are fragments of earlier census records.

Church Records. Roman Catholic registers, which usually start around 1800, are under the jurisdiction of local parish priests. However, the National Library of Ireland, Kildare Street, Dublin 2, has many of these registers on microfilm. If you plan a vacation in Ireland, you will want to spend some time at the National Library. It has a giant collection of family histories, historical journals, newspapers, and a manuscript collection of deeds, letters, rentals, and other papers relating to Irish families, all card indexed.

Census Records. Most of the early census records of Ireland were destroyed and are incomplete until 1901. (Many of the earlier census fragments are available on microfilm at the LDS Family History Library.)

Miscellaneous Sources. The Genealogy Bookshop, 3 Nassau Street, Dublin 2, has a free catalogue of current publications. Trinity College Library, College Street, Dublin 2, has a collection of parish and other historical records, some quite old. The Genealogical Office, Dublin Castle, Dublin 2, is part of the National Library, but it has its own extensive collection of pedigrees, armorial registers, wills, abstracts, family histories, and other material valuable to a genealogist. Most, however, are on LDS microfilm.

If you have enough ancestral information to search near your family's original home, you should not overlook local libraries, even in the smallest cities. Irish libraries often have much information to offer on local families.

There are many good books specializing in Irish genealogy. Two you should consult are John Grenham's *Tracing Your Irish Ancestors: The Complete Guide* and *Irish Family Names, with Origins, Meanings Clans, Arms, Crests, and Mottoes,* by Captain Patrick Kelly, republished by Gale Research Company, Book Tower, Detroit, MI 48226. For information about Irish Jews, contact the Irish Jewish Museum, 3-4 Walworth Road, South Circular Road, Dublin 8.

There are many Internet sites you will want to explore, but you can start with the Irish Family History Foundation at *www.mayo-ireland.ie/Roots.htm* and *www.aardvark.ie/cork/genres.html,* which has links to other sites including an audio program.

ITALY

Italian research is the most straightforward of any in Europe. If you know the town of origin of your ancestor, you are likely to be able to compile a full and authenticated pedigree without going much further.

There has been little or no centralization of records in Italy. Most civil registers, which were started in 1869, remain in the hometown, or *frazione,* the smallest civil division of government in Italy. The registers are kept in bound books on printed forms, and the information is unusually complete. Often the names of the paternal and the maternal grandfather appear on the record, because so many surnames are alike in one town. For example, in one northern Italian village with a population of 1,400 today, 850 people bear one surname. In another town in Sicily with a population of 6,000, 80 percent of the population share only seven surnames among them. Fortunately, for Italian ancestor hunters, the civil registers provide more than enough information to link each record to the right pedigree.

Census Records. The hometown archive contains a record called the *Anagrafe,* which is like a town census. The earliest of these dates from about 1885.

Passport Records. Passport applications were made at the local police station (*questura*) and those dated after 1869 are still with the police or the Prefect (*Prefettura*).

Probate Records. Wills filed within the past century will be lodged with the local notary, a job that is often hereditary in Italy. For wills older than 100 years you should write for information to Archivio Notarile, Ispettatore Generale, Via Flaminia 160, Roma.

Church Records. For early birth, marriage, and death records, the parish priest in your ancestor's hometown is the person to contact. In many cases, it will be difficult to get information without searching it out yourself (and you'll need to know Latin) or hiring a professional to do it for you. (In some places it is advisable to get permission of the vicar-general of the diocese and arrive at the parish church with a letter of permission in hand.) The difficulty does not lie with the priest himself but with the inaccessibility of the records, which may be hidden away in musty old lofts and which may be badly weathered or even destroyed by mice.

Immigration Records. There are very few emigration records in Italy, because quite a bit of the pre-World War I emigration was clandestine. But if your ancestor was listed in the U.S. 1920 census, you can get a citizenship date and then write to the U.S. Immigration and Naturalization Service, 425 I Street N.W., Washington, DC 20536 for Form G-639. This is a Freedom of Information Request, and if you can prove direct descent you will receive a copy of your ancestor's naturalization papers with a great deal of genealogical information in them.

Miscellaneous Sources. There are nine *Archivio di Stato* (state archives), in Rome, Naples, Palermo, Venice, Turin, Milan, Genoa, Florence, and Bologna, which have gathered some records of genealogical interest, in particular the *Leva*, or military conscription rolls of the nineteenth century. Contact the archives in the city that represents the province where your ancestor was born for these records.

In the U.S., you will want to contact POINT (Pursuing Our Italian Names Together), P.O. Box 2977, Palos Verdes, CA 90274, *www.xs4all.nl/~tardio/point.html*. They publish an annual directory, and you might discover someone else who is working on your family line along with his or her address. Another organization that can help you is Italian Genealogical Group, c/o Ms. MaryAnn Horn, 25 Vidoni Drive, Mt. Sinai, NY 11766, *www.netcom.com/~larosaf*.

Tom Alciere, whose "Tracing Your Italian Ancestry" (*www.phoenix.net/~joe/itans.html*) is a must-read for every Italian family historian, has these following additional suggestions:

1. When writing to a church, enclose a few dollars as a donation because records take time to search, and you want them to be happy to hear from you again.

2. If you know when an ancestor died, check newspapers for death notices either in person or using a local genealogist. Newspapers are usually on library microfilm in the area where they are published and often contain the names of siblings and their hometowns.

Several sites on the Internet will help you expand your search. Three are *www.italgen.com/main.htm*, *www.phoenix.net/~joe/*, and *http://genealogy.tbox.com:81/genatl/europe/aseurfj.htm*, each with many links to other sites of interest.

JAPAN

Because of the more recent immigration of most Japanese-Americans (since 1900), preliminary information from parents, grandparents, and relatives should help ancestor hunters pinpoint the ancestral hometown.

Birth, Marriage, and Death Records. When you have determined the home village, town, or city of your immigrant forebear, you should write for a copy of the household registration record *(Koseki)* for your family. It can be found in the *Mura-yakusho* (village office), *Gun-yakusho* (county office), or *Shi-yakusho* (city office).

If you find your ancestral village no longer exists, the LDS library in Salt Lake City can help you discover into what city the village was consolidated. (Because Japan is becoming a highly urbanized country, this process is happening more frequently.) You will need, if at all possible, to supply the library with transliteration or *Romaji* and also *Kanji* characters for the village place name. For people who have difficulty writing Kanji characters, the library does have available a Japanese form of request.

Miscellaneous Sources. For general information about Japanese national records, you should address your inquiries to the Kokwritsu Kokkai Toshokan (National Diet Library), 1-10-1 Nagatacho, Chiyoda-ku, Tokyo 100.

There are two genealogical societies in Japan that can give a great deal of help. One is Nihon Kakei Kyokai (Japan Genealogical Association), 8-4, 3-chome, Ginza, Chuo-ku, Tokyo. The other is Nihon Keifu Gakkai (Genealogical Society of Japan), 3, 2-chome, Nakatsu Hondori, Oyodo-ku, Osaka.

Try the Japan Genealogy Forum (*www.genforum.com/japan/*) to locate others searching for their Japanese roots. Another site to search is Japanese Genealogy Web Sites (*www.geocities.com/Tokyo/Temple/7622/index.html*) and Japan Queries (*www.geocities.com/Tokyo/Temple/7622/Queries.html*).

Two books are worth looking for: *Asian American Genealogical Sourcebook*, by Paula K. Byers (*www.books.com/scripts/view.exe?~0810392283*), for on-line order, and *A Student's Guide to Japanese American Genealogy*, by Yoji Yamaguchi (*www.books.com/scripts/view.exe?isbn~0897749790*), also for on-line order.

JEWISH ANCESTORS

Some years ago, an American woman visited Israel and placed small newspaper ads seeking relatives of her Russian-Jewish family named Shkolnik. Before she returned home, she received a call and an invitation to tea from her cousin Levi, who had changed his family name to Eshkol—and was prime minister of Israel. Such reunions, while not commonplace, are happening more and more. There has been an absolute explosion of interest in Jewish genealogy since 1980. Jewish family historians now have one of the best organized and most complete genealogical Web sites on the Internet at *www.jewishgen.org*, including links to many other fascinating Web pages you'll want to explore. One of these links is the Jewish Genealogical Family Finder. Type in your family name and place of origin, and you might find that some unknown cousin is already researching your ancestors. Click on *soc. genealogy.jewish*, a newsgroup (see chapter 10) of experts and family historians, and they'll give you personal help in your search. Also look under JewishGen ShtetLinks Project to see pictures, maps and read stories of Jewish communities, some destroyed, some still existing today.

While Israel is a Jewish nation, the Jews are not, of course, from this one country. If records of your Jewish forebears exist, they can often be found in the country of ancestral origin by using the same methods as a genealogist of any other origin. As usual, check with the LDS Family History Library before you begin individual research. They have recently filmed Eastern European Jewish records in Belarus, Bulgaria, Estonia, Hungary, Poland, Slovakia, and the Ukraine, as well as records in every other country where Jews once lived. Other records for eastern European Jewry can be located at the YIVO Institute, 555 West 57th Street, 11th Floor, New York, NY 10019, telephone 212-246-6080.

Despite the attempt by the Nazis to wipe out not only the Jews but also all records of Jewish historical existence, there are still many records of Jewish communities in Europe that survive. In Germany, particularly in the state of Württemberg (see address for Württemberg archives in the section on Germany in this chapter), Jewish family registers were kept from 1810, with genealogical information going back to 1750. Also contact Frank Mecklenburg, c/o Leo Baeck Institute, 129 East 73rd Street, New York, NY 10021, *www.jewishgen.org/stammbaum*, for help with German research. The LDS library has 2,100 microfilms of Jewish records, and filming in Germany is ongoing.

In Poland, surviving Jewish synagogue records for the years between 1810 and 1880 have been placed on microfilm and are available at the LDS library in Salt Lake City. There are over 2,000 microfilm reels, which encompass millions of records. You can access these records on microfiche or CD in the Family History Library Catalog, available at any branch. (Also see Polish archival information later in this chapter.)

In England, contact the Jewish Genealogical society of Great Britain, P.O. Box 13288, London N3 3WD, telephone 081-455-3323.

In the Netherlands, contact the Netherlands Society for Jewish Genealogy (Nederlandse Kring voor Joodse Genealogie), Mr. D Verdooner, Bosporus 8 1183 GH Amstelveen.

Some of the oldest Jewish cemeteries in Europe are a fabulous hunting ground for genealogical information. The Halnlein-Alsback cemetery in the German state of Hesse served twenty-nine Jewish communities; the Prague Jewish cemetery in the Czech Republic is the oldest in Europe.

The following agencies in Israel are piecing together European Jewish records and will respond to your requests.

1. "Yad Vashem"
Remembrance Authority
P.O. Box 3477
91034 Jerusalem, Israel
Telephone 02-751611
www.yad.vashem.org.il

2. Museum of the Diaspora
DOROT Genealogy Center
P.O. Box 39359
61392 Tel Aviv, Israel
Telephone 03-646-2062
www.bh.org.il

3. Central Archives for the
History of the Jewish People
P.O. Box 1149
91010 Jerusalem, Israel
Telephone 02-635716

4. Central Zionist Archives
P.O. Box 92
Zalman Shazar
91920 Jerusalem, Israel
Telephone 02-6526 155
www.wzo.org.il/cza/access.htm

5. Search Bureau for Missing
Relatives, P.O. Box 92
91000 Jerusalem, Israel
Telephone 02-612471

6. Israel Genealogical Society,
c/o Ester Ramon,
Rechov Harav Uziel 50,
IL-96 424 Jerusalem, Israel
Telephone 02-642-4147

Yad Vashem is the archive of the Holocaust and contains 1,000 *Yizkor* (memorial) books, which are histories of individual Eastern European Jewish communities. For more information, access *www. jewishgen.org/yizkor* or write to the address above. For further help with the special problems of tracing Jewish ancestors in Europe, contact the American Jewish Historical Society, 2 Thornton Road, Waltham, MA 02154, telephone 617-891-8110. For a list of other Jewish genealogical societies in the U.S., access *www.jewishgen.org/ faqinfo.html*. Also the U.S. Holocaust Memorial Museum is rapidly building its collection of genealogical materials and has recently microfilmed in the former Soviet Union and other eastern European countries. You can contact them at 100 Raoul Wallenberg Place S.W., Washington, DC 20024, telephone 202-488-0400 or access more information at *www.ushmm.org*. A beginning genealogist, just like you, has put together a Web page of places on the Internet that he found helpful, many in eastern Europe and former Soviet Bloc countries: *http://adams.patriot.net/~arielle/air/genlinks.html*. The passenger lists of 1850 through 1934, from Hamburg, Germany, the point of embarkation for many Jewish immigrants, containing the immigrants' hometowns, have been microfilmed, and are available at the LDS Family History Center and its branches.

Avotaynu: The International Review of Jewish Genealogy, P.O. Box 900, Teaneck, NJ 07666, telephone 800-AVOTAYNU (*www.avotaynu. com*), costs $29 for a year's subscription. An index of articles at their Web site will give you an idea of how helpful they'd be in your research.

MEXICO

Don't head for Mexico ancestor hunting unless you have thoroughly checked the LDS library in Salt Lake City. Its staff has filmed many of Mexico's civil and church records and may have just what you need. Check with your branch library for their "Research Outline for Latin America," which includes Mexico and all of Central and South America. Even if you do travel to Mexico, do not overlook the LDS branch libraries in that country. They will advise you how to proceed to solve your particular research problem. For their location, contact the Family History Library in Salt Lake City (see chapter 5).

Birth, Marriage, and Death Records. Local parishes have baptismal, confirmation, marriage, and death records from 1524 to the present. Mandatory civil registration has been the law since 1859 and includes the same general information as parish registers, with the exception that marriage certificates record the grandparents' names. These records are located in the Office of the Civil Registrar in each municipality.

Census Records. A special early census was taken (Spaniards only) in 1689, which listed name, birthplace, parents, grandparents, rank, and orders of chivalry bestowed. This census is located in the Mexican National Archive, Archivo General de la Nación, Tacuba 8, Segundo piso, Palacio Naciónal, Apartado 1999, Mexico City 1. The National Archive's publication department can be reached at: Departamento de Publicaciones, Apartado 1999, Mexico City, D.F. Modern census rolls exist from 1842 to the present and include standard census data plus religion, race, and Indian dialect. These census rolls are located in La Casa Amarilla, Mexico City.

Property and Tax Records. Property-tax records for the years 1542 to 1825 include the name, residence address, date of payments, and spouse's name. They can be found in the Archivo General de la Nación, address above. Land records from 1524 to the present are also at the Archivo General.

Military Records. Historical military records from 1524 to 1700 are at the Archivo General de Indias in Sevilla, Spain, and the Archivo General Military, Alcalá 9, Madrid, Spain. These documents usually contain names of parents, dates of commissions, and biographies. Modern military and some historical military records dating from 1600 to 1650 are at the Archivo General in Mexico City.

Immigration Records. Emigration records from 1519 to 1820 are located in the Archivo Histórico de Hacienda. Records from 1917 to the present are at the Archivo del Ex-Ayuntamiento (City Hall). Both are in Mexico City. Emigration records for the period 1820 to 1850, during the expulsion of the Spanish, are at the Archivo General.

Other emigration reports, called land entry records, are particularly valuable to Mexican-Americans. From 1903 to 1952 the names, ages, birthplace, and last permanent address were recorded for 1,500,000 immigrants at the El Paso, Texas, port of entry. These lists have also been microfilmed by the LDS library.

Miscellaneous Sources. Mexican Indian records are the oldest records in Mexico, dating from 900 to the present time, including the *Mayan Chronicles.* (In this country, you can find the chronicles at Brigham Young University in Provo, Utah.)

Other records, such as land and property grants to Indians from 1574 to 1700, are recorded in the Archivo General.

The Academia Mexicana de Genealogía y Heráldica in Mexico City has many family histories, with biographical and pedigree data, plus proofs of nobility.

The Mexican National Library has genealogical materials and

can be reached at Biblioteca Nacional de México, Instituto de Investigaciones Bibliográficas, Universidad Nacional Autónoma de México, Centro Cultural, Ciudad Universitaria, Delegación Coyoacán, Apartado 29-124, 04510 México. Also try a major genealogical library: Colonia Juárez Branch Genealogical Library, Colonia Juárez, 31009, Chihuahua, Chihuahua, México. In the U.S. you'll want to contact the Hispanic Genealogical Society, P.O. Box 810561, Houston, TX 77281; they publish the *Hispanic Genealogical Journal*.

For further reading, try *A Student's Guide to Mexican American Genealogy*, which you can order at *www.oryxpress.com/books/ftmex.htm*. For more Internet help try *http://users.aol.com/mrosado007/mexico.htm* for Hispanic genealogy resources.

NORWAY

About three million Americans are descended from Norwegian Viking ancestors, most having emigrated from Norway after 1825, with the peak year being 1883. This means that most of your progenitors do not reach back beyond Norway's modern records, so it should be fairly simple to pick up the trail if you've gathered the basic family history.

Birth, Marriage, and Death Records. Registers of vital statistics were first made compulsory in 1946, so most of the data for genealogical purposes must be gathered from parish registers.

Church Records. Norwegian parish registers record birth, baptism, marriage, and death, and in some instances movements into and out of the parish. Some registers date from 1600, but most are from 1700. According to law, parish registers are transferred to regional archives eighty years after the last entry. Here is a list of those regional archives with the regions they serve:

1. *Statsarkivet i Oslo* (also National Archives of Norway), Folke Bernadottes vei 21, Postboks 4015 Ulleval Hageby N-0806, Oslo, telephone +47 22 02 26 00 (for Østfold, Akershus, Oslo)

2. *Statsarkivet i Hamar*, Lille Strandgate 3, Postboks 533, N-2301 Hamar, telephone +47 62 52 36 42 (for Hedmark and Oppland)

3. *Statsarkivet i Kristiansand*, Vesterveien 4, N-4613 Kristiansand, telephone +47 38 02 55 11 (for Aust-Agder and Vest-Agder)

4. *Statsarkivet i Stavanger*, Bergelandsgt. 30, N-4012 Stavanger, telephone +47 51 50 12 60 (for Rogaland)

5. *Statsarkivet i Bergen*, Arstadveien 22, N-5009 Bergen, telephone +47 55 31 50 70 (for Hordaland, including Bergen, and Sogn og Fjordane)

6. *Statsarkivet i Trondheim*, Høgskoleveien 12, Postboks 2825 Elgasaeter, N-7002, Trondheim, telephone +47 73 88 45 00 (for Møre og Romsdal, SørTrøndelag, Nord-Trøndelag, and Nordland)

7. *Statsarkivkontoret i Tromsø*, N-9005, Tromsø (for Troms, Finnmark, and Spitsbergen)

8. *Statsarkivet I Kongsberg*, Frogsvei 44, N-3600 Kongsberg, telephone +47 32 86 99 00 (for Buskerud, Vestfold, Telemark)

Census Records. Norway has one of the oldest population rolls in Europe, dated 1664. These cover the rural districts only and list just men and boys or women engaged in farming. These early rolls and later official censuses from 1769 to 1900 are kept in the National Archives: Riksarkivet, Folke Bernadottes vei 21, Postboks 10, Kringsja 0862, Oslo 8.

The archives cannot make extensive searches but will offer advice, and if necessary, forward your request for information to the right agency. As always, if you want an answer, keep your inquiries brief and very specific: name, parish or town, and year of birth.

Probate Records. Probate registers going back to about 1660 are preserved in the regional archives (see addresses above) and show the registration, valuation, and division of real estate and property of all kinds left by the deceased. In recent years many have been indexed on cards.

Property Records. Property deeds back to about 1720 can be located in regional archives. Real estate books called *matrikler* will give you the names of owners of farms from 1665 to 1723 and are in the National Archives. Some older records from the Middle Ages have been printed as have those dating after 1838.

Immigration Records. Emigrant lists kept by the police of a number of districts are located in the regional archives. They show the name, home address, date of departure, destination, and name of ship. These lists may often prove to be the best starting point for genealogical inquiries. The Norwegian Emigration Center, Bergjelandsgaten 30, 4012 Stavanger, Norway, contains most of the published genealogical material in Norway. They will do research for a small fee.

Military Records. Those dating from 1650 are kept partly in the National Archives and partly in the regional archives, especially those in Bergen and Trondheim. The early ones are sketchy, but the later ones give much detailed personal information you are unlikely to find in any other source.

Miscellaneous Sources. For the very helpful "How to Trace Your Ancestors in Norway," write the Norwegian Information Service of the Royal Norwegian Consulate General, 825 Third Avenue, 38th Floor, New York, NY 10022, or access their Web site at *www.norway.org/ancestor.htm* to print out a complete copy. It contains a good overview of all the records in Norway and U.S. that a family historian needs to track down ancestors.

According to Norwegian authorities, the LDS genealogical library in Salt Lake City possesses film copies of all the principal family history records of Norway. The LDS Family History Library (see chapter 5) has published a research outline for Norway, which is worth having if for no other reason than its fascinating description of unique Norwegian naming practices.

Other sources in the United States you can check with for help in locating your Norwegian ancestry are the Sons of Norway, 1455 West Lake Street, Minneapolis, MN 55057, and the Norwegian-American Historical Association, Rolvaag Library of St. Olaf College, Northfield, MN 55057, *www.stolaf.edu/stolaf/other/naha/naha.html.*

Since most Norwegian emigrants were churchgoing Lutherans, you'll find helpful parish registers in the Archives of the Evangelical Church in America, 8765 West Higgins Road, Chicago, IL 60631, telephone 800-638-3522, Web address *www.elca.org/co/anatomy/ 2b.html,* and the Mortvedt Library, Pacific Lutheran University, Tacoma, WA 98447. You'll want to contact the Vesterheim Genealogical Center, 415 W. Main Street, Madison, WI 53703, and visit its museum in Decorah, Iowa 52101, which publishes *Norwegian Tracks.*

Finally, there is a strong literary heritage left by descendants of Scandinavian immigrants. Norwegian-Americans, in particular, can learn what the early days were like by reading O. E. Rolvaag's *Giants in the Earth.*

Another Web site of interest is Norway's Ministry of Foreign Affairs *http://odin.dep.no/ud/publ/96/ancestors/prep.html.*

REPUBLIC OF THE PHILIPPINES

Filipino immigrants began to arrive in this country after the U.S. annexed the Philippines in 1898. But since 1965, Filipinos have become the second largest immigrant group, after Mexicans. As with most recent arrivals, gathering enough family history to tie Filipino-Americans to their ancestral homeland should not be a problem.

The LDS Family History Library contains more than 40,000 microfilm rolls about the Philippines and its diverse peoples; indeed, it has almost *all* the country's civil records. It also has a valuable Research Outline you'll want to order. Obviously, you should go to your nearest branch library first. But there are other useful resources available, especially if you should visit the Philippines.

In Manila, go to the Manila Philippines Family History Service Center, Country Space 1 Building, Gil J. Puyat Avenue, P.O. Box 5026, Makati, Metro Manila. There you can obtain a list of LDS branches in the Philippines to help start your search. Also in Manila, the country's archives and records management office is located in the Philippine National Library, T. M. Kalaw Street, Ermita, Manila 2801.

Remember, most older genealogical records are written in Spanish, so you'll need a dictionary if you're not fluent. Some records are written in one of the almost eighty different dialects spoken in the Philippines. For help with culture, language, and genealogical records you should access the Mga Bayani Web site at *www.he.net/ ~skyeagle/ index.htm* and *www.worldaccess.nl/~radenmas/1-phil2.htm*. For a page of family historians researching their surnames, go to *http://members. aol.com/marcnepo/tribpurs/philgene/genelist.htm*.

For an overview of Philippine genealogy, you should look for *The Art of Ancestor Hunting in the Philippines*, by Luciano Santiago y Perez-Rivera, M.D.

POLAND

It has been estimated that about 30 percent of Americans can trace at least one of their ancestral lines into Poland. If you have such a Polish line, you'll want to first become familiar with Poland's troubled history so that you will know what country's records (Germany, Russia, Poland) to research. Some provinces have changed hands many times over the centuries.

The LDS church has filmed extensively in Poland, so be sure to check their Family History Library first. Vital records older than 100 years are in the Polish State Archives or its branches; those records less than 100 years old are in your ancestor's town hall (*Urzad Stanu Cywilnego*). You can approach genealogical research in Poland by getting in touch with one of the two central archives in Warsaw. One is for old records, the other for modern records (post-1945).

1. Old Records: Archiwum Glówne Akt Dawnych, ul. Dluga 7, 00-263 Warszawa

2. New records: Archiwum Akt Nowych, ul. Hankiewicza 1, 02-103, Warszawa

3. Film and tape: Archiwum Dokumentacji Mechanicznej, ul. Swietojerska 24, 00-202 Warszawa

In the summer of 1997, a devastating flood hit southwestern Poland, inundating the archives at Opole and Wroclaw. They will probably not be operational until 2002. For further information on these two archives, telephone the General Archive of Historical Records at (022) 831-54-91, ext. 39, or access their Web site at *http://ciuw.warman,net.pl/alf/archiwa/powodz/english.htm.*

The Polish Genealogy and Heraldry Society (Towarzystwo Genealogiczno-Haraldyczyne) Wodna 27 (Palac Gorkow), 61-781-Poznan, and the Association of Polish Nobility (Zwiazek Szlachty Polskiej, 81-701 Sopot 1, Skr. Poczt) accept memberships but do not do research. However, Polish archives provide a unique service for Americans with Polish ancestry. For a thirty-dollar deposit fee (fifteen dollars per hour, copies ten dollars) the Naczelna Dyrekcja Archiwów Pánstwowych, ul. Dluga 6, Skr. Pocztowa Nr 1005, 00-960 Warszawa, will research all Polish records for you and provide photocopies of all documents found. The total fee can amount to more than two hundred dollars, so this is not a step to be taken until other sources have been tried. (Payment in dollars by U.S. Postal Money order is acceptable.) Give them the fullest possible data on your ancestor and his or her family members, such as names, birth and death dates, marriages, spouses' names, and parents' names. The more you can give them, the less it will cost for the search. Correspondence in the Polish language is better, although English is accepted.

If you choose to do your own research, you will need to write in Polish. For a sample archive or parish letter in Polish access *http://members.aol.com/genpoland/certif.htm.* For a complete list of

Polish regional archives and their branches, go to *http://members.aol. com/genpoland/geninfo6.htm.*

Miscellaneous Sources. The Polish Embassy in Washington, DC, suggests that genealogists needing special help with problems of Polish ancestry contact Dyr. Hieronim Kubiak, Uniwersytet Jagiellonski, Instytut Badan Polonijnych, ul. Straszewskiego 27, 31-101 Krakow.

The LDS church has microfilmed archival records (about 6,000 rolls) in Poland and Protestant church registers as well. However, Catholic church records remain in their individual parishes or in ecclesiastical archives. All twenty-six archives with their addresses can be obtained at *http://members.aol.com/genpoland/geninfo6.htm.*

Societies in the U.S. you may want to contact are: the American Center of Polish Culture, Inc., 2025 "O" Street N.W., Washington, DC 20036, telephone 202-785-2320; Federation of East European Family History Societies, Charles M. Hall, President, P.O. Box 21346, Salt Lake City, UT 81421; Polish Nobility Association, Villa Anneslie, 529 Dunkirk Road, Anneslie, MD 21212; and the Polish Genealogical Society of America, c/o Polish Museum of America, 984 Milwaukee Avenue, Chicago, IL 60622. the PGSA Web site is located at *www.pgsa.org.*

For another helpful Web site, "Genealogy and Poland, A Guide," go to *http://members.aol.com/genpoland/genpolen.htm.*

RUSSIA

The former Soviet Union was composed of the following "states" and ethnic groups: Russia, Armenia, Azerbaijhan, Estonia, Georgia, Karelia, Kirgiz, Latvia, Lithuania, Moldavia, Tadzhikistan, Turkistan, Turkmenistan, Ukraine, Uzbekistan, and White Russia. For many years the Soviets did not respond to genealogical inquiries by private American citizens or by professional genealogists. Only recently have Russia and the other newly independent states been open to genealogical inquiries about their vital records, and there are still problems of language and money exchange. You may want to get the help of a professional.

Most of the immigrants from Russia between 1880 and 1920 were Jews escaping from pogroms and other violent anti-Semitism (see the "Jewish Ancestors" section, earlier in this chapter). After the revolution in 1917, immigration almost stopped until the breakup of the Soviet Union. Since 1991, Russians have again been flocking to the U.S.

Two organizations in this country that might be able to help you with biographical and family history information from their 1,000-volume library are the Russian Historical and Genealogical Society and the Russian Nobility Association, both at 971 First Avenue, New York, New York 10022. Another resource is the American Russian History Society, 1272 47th Avenue, San Francisco, CA 94107. The most extensive site on the Internet can be accessed at *www.friends-partners.org/oldfriends/info.html*. Although this is not strictly a genealogical site, it has many links to cultural information about Russia and other eastern European states, including museums, Russian language, business, and press coverage.

The German-Russian Genealogical Library has a Web site at *http://pixel.cs.vt.edu/library/odessa.html* to which you can link and search their repository of documents. For more information by mail, try the American Historical Society of Germans from Russia, 631 D Street, Lincoln, NE 68502 and the Federation of East European Family History Societies, P.O. Box 510898, Salt Lake City, UT 94151, e-mail *feefhs@feefhs.org*.

Two special Internet sites you'll want to explore are the World Gen Web site for Russian genealogy, at *www.dsenter.com/worldgenweb/Europe/Russia/index.html*, and the University of Pittsburgh's REESWeb site for Russian and eastern European studies at *www.pitt.edu/~cjp/rees.html*.

For professional genealogical research in Russia and the newly independent states, you should contact W. Edward Nute, Coordinator, Russian-Baltic Information Center—BLITZ, 907 Mission Avenue, San Rafael, CA 94901, telephone 415-453-0343, or access their Web sites at *www.dcn.davis.ca.us/go/feefhs/blitz/blitzih.html*, for a genealogy search order form, or *www.dcn.davis.ca.us/~feefhs/blitz/tetrad1.html* for a list of their genealogical and heraldic books. These are published in cooperation with the St. Petersburg Noble Assembly and the Archives of the St. Petersburg Branch of the Institute of History of the Russian Academy of Sciences, Dumskaya ulitsa, dom 3, Setazh, PEN, club Sankt, Petersburg, Russia 191011, telephone 812-312-14-40. BLITZ also sell copies of the Russian Genealogy Society periodical (*Izvestiya Russkogo genealogicheskogo obshchestva*) and have cemetery and Jewish records among others. BLITZ is helping the Russian archives computerize their records, which will make ancestor searching much easier than it is now.

In Belarus, the Association of the Belarusian Nobility can be reached at P.O. Box 124, Minsk 74, 220 074 Belarus, telephone 011 375 17 254 5800. If you telephone, be prepared to speak Belarussian, Russian, Polish, or German. An American genealogist in regular contact with the Central Historical Archives of Belarus is George Tarnowski, 2050 Spring Valley Road, Lansdale, PA 19446.

SPAIN

Although the number of immigrants from Spain to the U.S. is very low, centuries of Spanish occupation and intermarriage in Central and Latin America and the subsequent influx of immigrants from these countries means that a great many Americans have a Spanish line in their heritage.

There is not one but four principal national archives in Spain, each holding material of specific interest to American family historians of Spanish ancestry. The four archives are:

1. *Archivo de Simancas*, Responsible Provisional: José Luis Rodríguez, Carretera de Salamanca-Burgos, S/N, 47130 Simancas, Castilla-Leon, España, telephone 983/590003: here are military, naval, royal, and judicial records dating back to 1545.

Of particular interest is a tax list of residents of Castilla during 1752, giving surnames of parents and grandparents.

2. *Archivo Historico Naciónal*, Calle Duque de Lerma, 2, 45004 Toledo, Castilla La Mancha, España, telephone 91/5618005: Founded in 1866, these archives are the most valuable for genealogical study. Many historical records have three to five generations referenced; there are also documents of the Court of the Holy Inquisition from 1400 through 1800. The records are indexed.

3. *Archivo de la Corona de Aragón*, Director, Pedro López Gómez, Carrer Comtes, 2, 08002 Barcelona, Cataluña, España, telephone 93/3150211: These archives have cataloged some of the earliest legal, royal, and church documents in Spain, reaching back to the 1000s.

4. *Archivo General de Indias*, Director Pedro González, Avenida de la Constitución, 41003 Sevilla, Andalucía, España, telephone 95/4225158: These archives have a massive collection of 14 million reports on military and early land discoveries in the New World, and are very valuable records for tracing early Spanish-Mexican ancestry.

Church Records. For parochial archival information, contact Archivo Diocesano, Calle Beato Tomás de Zumarraga, 67, 01009 Vitoria-Gasteiz, Pais Vasco, España, telephone 945/248392. Spain has a treasure trove of early church parish records for Spain's 19,000 parishes. The most ancient church register in Spain is in the parish of Verdu and dates from 1394. For other parochial archives, access *http://user.aol.com/mrosado007/sparc.htm.*

Miscellaneous Sources. Here are some of the most important of Spain's Family History Centers. For a complete list, which runs to six pages, access *http://user.aol.com/mrosado007/spfhc.htm.*

1. *Andalusia.* Centro de Historia Familiar, Calle Sevilla 43, 11201 Algeciras, Cádiz

2. *Aragón.* Centro de Historia Familiar, Marqués de Montoliu 16 Bajo, 43002 Tarragona

3. *Asturias.* Centro de Historia Familiar, Calle González Abarca 43-47 Bajo, 33400 Aviles

4. *Basque country.* Centro de Historia Familiar, Calle Henao 53, 48009 Bilbao, Vizcaya

5. *Canary Islands.* Centro de Historia Familiar, Calle Maria Estrada 36, 35600 Puerto del Rosario, Fuerteventura, Islas Canarias

6. *Castile and Leon.* Centro de Historia Familiar, Calle Bartolomé Ordoñez 1 Bajo, 09005 Burgos, Castile-Leon

7. *Castile-La Mancha.* Centro de Historia Familiar, Calle Vicente Aleixandre S/N, 02006 Albacete

8. *Catalonia.* Centro de Historia Familiar, Calle Antigua de Valencia 49-51, 08913 Badolna

9. *Estremadura.* Centro de Historia Familiar, Avenida Ramón y Cajal 13, 06001 Badajoz

10. *Galicia.* Centro de Historia Familiar, Calle Bugallal Marchesi 5-BD, 15008 La Coruña

11. *La Rioja.* Centro de Historia Familiar, Plaza de las Chiribinas, S/N, 26004 Logono, La Rioja

12. *Madrid.* Centro de Historia Familiar, Calle Cuenca Esq. San Sebastián, 28804 Alcalá de Henares, Madrid

13. *Murcia.* Centro de Historia Familiar, Calle Jacinto Benavente 1, 30290 Cartagena, Murcia

14. *Navarre.* Centro de Historia Familiar, Ronda de Ermitagna 16, Parcela 20, sector 1, 31008 Pamplona, Navarre

15. *Valencia.* Centro de Historia Familiar, Calle Azorin, S/N, 3803 Alcoy, Alicante

Both Spanish and Mexican ancestor hunters may find the *Spanish Genealogical Helper* worth reading. It is published quarterly by the Augustan Society, 1617 West 261st Street, Harbor City, CA 90710, telephone 310-320-7766. Also of interest is the Spanish American Genealogical Association, P.O. Box 5407, Corpus Christi, TX 78405.

For a helpful reading list about your Spanish heritage, you should go to *www.familytreemaker.com/00000385.html.*

SWEDEN

Finn A. Thomsen, an authority on Scandinavian research, points out two interesting challenges to the Swedish-American ancestor hunter. First, many of the records made prior to 1875 were written in a Gothic script. Thus, you will have to learn to read in a new way, since some of the characters are completely different from the Roman alphabet. Second, there are some interesting surname customs in all Scandinavia and particularly Sweden. More than 40 percent of the current population share twenty names, all of which end in "son." Johansson alone accounts for one out of every fifteen Swedes. This means that it is very difficult for you to trace your Swedish ancestors by name. As you might guess, multiple sources are a must. As for the Internet, there are several Swedish sites to explore (see below), but unfortunately some of them are in Swedish.

In spite of those minor roadblocks, the rewards are great for the 12 million American descendants of Swedish ancestors who want to find living family in Sweden. About half (or 4 million) of Sweden's population are related to Americans.

Birth, Marriage, and Death Records. In Sweden keeping vital statistics has been the duty of the church. Every parish maintains these records whether or not the person sets foot in the church itself. Since the late 1600s, the parish clergyman has kept not only records of births, marriages, deaths, and confirmations but also records of arrivals and removals from the parish. Each parish also has records called *husförhörsläangder*, or household rolls, which are similar to a parish census.

Although some of these records remain in the parishes, most of the records more than 100 years old were transferred from their *län* (equivalent to our state) to regional archives called *landsarkiv*. A few cities have established their own archives called *stadsarkiv*. All are listed below with the areas they serve:

1. *Landsarkivet i Uppsala*, Fack 135, S-751 04 Uppsala (for the *län* of Stockholm, Uppssala, Södermanland, Örebro, Västmanland, and Kopparberg)

2. *Landsarkivet i Vadstena, Fack 126*, S-592 00 Vadstena (for the *län* of Öostergötland, Jönköping, Kronoberg, and Kalmar)

3. *Landsarkivet i Visby*, Fack 2142, S-621 02 Visby (for the *län* of Gotland)

4. *Landsarkivet i Lund*, Fack 2016, S-220 02 Lund (for the *län* of Blekinge, Kristianstad, Malmöhus, and Halland)

5. *Landsarkivet i Göteborg*, Fack 3009, S-400 10 Göteborg (for the *län* of Göteborg and Bohus, Alvsborg, Skaraborg, and Värmland)

6. *Landsarkivet i Hämösand*, Nybrogatan 17, Fack 161, S-871 24 Hämösand (for the *län* of Gävleborg, Västermorrland, Västerbotten, and Norrbotten)

7. *Landsarkivet i Östersund*, Arkivvagen 1 S-831 31 Östersund (for the *län* of Jämtland)

8. *Stadsarkivet i Stockholm*, Fack 22063, Kungsklippan 6, S-104 22 Stockholm (for the city of Stockholm)

9. *Stadarkivet i Malmö*, St. Petrigingen 7A, S-211 22 Malmö (for the city of Malmö)

10. *Stadsarkivet i Boris, Fack* 851-S-501 *Barås* (for the city of Boris, except for church records that have been transferred to *Landsarkivet* in Göteborg)

11. *Stadsarkivet i Västerås,* S-721 87 Västerå (for the city of Västerås, except for church records that have been transferred to *Landsarkivet* in Uppsala)

12. *Stadsarkivet i Örebro,* S-701 Örebro (for the city of Örebro)

13. *Stadsarkivet i Uppsala,* Uppsala kommun, Fack 216, S-751 04 Uppsala (for the city of Uppsala)

14. *Stadsarkivet i Gävle,* Gävle centralarkiv, Stapeltorgsgatan SB, S-802 24 Gävle (for the city of Gävle)

15. *Stadsarkivet i Karlstad,* Stadshuset, Drottninggatan 32, S-652 25 Karlstad (for the city of Karlstad)

16. *Stadsarkivet i Eskilstuna,* Kriebsensgatan 4, S-632 00, Eskilstuna (for the city of Eskilstuna)

17. *Stadsarkivet i Norrköping,* Norrköpings kommun, Stadsarkivet, S-601 81 Norrköping (for the city of Norrköping).

Property and Tax Records Material in the Riksarkivet (the National Archives), Fack, Fyrverkarbacken 13-17, S-100 26 Stockholm, dates back as far as 1540. Svensk Arkivinformation, Box 160, 880 40 Ramsele, will research and copy in the National Archives for a fee.

Immigration Records. Beginning in 1867, the police gathered complete information about passengers bound for America, including the destination in America. These records are indexed and available in the Göteborg *Landsarkivet,* the Emigrantinstitutet (House of Emigrants), P.O. Box 201, S-351 04 Växjö (*www.hv.se/forskn/migr/sei*), and the *Emigrantregistret* (the Emigrant Register), P.O. Box 331, S:a Kyrkogatan 4, S-651 05 Karlstad.

Military Records. All military records are located at the Krigsarkivet (the Royal Swedish Military Record Office), Banérgatan 64, 11588 Stockholm.

Miscellaneous Sources. For general information about Sweden's records you can contact *Riksarkivet* (the National Swedish Record Office), Fack, Fyrverkarbacken 13-17, S-100 26, Stockholm. Or contact *Statistika cent trabyrán* (the National Central Bureau of Statistics), Fack, Karlavägen 100, S-102 50 Stockholm. The National Association for the Preservation of Local Nature and Culture (Riksförbundet för Hembygdsvärd, Box 30193, S-104 25 Stockholm) was founded in 1916 to preserve traditional Swedish customs.

A sourcebook for Americans looking for Swedish ancestry, called *Cradled in Sweden,* by Carl-Erik Johannson, gives explicit directions for transatlantic research in Sweden, including an alphabetical index of all parishes and the *län* in which they are located.

Two genealogical societies can help you with specific problems in Swedish research. The first, *Personhistorika samfundet, Riksarkivet,* box 34106, S-100 26 Stockholm, publishes a magazine, *Personhistorisk tidskrift.* The second, *Genealogiska Föreningen,* Arkvigatan 3, Box 34106, S-100 26 Stockholm, publishes, *Släkt och hard.*

For a free copy of "Tracing Your Swedish Ancestry" and an interesting history of Swedish emigration to America entitled "Americans from Sweden," write to the Royal Swedish Embassy, Watergate 600, 600 New Hampshire Avenue N.W., Washington, DC 20037.

Also in this country, you should contact the American Swedish Institute, 2600 Park Avenue, Minneapolis, MN 55407, telephone 612-871-4907, which has Swedish-American Lutheran church records on microfilm, and the Swedish Genealogy Group, P.O. Box 16069, St. Paul, MN 55116, *www.mtn.org.mgs/branches/swedish.html.* This latter group has several publications and genealogy charts for sale and a newsletter, *Tidningen.*

On the Internet you should access *www.rootsweb.com/~wgsweden/* and *www.oz.net/~cyndihow/sweden/htm.*

SWITZERLAND

If you are descended from Swiss ancestors and are under twenty-two, you may still be a Swiss citizen. The law in Switzerland states that persons of Swiss ancestry, often those living for generations in a foreign country, can report to any Swiss government agency in Switzerland or in any foreign country before they are twenty-two years old and reclaim their Swiss citizenship. They may at the same time retain dual citizenship in any other country.

Under Switzerland's unique citizenship laws every Swiss is first of all a citizen of a community (village or city), and only by right of this community citizenship is he also a citizen of a canton (state), and last of all a citizen of Switzerland.

Each Swiss community has a genealogical records center for all its citizens, even those who actually reside elsewhere in the country. Hometown citizenship is inherited like a surname, so no matter where a person moves within Switzerland, his vital records are channeled back to the place where he is a citizen and entered into *Buergerregisters*.

The civil registrar of the town will, on request, prepare a *Familienschein*, or family record. Some of these records (in the canton of Bern, for example) go back to 1820, but most date from 1876, when such registration became law. Before 1876 the church maintained vital statistical records as in most other Western countries. Most of the church records date from 1600.

The Kantonarchive (there are twenty-six cantons, corresponding to our states, in Switzerland) have most church records on microfilm, but they do not provide research services. For a full list of canton addresses, access (*www.kssg.ch/chgene/into-f.htm*). Since these archives do not answer queries, you will have to go in person or hire a professional genealogist. Professional referrals can be obtained from the Zentralstelle für genealogische Auskunfte, Mr. Manuel Aicher, Vogelaustrasse 34, 8953 Dietikon ZH, Switzerland. If you want to hire a genealogist for a particular canton, access *www.webcom.com/~schori/ swis.html* for a list of professional genealogists throughout Switzerland—some English speaking, some not.

Because of the Swiss passion for record keeping from an early time, it is possible, especially in the case of noble families, to trace genealogies back to medieval times—even to Charlemagne. One of the exceptional genealogical achievements of all time is the pedigree charts of the Rubel-Blass family, prepared by Dr. W. H. Ruoff of Zurich. Dr. Ruoff traced the family back to the eighth century and documented 12,000 ancestors on 313 huge pedigree sheets.

The Library of the Genealogical Society of Switzerland, c/o Schweiz. Landesbibliothek, CH-3003 Bern, and the Heraldik & Genealogie, Atelier Galloway, Museggstrasse 25, 6004 Lucerne, could give you both genealogical and heraldic information. For general information about the country write or telephone the Swiss National Tourist Office, 150 North Michigan Avenue, Suite 2930, Chicago, IL 60601, telephone 312-630-5840.

You may want to contact the Family History Centers of the LDS church in Switzerland. Sectional branches of the society are as follows:

1. Wartenbergstr. 31, CH-4133 Pratteln, telephone +41-61-821 00 31

2. Herbstweg 120, CH-8050 Zurich, telephone +41-1-320 10 90

If you know from which Swiss community your ancestor emigrated, you should write directly to the civil registrar with your questions. If you do not know the community, you should consult the *Family Name Book of Switzerland (Familiennamenbuch der Schweiz)*, which should be in most libraries with sizable genealogical collections. This multivolume work, the magic key to Swiss genealogical research, has all present-day Swiss family names listed, with reference to the cantons in which they appear and the date on which they first appeared. In this country, you may want to subscribe to a quarterly newsletter for Americans of Swiss descent: *The Swiss Connection*, Ms. Marilyn A. Wellauer, 2845 North 72nd Street, Milwaukee, WI 53210. If you read French, a helpful Internet site is *www.kssg.ch/chgene/info-f.htm*.

If you didn't find your ancestral homeland listed in this chapter (or even if you did), turn to the next chapter and I'll show you how easy it is to dig up your roots in the great treasure trove of family history resources waiting for you in cyberspace, whether you have a home computer or not.

CHAPTER 10

Finding Your Roots in Cyberspace

THE COMPUTER was invented for genealogy! Ask enthusiastic family historians who use one and they'll swear that's true, although military and government agencies actually developed computers right after World War II for their own purposes. But it wasn't long before family historians began to use them to keep their family trees in order and create small databases of vital records. The LDS Church led the way in 1960, putting English parish registers on computer. Today they have *two billion* surnames computerized.

How many millions of genealogists keep their findings on a computer? I've heard that 40 percent of the forty-two million roots searchers do, but nobody knows for sure. I do know that just one of the many genealogical software programs, *Family Tree Maker*, has sold well over a million copies. There are also no numbers for how many family historians are searching for ancestors on the Internet, but the major Internet service providers (ISPs) report that genealogists are among the ten top users of America Online (AOL), CompuServe, and Microsoft Network.

Why is cyberspace genealogy so popular? The answers are simple. First, the Internet is the richest repository of information in the world, offering you the specialized knowledge of literally millions of experts and amateur genealogists. Second, the chances are great that someone out there on the Internet in Indiana, North Carolina, or England knows something about your family that you don't know, and is eager to share it with you—someone you probably wouldn't meet any other way. The second time I logged on to one of the AOL genealogy chat rooms and entered my family surnames, I met someone researching in my ancestral hometown. My first trip to the World Wide Web turned up a Barnes family Web site with information about ancestors who, family legend said, had "gone west in the 1840s and were never heard from again." A friend of mine, using CompuServe's tracing service, found his unusual name listed in a Cincinnati phone book, contacted the woman, and found an unknown cousin's widow. She had one-hundred-year-old family pictures she was willing to copy for him. You'll hear stories like these in every on-line genealogy chat room. You'll soon have one of your own. But first you need to understand a little about computers, genealogy software, the Internet, and how they combine to make ancestor hunting more rewarding (*thrilling* is not too strong a word) than you thought possible.

If you've never used computers or "surfed the Net," don't let the technology and strange terminology hold you back. All of us were "newbies" (computer talk for newcomers) once. It won't be long until you're talking the talk and trading e-mail addresses. At my last family gathering, I noticed that the favorite question was no longer "What line have you been tracing?" but "What's your e-mail address?"

Before we go on, let me reassure you that you won't necessarily have to invest in your own personal computer to search cyberspace for your ancestors. Public libraries across the country have been busy connecting to the Internet and offering this service free to patrons. Three-fourths of all libraries serving a population of 100,000 or more had Internet access by 1996, and most of the rest plan to be on-line by 1998. Even small libraries, serving 5,000 or less, are connecting at a rapid rate.

While getting out on the information superhighway from your library is free, there is apt to be a long waiting line. The librarian in my hometown's main branch says, "The minute we open, all forty computers are booked." And you'll have to pay for printouts (usually ten cents a page). Libraries also ask that you bring a fresh floppy disk to prevent the possible spread of computer viruses. And of course you'll have access only during regular business hours, which for many libraries are reduced these days due to budget cuts. If none of these strictures bothers you, then you're ready to go rooting on-line at your public library.

Still another path to the Internet is through your local copying business, like Kinkos, but expect to pay up to twenty cents a minute for using their equipment. For family historians who may spend an hour or more at a time on the Internet, the cost could be hefty. In my hometown, we also have a "cybercafe," which serves gourmet coffee with the Internet. Check with your local library or genealogy society for all the possibilities in your area.

Fortunately, almost every family historian has some access to computers these days, and Web TV is in the offing. But if you'd like the freedom of going on-line today whenever you want and staying there for as long as you want, or if you plan to use one of the CD-ROM genealogy programs, then you'll need to own a personal computer.

HERE'S THE COMPUTER EQUIPMENT YOU'LL NEED

Since you may be storing a large amount of data (several of the genealogy software programs have room for one million names), I recommend that you buy a Pentium II Processor–based system with 32MB of RAM, at least a 4.3-gigabyte hard drive, a CD-ROM drive with 16x speed, and a minimum 28.8-baud modem. This may sound like a foreign language if you haven't used computers before, but you'll soon catch on. For an explanation of computer terms go to *www.ancestry.com/ home/bestofgc/terms.htm*. There are also a number of good basic computer books—I like the Computers for Dummies series, which is well illustrated and will quickly bring you up to speed. You should be able to buy the computer outlined above for about $1,900; but prices for computers are falling, so shop around for the best deal. After you've done your homework, you'll probably decide that you want the fastest computer and largest capacity hard drive you can afford because you'll be using graphics in your family history book and it takes time and requires lots of computer space to load pictures and charts. Also, buy at least a 17-inch monitor (screen) to save your eyesight. I splurged and bought a 20-inch monitor, and I'm glad I did.

You may decide that you do not need sound and, strictly speaking, you don't. But I've found that the Web sites with sound, such as the Civil War sites that play music of the period, provide a fascinating and poignant environment for on-line genealogy.

You will definitely need a printer, either an inkjet or laserjet. Lasers are faster, putting out six to eight pages per minute as opposed to two to five pages for inkjets. Lasers do cost more initially than inkjets, but lasers cost far less to operate, last longer (I've had mine for nine years with one upgrade), and I think they deliver a better printout. If you plan to self-publish your family history book you'll need a laser. With an inkjet you'll get about three hundred pages for a thirty-dollar cartridge; with a laser, you'll get 3,000 pages for a seventy-dollar ink cartridge. The only reason to buy an inkjet is to control initial cost or if you plan to use color. Whatever printer you buy, look for high resolution, measured in dots—the more the better. And make sure you buy a printer that is compatible with the software you plan to use. The better your printer, the better your pages will look, especially if you're going to publish your own family history (see chapter 14).

Later you may want to consider investing in a scanner. A scanner reproduces most of your images, such as letters, maps, charts or photographs, and stores them in your computer for later printout. Scanners come in flatbed or the newer handheld varieties. Handheld scanners, as the name implies, are portable, and some family historians like them because they can be carried to libraries to scan in documents on the spot. I like the flatbed variety because I can scan in photos of my ancestors from existing biographical books (after receiving the proper permissions). Flatbeds are more expensive, but again prices are dropping and you can get a good one for under two hundred dollars.

At some point, especially if you plan to travel in search of your roots, you may want to consider a laptop computer. One also comes in handy at your local genealogical library because you can enter your finds immediately instead of taking hand notes and transferring them later.

As for word processing software, it's your choice. I use Windows 95 Microsoft Word version 7, but I have friends who use any number of other programs and are happy with them. I do strongly recommend a virus protection package if you're going on the Internet and plan to download some of the free genealogy shareware or attached files you'll find. (You wouldn't want cybervandals to wipe out your precious family history.) I use Norton Antivirus because it comes with on-line updates that are easy to access, but there are other good packages for you to choose. Later in this chapter, I'll cover the various genealogy program software you'll want to consider.

Don't forget to buy only equipment and software that have readily available and free technical support. If you're anything like me, you'll be calling the help lines several times in the weeks following your startup.

Yes, the right computer equipment is an investment, so you will probably want to see an actual demonstration of what you can do with it. For that, nothing beats making contact with your local genealogical society where you will find other family historians at all stages of their research in cyberspace ready to give you every tip and help you might need to make a decision and to get started.

THE RIGHT INTERNET SERVICE PROVIDER (ISP) FOR YOU

Literally hundreds of ISPs around the country can connect your computer to the Internet, the gateway to the World Wide Web, where a wealth of genealogical information awaits you. But there are several questions to ask yourself before choosing the right one for you:

Should I sign on with one of the national giants or a local firm? If you absolutely hate voice mail, you'll want a small, local service. They tend to have cozier customer relations, even real people who answer the telephone.

Will I want to use the Internet when I travel? If you plan to travel outside your home area, maybe to your ancestor's hometown or a distant library or courthouse, and want to use the Internet, your local provider will add a toll charge to your monthly bill. On the other hand, a national ISP often provides free numbers all over the country so you can always log on with a local call. (A friend of mine didn't know this and got a sixty-three-dollar telephone bill for three days of intermittent on-line use.)

What kind of ISP monthly plan should I buy? Genealogists always use the Internet more than they think they will. We're heavy-duty surfers, spending hours before we know it. Therefore pay-by-the-hour, e-mail only, or limited-use plans are not for us. I recommend the unlimited-use package, which usually costs about $20 a month. For this price, you'll also get extras, such as more than one e-mail address (one for other family members and one for your roots searching) as well as free space for your own Web pages (more later on this possibility). Ask the ISP you choose what the perks are for signing on. Some also have a period of free service, which allows you to see if you like them, a can't-lose proposition.

If you choose a local provider, you'll find them listed in your telephone book. If you choose a national ISP (probably best for serious ancestor hunters) you'll find a partial list below in alphabetical order. Each should provide you with free software and instructions on loading it into your computer. If you get stuck, call their help line and they'll walk you through it.

ISP	TOLL-FREE NUMBER
America Online	800-827-6364
AT&T Worldnet	800-967-5363
Concentric Networks	800-745-2747

Earthlink Network	800-395-8425
IBM Internet Connection	800-821-4612
Microsoft Network	800-373-3676
MCI Internet	800-550-0927
Mindspring	800-719-4660
Netcomplete	800-638-2661
Prodigy Internet	800-776-3449
Sprint Internet Passport	800-747-9428
Sprynet	800-777-9638

Some of these ISPs are huge, with millions of customers. You may want to see if their help lines will truly answer when you need them. Do a test. Call during the evening hours (Eastern time), their busiest, and see how long it takes them to answer.

A word about browsers: A browser is simply software that allows you to cruise the Internet and is built into your ISP program. Chances are you'll be using either Microsoft Internet Explorer or Netscape Navigator, the two largest, which boast "push technology" and bring Web information right to your desktop computer so you don't have to search through the Internet to find it. For most ancestor hunters, these browsers do the job. But there are alternatives, so called third-party browsers, which have advantages for some people. One called Opera is especially designed for disabled users who want to use keyboard commands instead of a mouse. Another, NeoPlanet, has TV-like channels to make surfing easier. Still another, Lynx, is for the technically advanced and is very fast. There are literally hundreds of these alternative browsers, some made to run in front of other browsers. For an update on most browsers and their capabilities, go to *http:/browser-watch.internet.com.*

Now that you have your computer and you've connected to an ISP, you're ready to launch yourself into cyberspace genealogy. Get ready for the ride of your life.

FIRST STOP: ISP GENEALOGY FORUMS
AND CHAT ROOMS

All major ISPs have genealogy forums, which have chat rooms on specific topics such as Irish Passenger lists or New England research, a beginner's page with a tutorial, and various other aids for the family historian. To access America Online's (AOL) Genealogy Forum (see below), log on to AOL and click on Find, which takes you to Find Central. At Find Central, click on Find It on AOL, type Genealogy Forum, click on highlighted Genealogy Forum, then Go There.

On the main page, you'll see a Resource Center, five chat rooms, a Message Center, Surname Center, Forum News, Dear Myrtle (a genealogist's daily column), and a listing of new genealogy Web sites to explore.

CompuServe has two forums, the Genealogy Forum and the Genealogy Support Forum, the latter with representatives of various genealogy services (software, publishing, professional help) to answer your questions.

Microsoft Network has a Genealogy Forum, which opens with a new screen every day.

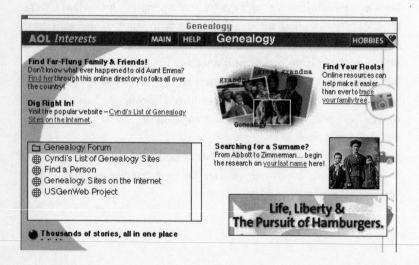

Topics in chat rooms change regularly. On one day in one AOL chat room, chats started at 9:00 A.M. and went on past midnight (all Eastern time), covering such subjects as LDS Family History Center, German/Eastern European research, Georgia, Native Americans, Dutch, Indiana/Illinois/Iowa and French language SIG (special interest group), among a number of others. On any day at any time of the day there could be something of vital interest to you, so when you log on to your ISP be sure to check the Genealogy Forum home page to see what's happening.

GENEALOGY NEWSGROUPS, LIST SERVERS, AND BULLETIN BOARDS

There are a great number of Usenet newsgroups, list servers, and bulletin boards, easy systems of posted messages and replies, devoted to genealogy. Since there are more than 20,000 newsgroup topics, you'll want to narrow your search to just genealogy. You can get a current listing of newsgroups by accessing either *http://Tile.net/news* or *www.yahoo.com/news/usenet*. Yahoo is a search engine (see later in this chapter), but several other search engines can search for Usenet newsgroups as well. Another good tool is Deja News (*www.dejanews.com/forms/dnq.html*). It has an archive database, which is searchable by keyword or phrase. This allows you to access current or past postings back to 1994. For example, type in "Germans from Russia" or better yet your special area of interest, and you will get a listing of everything in the database that corresponds. Another good source for genealogy newsgroups is the constantly updated list at *http://members.aol.com/johnf14246/gen_mail_general.html*, which contains precise information on how you can subscribe to the lists. Yet another Web site you should check is *www.liszt.com*.

What exactly are newsgroups, list servers and bulletin boards? Think of them as giant electronic genealogy centers. Members read messages; respond with their own posts, questions and queries; and in this way converse with hundreds, even thousands, of other people interested in the same subject.

The best known of the newsgroups and lists with more than 7,000 subscribers is Roots-L. It has a surname list and maintains a FAQ (frequently asked questions) section. For more information about Roots-L, go to *www.infobases.com/roots-1/qtemp01.htm.* I've listed Roots-L and other important genealogy lists below with their e-mail addresses so that you can subscribe. When I began to subscribe to lists, I got one response in two minutes, but most took a day or two. Follow the subscription instructions exactly and keep the information in your welcome package (which will come to your e-mail address) on file. I printed it out and put it in an Internet binder I keep by my computer. If you go on vacation, you'll want to unsubscribe temporarily because the volume of messages can overflow your e-mail box capacity. Some newsgroups and mailing lists charge a small fee, but most do not. Quite a few bulletin boards do charge. For a list of more than fifty specialized discussion groups by state, go to *www.wp.com/genealogy/page80.html.* For a complete list of genealogy bulletin boards, go to *http://genealogy.org.80/PAF/www/gbbs/.*

To subscribe to the following newsgroups and list servers, simply send the words in the To Subscribe column as the text in the body of the message to the e-mail addressing following. If there is nothing in the To Subscribe column, send an e-mail or telephone in the case of bulletin boards and ask for subscription information.

The list on page 207 scarcely begins to tell the story. There are Usenet newsgroups, list servers and bulletin boards for almost every genealogical interest, and you can easily dig them out at DejaNews (see above) or use one of the many search engines I'll talk about later in this chapter. With this information, you should be able, in a relatively short time, to subscribe to lists that will feed you information on your major genealogy interests on a daily basis. Expect a lot of e-mail.

In the unlikely event that you do not find the one list you need—say you're researching an ancestor who was an Italian "sandhog" during the building of the New York subway—consider creating a list of your own. It doesn't take a lot of special equipment or know-how, but

List	To Subscribe	E-mail Address
Roots-L	Subscribe	ROOTS-L-request@rootsweb.com
Adoptees	subscribe adoptees firstname lastname	listserv@sjuvm.stjohns.edu
Afrigeneas	Subscribe afrigeneas firstname lastname	listproc@msstate.edu
Deep-South-Roots	SUB	MAISER@rmgate.pop.indiana.edu
Far-West-Roots	SUB	MAISER@rmgate.pop.indiana.edu
GenChat	subscribe	GEN-CHAT-L-request@roots web.com
Gen-Medieval	subscribe	gen-medieval@mail.eworld.com
Gen-Newbie-L	subscribe	GEN-NEWBIE-L-request@rootsweb.com
JewishGen	SUBSCRIBE JEWISHGEN firstname lastname	D/dratwa@mjb-jmb.org
La-Cajun-Roots	SUB	MAISER@rmgate.pop.indiana.edu
Mormon-Index	subscribe mormon-index	Majordomo@lists.panix.com
Northeast-Roots	SUB	MAISER@rmgate.pop.indiana.edu
Quaker-L	subscribe	quaker-roots@rmgate.pop.indiana.edu
Research-HowTo	subscribe	RESEARCH-HOWTO-L-request@rootsweb.com
soc.genealogy.computing		GENCMP-L-@rootsweb.com
soc.genealogy.german		GEN-DE-L-@mail.eworld.com
soc.genealogy.slavic		gen-slavic@mail.eworld.com
soc.genealogy.surnames		GENNAM-L-@mail.eworld.com
soc.genealogy.uk+ireland		GENUKI-L-@mail.eworld.com
Texahoma-Roots	SUB	MAISER@rmgate.pop.indiana.edu
Cat Eye Bulletin Board	about West Virginia	304-592-3390
Instant Relatives BB	Salt Lake City	801-446-5374
KC GeneSplicer BB	Kansas City, Kansas	913-648-6979
Pot of Gold	BB Huntsville, Alabama	205-650-0998
Roots & Branches BB	Billerica, Massachusetts	508-670-9053
Genealogy of San Francisco BB	San Francisco	415-584-0697

it will help to have some expert advice. You'll find it on the newsgroup creation page at *www.math.psu.edu/barr/alt-creation-guide.html* and on *www.connect-time.com/tutorials/creatnews.html*. Your idea must undergo a mandatory discussion period by Usenet list users, and if it receives 100 yes votes, you'll have a *soc.italiansandhogs* newsgroup of your own.

Now Let's Go to the World Wide Web

The first time I logged on to AOL (my ISP), clicked on Find and typed the word "genealogy," then clicked on Search, I was transported to the World Wide Web and shown 94,881 matches. I was overwhelmed! It would take months to check that many Web sites to see which ones might have what I needed. At this point many genealogists, myself included, take an Internet class at their local adult education center. And one of the first things you learn is how to narrow your search. I'll give you some tips here, but every ISP (and every search engine) has a tutorial on how to do this and it's worth reading. If you want to go further with self-study try "Getting Started on the Internet" at *www.ci.berkeley.ca.us/bpl*, the University of California at Berkeley library Web site. Here's how to begin narrowing your genealogy search.

1. Searching for a phrase: if I want to search for *Barnes family* and don't want to look through thousands of Web pages with each of those words somewhere on the page, I simply put quotes around the phrase— "Barnes family"—and my computer will only return Web pages with that exact phrase.

2. Using plus (+) signs: if I want to narrow my search even further, then I put a plus sign in front of those words I always want returned in Web pages, such as *+Barnes+family+West Virginia*.

3. Using minus(-) signs: if I put a minus sign directly in front of a word, such as *+Barnes+family+West Virginia-Marion County*,

I will not have to scan Web pages that I may have already searched.

4. Using Boolean Operators: This is simply computer talk for using the words *AND, OR, AND NOT* and the sign for parentheses (). Here's how they work. *Barnes AND family AND Harrison County* will bring me documents that contain all these words. *Barnes OR Harrison County* will give me documents containing either the words Barnes or Harrison County. *Barnes AND NOT Marion County* will give me Barnes without Marion County references. And finally, parentheses () are used to group words. To find Web pages that contain the word *Barnes* and either the word *Harrison* or *Marion*, type *Barnes AND (Harrison OR Marion)*. Remember, these Boolean Operators will not work for you unless they appear in all CAPS and have a space before and after.

5. More like this: if you're getting more results than you can possibly search, you'll find the phrase *More Like This* next to the Web link that most closely matches what you want. Click on this, and you'll refine your search again.

As with most new things, searching the World Wide Web looks a bit more complicated than it is. Try each of these searches on a family history question of your own, and you'll soon see how it works.

Search Engines

There are more than 1,200 search engines on the Web. But the ones below are the best general search engines and their Web addresses. A Web address is called a URL (Universal Resource Locator) and must be typed exactly as written or you will not go to the site. (Computers are not smart enough to know what you should have typed.) Remember that each of these search engines has a Help file. Click on it and you will find out just what this search engine will do for you and how best to use it.

SEARCH ENGINE	URL
Alta Vista	*http://altavista.digital.com*
Excite	*www.excite.com/*
HotBot	*www.hotbot.com/*
InfoSeek	*www.infoseek.com/*
Lycos	*www.lycos.com*
Mamma	*www.mamma.com*
Magellan	*www.Magellan.net*
WebCrawler	*http://wcl.webcrawler.com/*
Yahoo	*www.yahoo.com*

Go to each of these search engines and type Genealogy in the search box. See what you get. Then go back and narrow your search to your special interest and see what is returned to you. In a short time, you'll have favorite search engines because you'll get more from them.

You can also get a list of specialized search engines using Alta Vista. Go to *http://altavista.digital.com* and enter this in the search box: "Specialized Search Engines." You'll get several dozen responses. Also try the Clearinghouse of Internet Subject Guides at *http://www.clearinghouse.net/chhome.html*. Another helpful site, which evaluates search engines and gives you their particular research strategies, is *http://weber.u.washington.edu/-helenew/webeval.html*.

For the latest on search engines that can find genealogy (search engines are constantly changing), go to *http://feefhs.org/sesearch.html*.

My Favorite Genealogy Sites on the World Wide Web

There's no question that everybody's favorite Web site for genealogy is the one that Cyndi Howells, Washington State housewife and avid genealogist, started in 1996. Almost alone, in little more than two years, she amassed information that is now spread over 300-plus Web pages with 31,000 links to almost every imaginable area of interest to the family historian. That this work is simply a labor of love makes the immense amount of effort that went into this site all the more amazing. I think of her as an example of the best of family historians, who desire to share what they discover with other roots searchers. You'll want to visit her home page at *www.cyndislist.com* and see for yourself. Plan to spend some time because there is just so much to access, and you won't want to miss a thing. You'll find yourself coming back over and over again, because Cyndi adds a thousand new links every month. Below are some of my other favorites. You'll find your own and when you do, bookmark them (check your ISP Help List to learn how to bookmark), so that you can go straight to them without typing the URL every time.

A Barrel of Genealogy Links: lots of military and everything else
http://cpcug.org/user/jlacombe/mark.html

Afrigeneas: African-American genealogy
www.msstate.edu/archives/history/afrigen/

AGLL: genealogy products and services
www.agll.com

Ancestry: library, databases, maps, shopping, beginners' classes
www.ancestry.com

Best Genealogy Links on the WWW: Twenty-three pages of links to almost everything
www.geocities.com/Heartland/1637

Encylopaedia Britannica: links to royal genealogies and more
www.ebig.com

Canadian Heritage Information Network: in French and English
www.chin.gc.ca/

Carrie's Adoptee & Genealogy Page: lots of links to other adoptee sites
www.mtjeff.com/~bodenst/page3.html

Computers in Genealogy: a UK site about their publication
www.gold.ac.uk/~cig/

Embassies in the United States
www.embassy.org/embassies/eep-1100.html

Everton: the must-read *Genealogical Helper* on-line plus
much more
www.everton.com

Federal Agencies: Internet sites
www.lib.lsu.edu/~kiran/maryjanesearch/search.html

Genealogy Home Page: listing of Family History Center
branches
www.genhomepage.com/

Genealogical Journeys in Time: a family home page that has
become huge
http://ourworld.compuserve.com/homepages/Strawn

Genealogy Resources on the Internet: lists just about
everything
www.umich.edu/~cgaunt/gen_intl.html

Genealogy ToolKit: hotlinks to useful Internet sites
http://feefhs.org/webm/webtools.html

Helm's Genealogy Toolbox: European research gems
http://genealogy.tbox.com:81/genatl/europe/aseurfj.htm

Journal of Online Genealogy: free on-line newsletter
www.onlinegenealogy.com/

Library of Congress: research tools for professionals
http://lcweb.loc.gov/homepage/lchp.html

LibWeb: links to many different library Web sites
http://sunsite.berkeley.edu/LibWeb

Lineages, Inc.: services and publications
www.lineagesnet.com

Look-It-Up: 109 dictionaries (641,723 words)
www.onelook.com

Map Find: interactive maps
www.vtourist.com/webmap

New England Historical Genealogical Society: New England area and more
www.nehgs.org

North American Genealogy Resources: state-by-state help
www.genhomepage.com/northamerican.html

Online Genealogical Database Index: exciting access to surname databases
http://silyg.doit.com/genweb/

National Genealogical Society: the oldest of them all
http://genealogy.org.NGS/

People find: search for address information
www.yahoo.com/search/people/phone.html

RAND Genealogy Club Home Page: employees' club with searchable data
www.rand.org/personal/Genea

Societies & CIGS: links to genealogical societies worldwide
http://genealogy.org/~gwsc/gwscintl.htm

Treasure maps: e-zine (electronic magazine) with back issues to download
www.firstct.com/fv/tmaps

USGenWeb Project: a huge database
www.usgenweb.com

U.S. Government Agencies: links, links, and more links
http://galaxy.einet.net/galaxy/Government/Government-Agencies.html

U.S. State Governments
www.yahoo.com/Government/States/

This is not a complete list of Web sites devoted to genealogy. That would take a whole book by itself. But each of these sites is a great entry point, which will allow you to travel into deep cyberspace genealogy, and help you gather your ancestral family together. Happy searching!

USING GENEALOGY CD-ROM PROGRAMS

When I first started my family history search, I used a system of binders and shoe boxes and hand-printed charts to keep my information and documents in order. It was a good system until the computer came along. While I still need boxes and binders to store my primary documents, it's a lot easier and a great deal more fun to use a computer genealogy program to chart my genealogy and bring order into the lives and deaths of hundreds of forebears. These programs also simplify the production of a family history book.

There are dozens of genealogy software programs. Here are a few I can recommend along with the benefits of each.

Family Tree Maker is a CD-ROM with huge storage capacity that includes a 150-million surname search file called Family Finder. If you find an ancestor, the program will tell you where to look for even more information. The rest of the program is menu driven so that you can begin creating your family charts at once. It also allows you to add extra data beyond names and vital dates, such as high-school graduation and medical information. You can also print out attractive family trees along with adding graphics, sound, and video. It has its own built-in tutorial to make all this possible. *FTM* will even help you set up your own Web site. Created by Broderbund, telephone 800-474-8696, this company also sells a number of archive CDs such as Civil War military records and many volumes of *World Family Tree* in German, Spanish, French and Italian, as well as English. To download a demonstration version of this genealogy program and for more general information, go to their Web site at *www.familytreemaker.com/*. The deluxe version is one of the most expensive genealogy computer programs at about $90 (discount stores), but I think it's worth it.

Brother's Keeper is a great Windows shareware (free) program for beginners, and you can download it from *http://ourworld.compuserve.com/homepages/Brothers_Keeper/*. It allows you to print a variety of charts, can hold one million names, attach pictures to people, print multipage ancestor charts, and much more. What a bargain!

Ancestral Quest is a highly rated (#1 by *Everton's Genealogical Helper*) program and costs about $50. It has an atlas and genealogy source sites, and shows you the basics. For more information and an on-line brochure, go to *www.ancquest.com/*, or telephone 800-825-8864.

Family Origins can be downloaded on-line. It contains a photo pedigree chart and creates many reports up to and including a family history book. You might want to use the relationship calculator if you get many-times-removed cousins mixed up. Created by Parsons Technology, telephone 888-883-0791 (*www.parsonstech.com/software/famorig.html*), the program is inexpensive at $29 and helps you create your own Web pages.

Reunion is the family tree software constructed especially for Macintosh users, although they do have a Windows version. It has graphic forms to build family group sheets, a date and a relationship calculator, plus much more for a $99 price tag. To learn more, telephone Leister Productions at 717-697-1378 or access *www.leisterpro.com* for reviews, new features, and links to the Web pages of users.

Although each computer genealogy program has its strong points and will do the job, no one program fits every genealogist. I'm happy with *Family Tree Maker*, but I know genealogists who swear by *Ancestral Quest* and the other programs I've mentioned. As usual, when making an important purchase you should do your research and get recommendations from satisfied users. For current reviews, go to ComputerLife Online at *www.zdet.com/complife/fea/9612/gene8.html.*

SHARE YOUR FAMILY WITH THE WORLD AT YOUR OWN WEB SITE

Once you've organized your family history in a computer program, you could share your pedigree charts, photos, and stories with the rest of the world on your own World Wide Web site. This isn't showing off. It's a part of your search for ancestors. If you include your e-mail address, people who are looking for your surname on the Web and who visit your home page can send you a message—maybe you'll both find an unknown relative.

For an example of a personal home page on the Web go to *www.doit.com/tdoyle/* for Tim Doyle's Home Page. He has links to the home pages of his parents, nephews, and nieces, as well as his own genealogy, photos of his grandfather, a computer genealogy program he wrote himself, and more. For links to other interesting home pages to look at before you plan yours, go to *http://monticello.avenue.gen.va.us/lmccug/gen-cig.html.*

There are several ways you can create your own genealogy Web site. First, find out if your ISP offers you a free Web page or pages as a perk for signing with them: call customer service and ask if they provide Web page space and how much space you can have. Also ask them if they have any help files or guidelines, even a Web page template, that can help you get started. If you're using *Family Tree Maker* or *Family Origins* computer programs, they have home page construction built into their software and offer you space and a link to their own Web site. More computer genealogy programs are offering this service all the time, and I suggest you take advantage of these programs if you want your family history on the Web.

If you don't wish to create your own Web page, there are companies who do this for you for a fee; they will even maintain your site, adding or subtracting names or photos as you direct. One of these to explore is Genealogy Roots Corner at *www.coast-resources.com/roots.htm*.

Before you begin your own Web page, I suggest you visit Cyndi Howells's Genealogy Home Page Construction Kit (*www.cyndislist.com/construc.htm*). She has included just about every bit of information you'll need to plan, write, illustrate, and then get your Web page advertised on or linked to search engines, other genealogy sites, newsgroups, and lists. For additional information on cyberpublicity go to *www.connect-time.com/tutorials/promote.html*.

If you don't want to learn about Web advertising, you can hire an announcement service to do it for you. Announce-A-Site (*www.webplaces.com/new/index.htm*) charges only $12 to add your page to fifteen search engines. For a wider distribution you'll pay $249 to Central Registry (*www.CentralRegistry.com/*) to announce your site to 400 search engines.

Remember, there are millions of Web sites and new ones going up at the rate of one a minute so you'll need to let everyone know that you have one. Don't be modest. After you've advertised your arrival on the Web, include your Web address (URL) in everything you write, post, or e-mail.

A Word About Netiquette

Genealogists use a lot of e-mail and are often in real-time chat rooms, so it's a good idea to learn the basic rules of computer etiquette that your mother never knew. For example. NEVER TYPE IN ALL CAPS. It's considered shouting, and you can see why. Next, because you're faceless, it's a great deal more difficult to get your points across without offending, especially if you're disagreeing. After all, you're expressing emotions without being able to show by body language that you're still friendly. Netiquette gets around this problem with emoticons, a series of symbols that acts as behavioral shorthand on the Net. For example, a grin is written as (:), a big grin as (:D), and a hug as (()). (Turn this page on its side so that you can see the meanings.) Other shorthand symbols are IMHO, in my humble opinion and BTW, by the way. There are many more, and you will find favorites in every chat room. Check Arlene Rinaldi's Web site at *www.fau.edu/rinaldi/ netiquette.html*, which will give you additional on-line etiquette short-cuts.

By now you're probably thinking that cyberspace is almost too good to be true. Never has so much knowledge been available to every family historian. This said, there's an obvious caution that you've probably already thought of yourself: Not every piece of information you find will be accurate; after all, human beings posted the information and humans make mistakes. If you come upon factual material about an ancestor that seems wrong or doesn't jibe with other primary records you have, then believe your records. Be cautious, yes, but be ready for one of the most exciting experiences of your search for family. I put my time in cyberspace right up there with walking the streets of my ancestors' Irish village. It has the same feel of discovery.

And now let's go from the new age of cyberspace back to the days when one of your ancestors may have worn a coat of arms.

Does Your Family
Have a Coat of Arms?

ONE DAY a secretary at the Jomar Advertising Agency in Memphis, Tennessee, opened a letter addressed to "Jomar Adv. Agy."

"Good news for the Agy family!" it cried. "Did you know that the family name Agy has an exclusive, and particularly beautiful coat of arms?"

The Agy family, the letter went on, would now have its arms exactly reproduced with "regal red flocking."

Perhaps you, too, have received one of these "personal" computerized letters, for there are many mail-order arms companies flooding the country with them. While there is nothing wrong with having a mail-order wall plaque with your family name on it just for the fun of it, you should be aware that it is probably not authentic.

Still, a genealogist friend of mine has collected several family crests from ancestral lines he has researched, and though he realizes the chances are slim that these arms were actually granted to his ancestors, they still dramatically and decoratively reflect his interest in family history.

If you want to display arms on your wall for the fun of it, as my friend has, look up your surname in a book of arms (called an "armory") for your ancestral country (you'll find many armories in genealogical libraries), and copy the coat of arms on a piece of paper.

When your friends ask about this intriguing decoration, you can say, "Oh, those arms belong to someone with my surname a long time ago." An honest answer and heraldically correct—caveat auditor.

Many countries have a heraldic tradition, but in most cases, coats of arms were issued to *individuals* rather than families. Under most heraldic rules, only first sons of first sons of recipients of coats of arms may legally bear their ancestors' arms. Younger sons may use a version of their fathers' arms, but the rules of heraldry are that they must be changed ("differenced"). If the possessor of a coat of arms (called an "armiger") dies without male heirs, his daughter may combine her father's arms with her husband's arms (called "impaling"). There are many more such ancient rules, but these give you the general idea.

Heraldry for Genealogists

The idea of using distinguishing marks on weapons or clothing is as old as fighting men. Greeks used them on their shields centuries before the Middle Ages, and African warriors painted hereditary designs on their hide-and-wood shields. But it was in medieval Europe that this form of military decoration reached the flowering that has come to be known as heraldry.

Heraldry probably began among the English in the early 1100s and came about because, during the Crusades, men from many countries were thrown together on the battlefield and needed quick, nonverbal ways of identifying friend or foe—a problem accentuated by the fact that armor had by then become so sophisticated that closed helmets prevented facial recognition during hand-to-hand combat. English knights gradually added other identifying marks to their armor, and their fashions were soon adopted by most of the rest of Europe. Distinguishing crests were placed atop helmets, because the shield was not always visible in battle; a cloth coat (surcoat) on which the

"KNYCHTHEDE IS A GREIT HONOUR"

What is all this fuss about knights and coats of arms? Who were these ancestors and what did all this mean to them? To answer these questions, here is a noble explanation of the meaning of knighthood, written in 1456 by a Scottish knight, Sir Gilbert of the Haye. If our ancestors lived up to a fraction of their code, they are worthy of our pride.

Knychthede is a greit honour [he wrote—and hereafter I'll translate into modern English] married with a great servitude, that insomuch as a man has a noble creation and beginning, he has honor, insomuch as he is bound to be good and agreeable to God he is bound to him that does him honor. Unworthy is he to be lord and master that never knew what it was to be a servant.

The office of knighthood is to maintain and defend widows, maidens, fatherless and motherless children, poor miserable, pitiable persons, and to help the weak against the strong and the poor against the rich, for ofttimes such folk are despoiled and robbed and their goods taken and put to destruction for want of power and defense.

He that has none of these virtues is not a true knight and should not be accounted as one of the order of knighthood.

Where honor is not kept, order goes backward.

knight's arms were sewn was worn over the armor, becoming literally a coat of arms.

During the thirteenth and fourteenth centuries, coats of arms became more elaborate and numerous—so much so, in fact, that they created the need for heralds: experts who memorized the arms of each man. Heralds acted as "masters of ceremonies" during knightly tournaments and announced each contestant by name as he rode into the arena.

Of course, each knight tried to make his arms unique, but duplications inevitably occurred, resulting in court battles and some bloodier fights as well. By 1418 it was apparent that some kind of royal regulation was necessary. In 1419 Henry V of England forbade anyone to assume arms unless by right of ancestry or as a gift from the crown. Later in the century, Richard III sent the heralds, now royal authenticators of arms, into the shires on what were called "visitations." These visitations were held about once every generation for almost two centuries for the purpose of officially verifying, listing, or denying arms in use.

Heraldry early developed its own language—largely Norman French, the court language of the time—which is still in use. A description of a coat of arms is called a "blazon" and is written in the same way as it was over 500 years ago.

For example, if your coat of arms has a silver horizontal dividing line on a red shield with three five-pointed stars and three gold lions' heads, your blazon reads: *Gules, on a fess argent between three lions' heads Or, three mullets of the first.* Even the most complicated blazon is usually only one sentence long, like this one.

Figure 9 is a simplified explanation of the different parts of a coat of arms. The main component is the shield (*escutcheon*) upon which certain decorative devices, called *charges*, are placed. On top of the shield is the *crest*, sometimes an animal; and as part of the crest, a helmet and mantle, a fancy representation of the protective cloth (surcoat) knights once wore. The last main element of a coat of arms is the *motto*—which may be in any language but in England is usually in Latin.

There are more than 100,000 English arms (including Wales and the six northern Irish counties) on the rolls of the Royal College of Arms in London today. Scottish heraldry is a separate institution and is governed by different traditions and rules. Although there is a continuing interest in heraldry in Germany, France, and Italy, there is no ongoing heraldic system, primarily because there has been no monarchy for some time. Spain is the exception. Although only recently a monarchy again, it has done a much better job of maintaining heraldic records.

FIGURE 9
HERALDIC COMPONENTS AND "TINCTURES"

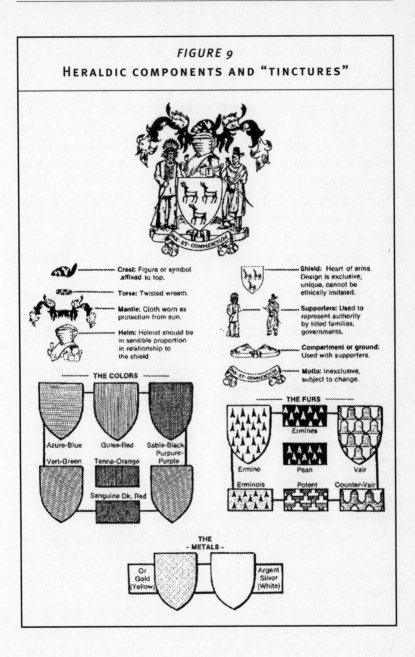

Crest: Figure or symbol affixed to top.

Torse: Twisted wreath.

Mantle: Cloth worn as protection from sun.

Helm: Helmet should be in sensible proportion in relationship to the shield.

Shield: Heart of arms. Design is exclusive, unique, cannot be ethically imitated.

Supporters: Used to represent authority by titled families, governments.

Compartment or ground: Used with supporters.

Motto: Inexclusive, subject to change.

THE COLORS

Azure-Blue | Gules-Red | Sable-Black
Vert-Green | Tenne-Orange | Purpure-Purple
Sanguine Dk. Red

THE FURS

Ermines
Ermine | Pean | Vair
Erminois | Potent | Counter-Vair

THE METALS

Or Gold (Yellow) | Argent Silver (White)

A COAT OF ARMS, WITH OR WITHOUT
A PRINCE IN YOUR PAST

If you are among the 82 percent of Americans with at least one line stretching back to England, Wales, Scotland, or Ireland, your ancestor, no matter how humble, may have had noble blood and may have had arms registered in his name. You may even have an ancient king concealed high in the branches of your family tree, like two of our former presidents. Abraham Lincoln, although born of poor parents in a log cabin, was descended from King Edward I of England. And Richard M. Nixon is actually twentieth in line of descent from King Edward III, who also had problems during his reign—the Hundred Years War and the Black Plague. Although this sounds like a very special pedigree, the truth is that there are well over 100,000 persons of English background living today in England and the United States who are known descendants of Edward III, who in turn was related to most of the main royal lines of Europe in the Middle Ages.

The reason so many average Americans of English descent have such exalted pedigrees, according to British heraldic expert L. G. Pine, is that in Continental Europe royal family circles kept very much to themselves and formed a kind of marriage trade union. The same thing happened with the nobility, so that they would not be contaminated with commoner folk. In England and Scotland, however, these rules were not observed, so that from royalty to peasant, there were degrees of relationship over several generations. Consequently, many distinguished connections turn up in families of just plain folk.

A kingly ancestor, therefore, is highly probably for anyone with many English lines, and it can be a lot of fun to find out. If you are of European descent, however, unless you have a family tradition that indicates some title in your ancestry, there is not a great chance that you have a coat of arms. The European nobility and royalty rarely intermarried with the commoner folk—those who became the principal migrants to America. Nevertheless, you may want to check out a family rumor.

If your ancestors did not have royal blood, that does not necessarily mean your forebears did not have a coat of arms—at least not in England. If you find one with the abbreviations Gent. or Esq. (for Gentleman and Esquire) after his name, it is an indication he was a bearer of arms.

Some printed sources for Americans with connections to English royal lines are *Burke's Presidential Families of the United States of America*, *Ancestral Roots of Sixty Colonists* by Weis and Sheppard, *The Magna Carta Sureties* by Adams and Weis, and *Living Descendants of Blood Royal* by Adams and d'Angerville. National societies interested in proving royal ancestry for Americans are Descendants of the Illegitimate Sons and Daughters of the Kings of Britain, c/o Brainer T. Peck, Lakeside, CT 06758; and the Augustan Society, 1617 West 261st Street, Harbor City, CA 90710.

There is a way for Americans to have a coat of arms other than through inheritance or grant from a foreign power. Private U.S. heraldic institutions, which are businesses not chartered by the government, will design heraldic devices in the ancient manner to order. Such coats of arms may then be copyrighted to prevent their being used by others, and you have the modern equivalent of a medieval grant of arms. If it all seems a bit silly, it is no more so than the way arms were originally granted by some European countries.

Coats of arms can be purchased for about $100 from The American College of Heraldry, Box 29347, New Orleans, LA 70179. Another business that sells coats of arms to Americans is the Augustan Society, mentioned above.

These and other organizations are seeking to register the use of arms in this country, but unlike the College of Arms in England, they have no legal standing and are unable to enforce the registration of your arms.

HERALDIC INSTITUTIONS WORLDWIDE

In the rest of this chapter I have tried to describe the heraldic traditions of most of the countries that provided the United States with immigrants. But the fact is that the British Isles and Western Europe took heraldry far more seriously than did the rest of the world, establishing offices of heraldry that have survived the centuries. Other countries that at one time had heraldic traditions, such as Hungary, Russia, and Lithuania, legally banned such activities while they were part of the Soviet Bloc. However, information is now becoming available again. If the heraldry of your mother country isn't described in this chapter and you are still determined to search for a coat of arms, try writing to the country's embassy in Washington, DC. (Check with a reference librarian for their address or access the country's Web site at *www.embassy.org/embassies/eep-1100/html*. They may be able to direct you to a historian or university with an interest in heraldry.

Austria

There never was a central bureau in Austria expressly for the purpose of granting arms. After 1760, laws forbade anyone outside the nobility from bearing arms. Arms granted by the king or emperor are included in general genealogical records in Austrian state archives. In 1919, the official use of arms was forbidden and has since become a part of the country's constitution. If you would like to see the state arms of modern Austria, go to *www.heraldica.org/topics/national/autriam.htm*.

Belgium

The Belgian constitution provides that the king may confer titles of nobility, and 761 titles exist from before 1795. The Heraldic Council of Belgium, operating since 1844, verifies noble titles and coats of arms. Address your questions to Le Conseil Héraldique, 85 Rue du Prince

Royal, Brussels. For more information access *www.heraldica.org/topics/ national/belgium.htm.*

British Isles: England, Wales, and Northern Ireland

All coats of arms in England, Wales, and the six northern counties of Ireland are granted through the Royal College of Arms in London. (Scotland has a separate registry, described later in this chapter.) The heralds at the college have original records of arms going back to the times of the first visitations in 1484 plus all the arms recorded in the more than 500 years since.

Unless you are going to be in England for an extended visit, there is little chance that you can have your ancestor's arms assigned to you (or new arms granted) during your vacation. It is best to get the investigation started well in advance of your trip. In any event, you will not be allowed to search in the College of Arms for your own records. These documents, most of them priceless, are considered the property of the heralds (officers of the Queen's Household).

If you are not planning a trip abroad, you can conduct all your business with the heralds by writing or calling the Officer in Waiting, the College of Arms, Queen Victoria Street, London EC4V 4BT, telephone +44 171 248 2762 (*www.kwtelecom.com/heraldry/collarms/*).

There are three conditions under which you can be granted arms:

1. If you are one of those rare individuals who can document that you are a direct descendant of an armigerous ancestor in an unbroken succession of first sons (or heirs), you can have your ancestor's arms assigned to you.

2. If you can prove descent through any other son of an armigerous ancestor, you are entitled to "differenced" arms.

3. You can apply for (buy) an entirely new grant of arms if you are of English or Welsh descent. (Charges for searching records and granting arms range up to several hundred dollars.)

When you are granted a coat of arms, it is designed by a herald in consultation with you, researched to make certain it is original, and then depicted by artists on vellum in colors and gold.

About fifty Americans every week visit or write to the College of Arms, curious to know whether they have a coat of arms. To familiarize yourself with the records at the college, you should take a look at *Records and Collections of the College of Arms* by Sir Anthony Wagner, a former herald. You can find this book in most large English libraries, the Library of Congress in Washington, D.C., the New York City Public Library, and the Newberry Library in Chicago.

The Heraldry Society at 28 Museum Street, London WC1A1LH, is a heraldic organization particularly friendly to Americans. Its quarterly magazine, *The Coat of Arms*, is well worth its price of five dollars per year.

If you are interested in hiring an English professional to help you establish your right to arms, you should contact the Institute of Heraldic and Genealogical Studies, 79-82 Northgate, Canterbury, Kent CT1 1BA, telephone 01227-768664, or access *www.cs.ncl.ac.uk/ genuki/IHGS/*. (You should always include International Postal Reply Coupons when writing for a research quotation.) For a publisher of books on heraldry in the U.K., write to Heraldry Today, Parliament Piece, Ramsbury, Wiltshire SN8 2QH, telephone +44(0)1672 520617, or e-mail *heraldry@heraldrytoday.co.uk*. For a list of available publications, access *www.heraldrytoday.co.uk/default.htm*.

Scotland

According to professional genealogist, L. G. Pine, there are at least 50,000 spurious coats of arms in use in England today. Not so in Scotland. The system of heraldry in Scotland is probably the most simple and well governed in the world. Since 1672, the Lord Lyon (the name derived from the rampant lion on the arms of the royal line of Scotland) has had full legal control of all coats of arms. Use of a coat of arms not granted by the Lord Lyon can bring a jail sentence or fine even today, just as it did 300 years ago. A Lyon Register that now fills some fifty volumes ensures that no person may legally use arms that have not been registered in his own name.

If you are a descendant of a Scottish armiger, you can petition the Lord Lyon for a grant of your ancestor's arms. If you do not have an ancestor who was granted arms in his lifetime, you must petition to obtain a grant of arms for *that ancestor*. Then you can apply for the reassignment of those arms to you, if you are an heir, or another version of the arms if you are descended from a younger son. This double procedure, which is more expensive, is often the only way Americans can obtain armorial bearings in Scotland where none has previously existed.

The Scottish system does not exclude women. Arms can be granted to appear on a lozenge (diamond-shaped shield) if the woman is an heiress of a chief of a clan or of noble family. After marriage, she may continue to use her own armorial design or have it impaled (combined) with her husband's arms.

To check on your Scottish coat of arms you should write or visit Court of the Lord Lyon, Lyon Office, H.M. New Register House, Edinburgh EH1 3YT.

A former Lord Lyon, Sir Thomas Innes, has written what many consider to be the best book on Scottish heraldry, *Scots Heraldry*, which is in many major library and genealogical collections in this country.

Also of heraldic interest to those of Scottish ancestry is clan and tartan information. For an accessible data base of over 2,000 tartans go to *http://digiserve.com/heraldry/scottish.htm* and the Gathering of the Clans Web site at *www.tartans.com/*. The Scottish Tartans Society can be reached at Port-Na-Craig Road, Pitlochry, Scotland PH165ND.

Denmark

There is no central bureau in Denmark that corresponds to England's College of Arms. Arms are taken today only in conjunction with a high Danish award, such as the Order of Dannebrog. For ancient arms, the book *Danmarks Adels Aarbog* shows illustrations of coats of arms. To locate this book, write to the Danish National Archives: Rigsarkivet, 9 Rigsdagsgården, DK 1218, Copenhagen K. For a history and description of royal Danish arms, go to the Internet at *www. heraldica.org/topics/national/denmark.htm.*

Finland

Coats of arms belong only to noble families who are members of the House of the Nobility. During Finland's troubled history, nobility was granted by Sweden, Russia, and even the Holy Roman Empire. Since 1919 no new nobles or arms have been created. You should address your questions on heraldry to the House of the Nobility, Riddarhusgenealogen, Riddarhuset, Helsinki. For examples of various Finnish coats of arms access *http://virtual.finland.fi/finfo/english/vankeng.html.*

France

France, like many republics, does not recognize heraldry except when it constitutes a seal for a town or a trademark for a product, such as a wine or an automobile. But, of course, France has a rich heraldic tradition from the Middle Ages. It was the French king Charles IV who established the world's first college of arms in 1406, an office now long defunct.

The major source of heraldry in France is the *Grand Armorial of France,* by Henri Jougla de Morenas, an encyclopedia of 40,000 coats of arms, which can be located in many LDS branch libraries.

The principal heraldry society in France is Société Française d'Héraldique, 113 Rue de Courcelles, Paris.

For information on French Heraldry on the Internet go to *www.heraldica.org/topics/france/index.html.*

Germany

For the records of German coats of arms, address Deutsches Wappenrol Bureau, Bonn.

For information about an ancestor who was a member of the German nobility, write Deutsches Adelsarchiv, Schonstadt, Germany. Also check with Der Herold, Verein für Heraldik, Archivstr. 12-14, Berlin D10033.

The records of the *Edda* (Iron Book of the German Nobility) are deposited in the above three archives.

For the complete story of German heraldry and nobility, consult the *Genealogisches Handbuch des Adels*, by Forest E. Barber, in the Library of Congress.

A database of German noble families can be accessed at *www.informatik.uni-erlangen.de/html/ww-person.Engl.html*. Another site of interest is *www.geocities.com/Colosseum/1959/wappen.html*.

Republic of Ireland

Although the office of the Chief Herald of Ireland dates from only 1943, all the surviving Irish heraldic records from the centuries of English occupation can be checked for your ancestral arms by addressing The Chief Herald of Ireland, Genealogical Office, 2 Kildare Street, Dublin Castle, Dublin 2. Some of these records date from the reign of the English king Richard II in the late 1300s. Most of these ancient arms have been photostated for the College of Arms in London, since there are so many family ties between the two countries.

Irish arms, in a way, are family arms in that the Chief Herald will grant you the arms of the chief of your name if you can show that you are descended from him or one of his ancestors.

A good source to consult is Burke's *Irish Family Records*, published by Burke's Peerage and located in most genealogical libraries. For Irish heraldry on the Internet, go to *www.finearts.sfasu.edu/uasal/heraldry.html*.

Italy

In 1947, noble titles were abolished, but those granted before the Fascist era beginning in 1922 were recognized as part of a family's name.

In one way titles are still taken seriously since there is a hefty fine for illegally using a noble title, and there is a continuing interest in the history of the nobility and in heraldry.

For professional help in researching your Italian ancestors who may have been entitled to arms write to Luigi Mendola, Araldica, Istituto Genealogico Italiano, Presso Casati-Mendola, Via M. D'Azeglio, 9-B, 90143 Palermo.

The Library of Congress contains several books on Italian heraldry which you may find helpful: *Bibliografia Araldica e genealogica d'Italia* by Giustino Colaneri and *Dizionario storicoblasonico delle famiglie nobili e notabili italiana estinti e fiorenti* by Giovanni di Crollalanza.

For several articles and tips on researching ancestral nobility in Italy access *www.italgen.com/main.htm.*

Japan

In Asia, Japan alone had a highly developed heraldry tradition, starting in the eleventh century. Today, ancient family crests—plum flowers, bamboo leaves, cranes—are in use everywhere as trademarks on the products and shops of industrial Japan. (Mitsubishi has a crest of three diamonds.)

As in Europe, Japanese heraldry had its root in the need for instant identification between military friends and foes. Gradually, however, the crests (called "mons") went home with these early warriors after battle and became family symbols.

For many years, the family crest was the prerogative of the nobility and high-ranking soldiers (Samurai), but about 1600, during a more peaceful era that lasted until the middle of the nineteenth century, commoners began to design and use family crests. At first they were used on soldiers' shields and ceremonial kimonos, then on lanterns and lacquerware, and today, not surprisingly, on shops and products. Of course, there were restrictions based on custom. The three-leafed hollyhock was reserved for the Tokugawa family, and the sixteen-petaled chrysanthemum was considered the exclusive property of the imperial family.

There are 200 basic patterns of crests surviving today, with some 4,000 variations. Many are lovely representations of nature—three gingko leaves, wild cherry blossoms, a Korin-style crane.

For help in locating your family crest write to the National Diet Library, Kokwritsu Kokkai Tochokan, 1-10-1 Nagata-cho, Chiyoda-ku, Tokyo 100. For an illustrated book, check your bookstore for *Japanese Design Motifs; 4,260 Illustrations of Heraldic Crests* by Matsuya, part of the Dover Pictorial Archive series.

Jewish Heraldry

Jews in Europe have been using coats of arms since the fourteenth century, and although some noble Jews placed menorahs or other symbols on their arms, most with their eagles and lions and griffins could not be distinguished in appearance from any other arms. For your Jewish noble ancestors, you'll need to do good heraldic research in your ancestral homeland. An excellent article on Jewish heraldry can be found on the Internet at *www.heraldica.org/topics/jewish.htm.*

The Netherlands

Any individual may adopt a coat of arms in Holland. There is no regulation and no official registration.

Norway

There have been no titled families in Norway since 1814 and no registration of heraldic arms since 1821. Individual Norwegians may adopt a coat of arms at will, although there is no extensive history of heraldry in the country. There is a tradition called *bumerker*, special emblems used to mark tools or used as signatures, which can be an addition to any family history.

For heraldic information write Universitetsbiblioteket i Oslo, Drammensveien 42, 0255 Oslo 2.

Poland

Many of Poland's records were destroyed during World War II. Those that survive are at the main historical archives, Archiwum Glowny Akt Dawnych, ul. Dluga 7, 00-263 Warszawa.

Nobility and heraldry were not politically popular during the Communist era, but many Polish-Americans searching for their coats of arms can get help from the Polish Genealogy and Heraldry Society (Towarzystwo Genealogiczno-Heraldyczyne) Wodna 27 (Palac Gorkow), 61-781 Poznan, Polska, and the Association of Polish Nobility (Swiazek Szlachty Polskiej, 81-701 Sopot 1, Skr. Poczt.79. Their U.S. representative, Dave Zincavage, can be reached by e-mail at *JDZI@delphi.com* or *GFSJDZI@aol.com*. A helpful book can be found in the Library of Congress under the title *Herbarz polski*, by Kaspar Niesiecki.

Chevalier Suligowski, an expert on Polish heraldry, explains that Polish coats of arms, unlike European heraldry in general, can often represent a "clan" or tribe with more than one family in it. On the whole, he says, the rules of Polish heraldry were much less rigid than the rules on arms developed in Western Europe. As a result the nobility, consisting of more than 40,000 families, used about 7,000 arms.

Portugal

Few records of ancient Portuguese arms survived the devastating earthquake of 1755. Those that remain are in the National Archives. Address your queries to Arquivo Nacional da Tôrre do Tombo, Largo de S. Bento, 1200 Lisboa. For a genealogical group in the U.S. write to Portuguese Ancestry, Rosemarie Capodicci, 1155 Santa Ana, Seaside, CA 93955. For a research syllabus, send $7 to Doug da Rocha Holmes, 2701 Corabel Lane #34, Sacramento, CA 95821, telephone 916-489-9599.

Russia

Three major resources for Russian heraldry are in the Library of Congress: *Department gerol'dii* (eighteen manuscript volumes) and *Alfavitnyi spisok familiiam*, plus *Armorial de la noblesse de Russie* by Igor V. de Tretiakoff.

You might also want to contact the Russian Nobility Association, 971 First Avenue, New York City, New York 10022, or the St. Petersburg Noble Assembly, Dumskaya ulitsa, dom 3, Setazh, PEN, club Sankt, Petersburg, Russia 19011, telephone 812-312-14-40.

Spain

The archives of Spain, in spite of losses during the civil war of the 1930s, are marvelously full of information about the heritage of Spanish nobility and heraldry. Nevertheless, there is no central college of arms as in England. This makes hunting for your ancestor's arms more difficult. On the other hand, your search has a good chance of success. There were 500,000 noblemen (*hidalgos*) in Spain at the end of the 1700s, which means there are literally millions of their descendants entitled to display ancestral arms.

Most national archives in Spain have records of *hidalgos* (see chapter 9). Manuel Carrion Gutiez, the secretary general of the *Biblioteca Nacional* in Madrid, suggests two sources other than his library for Americans of Spanish descent searching for their family's heraldic tradition. They are (1) Instituto Internacional de Genealogía y Heráldica, C/Atocha, 94, Madrid and (2) Asociación de Hidalgos, same address.

The major sourcebook of Spanish heraldry is *Heraldic and Genealogical Encyclopedia: Spanish-American* in the Library of Congress in Washington, D.C. It contains the arms and genealogies of many families in Spain and Latin America.

Two professional genealogists in this country researching Spanish heraldry are: Susan Ybarra, 3776 South 575 West, Salt Lake City, UT 84115 (*www.iosphere.net/~jholwell/fam-find/spa/9701072.html*) and

Jose A. de la Torre, Rootsearch, 999 Ponce de Leon Boulevard, #600, Coral Gables, FL 33134 (*heraldry@deltaintl.com.*)

Sweden

Only those of the noble class received arms. Today, the traditions of heraldry are governed in Sweden by an official board called the Riddarhusdirektionen (the Directorate of the House of the Nobility). This group approves coats of arms for flags, towns, and individuals.

For heraldic information, write Riksheraldiker, Riddarhuset, P.O. Box 2022, S-103 11, Stockholm.

Switzerland

Switzerland, where anyone may adopt arms at will, has a long tradition of heraldry. Write for information concerning your ancestor's arms to Archives Héraldique Suisses, Chemin du Parc de Valency, 11 Lausanne.

For professional help in Switzerland write or call Studio Galloway, Libellenstr. 65, 6004 LU, telephone ++41 - (0)41 420 38 48 or access them at *www.firmnet.ch/galloway/heraldik_e.html.*

If you visit Zurich, you will want to visit the Burgerbibliothek (Citizens' Library), which contains the oldest original roll of arms from the sixteenth century. To learn more about this treasure from the past, go to *http://people.delphi.com/ivanor/zroaen0.htm.*

CHAPTER 12

Your Family Health History

A FEW YEARS AGO the *Times* of London ran a picture of Lady Jane Howard, born in 1945, alongside a portrait of her ancestor Queen Catherine Howard, born in 1521. The family resemblance was striking. The *Times* also showed that Viscount Robert Devereux, born in 1932, was a dead ringer for an earlier Robert Devereux, born in 1566, who was reputed to be the lover of Queen Elizabeth I.

Now, most of us do not have portraits of ancestors five centuries back, but if we did we might find remarkable resemblances caused by a family's dominant genetic code being transferred from one generation to another—Great-grandma's nose, for instance, or G-great-grandpa's red hair. You might even inherit webbed toes. But physical characteristics are not the only things we inherit, and in this chapter we'll explore how investigating your background can help you understand something about your health, both physical and emotional.

CHARTING YOUR FAMILY MEDICAL HISTORY

Over 15 million people in the U.S. suffer from 1,500 genetically caused diseases such as cancer, osteoporosis, hemophilia, cystic fibrosis, Down's syndrome, diabetes, Addison's and Parkinson's diseases, glaucoma, muscular dystrophy, thyroid problems, Alzheimer's, and night and color blindness. Substance abuse can appear to run in families as well as obesity, but we don't know for certain if this is genetic or learned behavior or a combination. What we do know is that genetic research is in a period of explosive discovery; diseases we don't think of as genetically linked today may be found to be so tomorrow. I suggest you take down *all* health information for the future as well as the present. Whichever it is, genetic or not, you'll want to be aware of patterns in your family health history so that you can guard against repeating them by taking diagnostic tests or changing your lifestyle. The closer your kinship, the more care you need to take. Your parents, children, and siblings are called first-degree relatives and share 50 percent of your genes. Your grandparents, aunts, uncles, nieces, and nephews are second-degree relatives and share 25 percent of your genes. Your third-degree relatives, such as your great-grandparents and cousins, share 12.5 percent of your genes.

Inherited diseases can be transmitted through groups, as well as through individual family trees. The disease known as Tay-Sachs is peculiar to American Jewish children of Eastern European ancestry; sickle-cell anemia to African-Americans of West African heritage; cleft palate to Japanese; clubfoot to Maoris; Machado/Joseph's disease to Portuguese; and Cooley's anemia, or thalassemia, to Italians and other people of Mediterranean stock. (For a nontechnical and highly readable explanation of what genetics means to the individual, consult *The Human Pedigree,* by Anthony Smith, and *The Heredity Factor,* by Dr. William L. Nyhan.) For an on-line printout of symptoms and treatment for any number of genetic disorders as well as nongenetic problems, go to the American Medical Association's Medline Web site at *www.invivo.net/bg/medicine.html* or the Health Sciences Center Library of Emory University MedWeb site at *www.cc.emory.edu/ WHSCL/medweb.html.* For information on gene-linked breast and colon cancer for Jewish women of Eastern European heritage, go to *www.jewishgen.org* and click on Health:Heredity.

Why are genetically transmitted illnesses important to the genealogist? William H. Carlyon, former director of health education for the
American Medical Association, believes it is important not just to family historians but to everyone. It would be diagnostically valuable, he
says, for every American to be concerned with his or her family history
of illness. For instance, a healthy, athletic friend of mine was shocked
to have his weak spells and extreme thirst diagnosed as diabetes.
"There's no diabetes in my family," he insisted. When his doctor suggested he check with relatives, his mother confirmed that a grandfather had died of the disease.

If there were such a thing as a medical census, and the census
taker asked you what your great-grandmother died of, would you
know? Chances are you would not, because families tend to avoid
such subjects. To take one unusual example, in *Jody*, newspaper writer
Jerry Hulse's book about his wife's hereditary illness, doctors had to
know whether Jody's parents had suffered from stroke or diabetes before they could perform a delicate, life-saving operation on her brain.
Since Jody was adopted, she had no information about her natural
family's medical history. The successful search for her mother provided vital medical clues that saved Jody's life. While few cases are so
extreme, it could prove invaluable someday for you or a member of
your family to know your family's medical history. Another book, *Genetic Connections*, by two nurses, Danette L. Nelson-Anderson and
Cynthia V. Waters, will help you document your health history with a
series of work sheets if you don't care to make your own.

It is not too difficult to obtain medical history three generations
back, and most of us can get some information for the fourth generation as well. That is over 100 years of your family's health history. Making a point to seek such information often gives insights into family
"behavior."

A woman friend of mine had been warned by her mother never to
lift anything heavy. "Something might break loose inside," she said,
"and it could kill you." My friend passed along the same advice to her
daughter, without really understanding why. Later she researched her

family medical history and found that her great-great-aunt had seen a heavy carriage fall on her younger brother, and with strength born of desperation, had lifted it off him. He survived, but she died days later of internal hemorrhaging, leaving behind a health lesson for four generations of women in her family.

If, after compiling your family medical history, you find that heart attacks, cancer, or any hereditary diseases predominate, you should share this part of your genealogy with your doctor as well as the rest of your family. One family researcher found three generations of cancer among the female members of her paternal line, which alerted her to be especially watchful for cancer signs in herself and to make sure to have an annual physical examination. Her husband, whose medical history showed a series of early strokes for both male and female family members, modified his diet and brought his blood pressure down.

If you make a point of collecting your family's medical history— long illnesses, causes and dates of death—you may gain insights into your own health patterns. Certainly you will be able to deliver into your doctor's hands a valuable diagnostic tool.

CHARTING YOUR FAMILY PSYCHOHISTORY

Not too long ago, I received a distraught telephone call from my cousin's wife, a woman I'd never met. "I know you've researched the family's health history," she began, then went on to describe the troubling behavior of two members of her family. "Have you come across any mental problems in your research? None of the rest of the family will talk about it."

I had documented not only a history of bipolar affective disorder (manic depression) in the family but also of Tourette syndrome, which is sometimes associated with that mental health problem. I was also able to tell her stories of long-dead family members who displayed symptoms, according to family legend, long before modern medicine had diagnosed or learned how to treat these conditions successfully.

Have you ever wondered why you behave the way you do? If you would like to understand yourself better, perhaps you should take a close look at your family's emotional behavior patterns over the last few generations.

In recent years there has developed a new field of study called *psychohistory*. One of the experts in this field, Dr. Mary Matossian of the University of Maryland, explains that a family is an emotional system, with each member developing a pattern of behavior toward every other member of the family. If we examine these relationships back through many generations (five is preferred, but three is sufficient), we can often find patterns of behavior recurring. Your research should not become just a hunt for family faults and foibles; you should also try to uncover cases of accomplishment and perseverance in the face of disaster, for the qualities that led to such deeds are an important part of your genetic inheritance, too.

The signs of an emotionally successful family, according to Dr. Matossian, are as follows, (1) good ties with cousins, uncles, aunts, grandparents; (2) parent-child relationships that are warm and affectionate; (3) well-defined roles for individual family members; (4) families where strong, stable members come to the aid of those who need help; (5) families that keep track of one another, giving support and encouragement all through life.

Americans have long prided themselves on being a nation of rugged individualists, she points out, but the truth is, most of us have derived our strength from our families. Thus, the more we know about our forebears, the more we really know about ourselves.

What kind of family emotional patterns should you look for? Here is a list of questions to ask to help chart your family's psychohistory. You will already know the answers to some of them from previous chats with your older family members. But for other questions, you may have to pry very gently for answers from those older relatives whom you know most intimately.

1. How did your grandmother get along with your mother, and her mother with her daughter?

2. How did your grandfather get along with his father and his father with his son?

3. Who was Father's favorite child and which child did Father discipline most?

4. How well does your generation get on with cousins, uncles, aunts, and grandparents?

5. What is the family's attitude toward its older members?

6. Does your family have a history of prodigal sons and scapegoats?

7. Are there bad-luck stories of fortunes nearly made?

8. Are there alliances and counteralliances between branches of your family tree?

9. Does your family have a long history of either dominant mothers or dominant fathers?

10. Does your family include an unusual number of marital separations, divorces, aggressive or violent individuals, or mental illness?

11. What types of family conflicts occurred and what was the family's response to them?

12. How were family members ranked in terms of family prestige by sex, age, ability, profession, or money?

13. Did your family pull together and help one another in times of trouble?

After you have gathered sufficient information, you may want to try charting your family's emotional history, in the way that Dr. Matossian has charted the psychohistory of the royal English Tudor family. The Tudor chart (see Figure 10) reveals strong patterns of family ambivalence and conflict.

Here is a narrative key to Dr. Matossian's code:

1. Strong positive bond—strong feelings of love and admiration.

2. Distant relationship—between people who do not talk about any subject that might be anxiety provoking (they discuss the weather).

3. Positive bond—less intense love and admiration than item 1.

4. Imaginary bond—relationship between two people closely related by blood who know each other only slightly or not at all (or a relationship between a child and parent who died when the child was an infant).

5. Ambivalent bond—the simultaneous existence of conflicting emotions of love and hate.

6. Conflictual bond—relationship between people who fight a lot; but they get something out of fighting, since they keep at it; they are bound together.

Using this method of diagramming relationships, you will be able to draw a schematic of your own family's emotional system.

If you would like to see how a psychiatrist develops an individual's psychohistory, I recommend the book *In Search of Nixon: A Psychohistorical Inquiry,* by Bruce Mazlish, a Massachusetts Institute of Technology professor. You may be able to apply some of his techniques to your own family chart. To explore a variety of mental health issues, check the Emory University mental health Web site at *www.gen.emory.edu/MEDWEB/mentalhealth.html.*

What does psychohistory mean to you? Until now you have been concerned with the questions "Who am I?" and "Where did I come from?" Charting your family's psychohistory can answer an important third question: "Why am I the kind of person I am?" While this is not a question everyone wants to explore, I believe psychohistory can give today's family history a depth never known before. It will show you

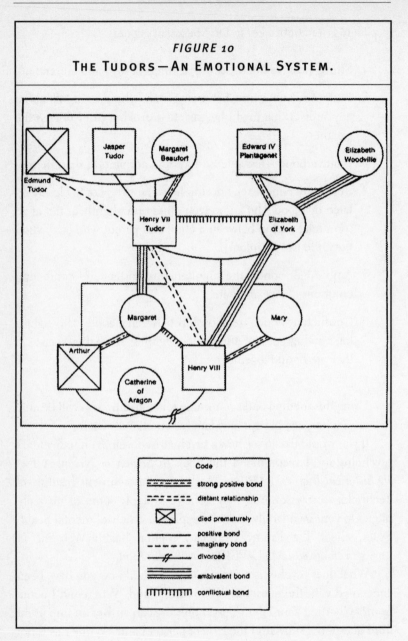

FIGURE 10

THE TUDORS—AN EMOTIONAL SYSTEM.

how your ancestors thought and felt, and it will help you challenge destructive family emotional patterns and shore up positive ones.

If you want to explore this fascinating and potentially lifesaving subject in all its detail, I recommend Carol Krause's *How Healthy Is Your Family Tree?*

CHAPTER 13

Family Gathering: How to Unite Your Newfound Family

ONE SPECIAL REWARD of ancestor hunting is sharing a common blood bond with others in your extended family. You are a part of them and they are part of you. While some people may simply not want to know their great uncles or second cousins, others will find their holidays, their vacations, and their lives in general given extra dimension and pleasure if they reunite with their extended families.

After you have been collecting family history for a while, you may want to try collecting—getting together—the family itself. You can start with brothers and sisters, parents and grandparents, aunts and uncles. Before you know it you'll have a family association, a group of many families of the same name joined together. In fact, there may already be a family association organized for your surname, for there are presently thousands of American families united in this way. For example, the Tolman branch of my family has 10,000 members and employs several of them as full-time family genealogists. Check your library for the annual issue of the *Genealogical Helper*, 3223 South Main Street, Nibley, UT 84321, telephone 800-443-6325, *www.everton. com*, for their listing of family associations, including their addresses and the names of their newsletters.

For family reunion information on the Internet, try ReunionNet (*www.reunited.com*) or write Suite 400, 318 Indian Trace, Fort Lauderdale, FL 33326, or telephone 954-389-3636. If you don't find your surname there, try Yahoo (the Internet search engine), which has a Family Reunions site at *www.yahoo.com/Society_and_Culture/ Reunions/Families/*. Just enter your family name and click on Search.

Reunions magazine, P.O. Box 11727, Milwaukee, WI 53211, telephone 414-263-4567, sells mailing lists of family reunion organizers— yes, there are professionals doing this work. It's quite a big market, since over 200,000 families have reunions annually, and with the baby boomer generation beginning to search for their family history the market can only grow larger. If you find your surname in *Genealogical Helper* or *Reunions* or on the Internet, by all means get in touch with your relatives. If you cannot find an already organized family association, you might want to consider starting one. (I'll show you how later in the chapter.)

GETTING TO KNOW YOUR EXTENDED FAMILY

The way to start getting to know your extended family is through a summer or holiday family reunion. It's a good idea to start planning the reunion well in advance—a year ahead, if you can—and pick a place centrally located for most family members, with sufficient accommodations and children's play areas close by. Of course, it's even better if you can hold the gathering near an old homestead or other historical place associated with the family; but if not, most reunion organizers find that attendance improves if the reunion is held in a resort area or near family attractions or sports activities.

On the day of the reunion have Pedigree Charts and Family Group Sheets available (blank or filled out) and set out displays of family photographs, medals, or other family heirlooms. The program itself should include some get-acquainted time, a chance to tell family stories, an informal talk by someone on some aspect of the family history, and a reunion photograph. (Don't forget your tape recorder or video camera when Grandfather begins his stories. You may have heard them, but your grandchildren will appreciate them in years to come.)

After your first family reunion, you may want to try something more elaborate the next time. According to Reunion Research half of all family reunions last three or more days, while 22 percent last two days and are attended by an average of 100 people. (African-American reunions are even larger with an average of 150 participants.) You can see that this would require more planning for accommodations (only 15 percent of attendees stay with relatives), meals, and entertainment. Food is a major part of every family reunion, a kind of ultimate Thanksgiving—especially if it includes old family dishes and recipes. I've never forgotten my Aunt Anna's apple butter on biscuits or Aunt Flora's pecan pie, and I treasure those recipes in their handwriting.

Besides the fun and good feelings a family get-together can generate, reunions are a good place to enlist other relatives in your ancestor-hunting projects. You may also be able to solve some family history mysteries. Most relatives have terrific family stories that need only the stimulus of a story-telling session to pry loose. In addition, you can discover a great deal of family folklore, unique to your family and no other—traditions, favorite expressions, humorous and memorable incidents. Preserve them in writing or on tape. They will help you fill in the map of the past.

In America today there is a renewed and growing sense of the importance of family relationships. Children, in particular, respond positively to family reunions because they receive the strong message that they are part of a family with a heritage, a family that cares about itself. You'll want to include special children's games and genealogical sessions. And don't forget the all-important T-shirt printed with the family name; every member will want one.

How to Organize a Family Association and Publish a Newsletter

If you cannot find an already organized family association (after checking the *Genealogical Helper*), why not start one? Just as your Pedigree Chart starts with you, so does your family organization.

How many generations back and how many names does the family association cover? It will follow only one surname line, probably at least back to the immigrant ancestor (called the "family progenitor"). If it is a not-so-common name like Eddy, it may well take in all the Eddys in the United States and trace back to some ancestors overseas. If it is a more common name like Williams, you may want to establish your family association as "The Descendants of Jesse Williams" or whatever your immigrant forebear's name was.

With your own immediate family you already have the nucleus, and if you have been gathering your family's history from relatives you have probably got a good family address file already started. Visit every relative who lives close to you; personal contact is the best way to build enthusiasm, get their ideas, and solicit their support. Write to every family member you cannot talk to personally, and get the names and addresses of other relatives, no matter how distant. You will be surprised how fast your mailing list will expand.

Of course, in many of today's far-flung families, it is difficult to visit people, but a family association can still be started by telephone, correspondence, and even these days by e-mail. The Linder Family Association, according to its organizer, Shirley Linder Rad, was started entirely this way. The first family officers lived in Texas, New Mexico, and Utah, and did not meet until they held a national convention eighteen months after organizing. By this time the Linder Family Association had grown to over 100 members from thirty-seven states. Five years later, the Linders had collected more than 700 Family Group Sheets for its 2,000 members.

In the beginning, you may be all your family association's officers rolled into one. But just as soon as possible, the work should be divided and a governing board of sorts established. Communications should be opened with the rest of the family, money raised, and a family reunion planned. A family association history book should also be started to follow the surname line back to the immigrant ancestor and beyond.

To get in touch with as many family members as possible to tell them a family organization is being started, it is best to put out a newsletter—something more official-looking than the average letter—to let them know you're serious. (You can give it a fancy name such as *Carswell Chronicle* or *Sparkman Family Tree*, or a cute name such as *Koch Kith and Kin*, or *Long Line*.)

The main idea is to imbue your first few issues with your own enthusiasm so that others will be interested in organizing, working, and in making financial contributions to the family association. You should provide dues information and a clip-out coupon in each issue to make it easy for them to join.

Include stories of some of the goals of the new organization such as reunions, the collection of family history, even the compilation of family recipes (Walter's Publishing of Waseka, Minnesota, publishes over 3,000 family association cookbooks annually). Try anything you think will pique the interest of your cousins. Show family members right from the start that the publication will help them put together their own branch of the family tree. Publish a few photos of early forebears or of family heirlooms. Write a story about one of the family's common ancestors who turned up in your own research, or about the family coat of arms (if any), or the origins of the family name. In later editions invite other members to contribute family history stories; tell about births, deaths, and marriages among the members; give reunion news and have a column that puts members working on their personal genealogy in touch with one another.

The biggest problem facing most new family associations is money. A common error is to set membership dues too low. It is difficult to publish and mail a newsletter four times a year (the usual number) for much less than $15 per subscriber. Even this price will do no more than take care of essentials and will not help you build the family treasury for ultimate publication of a family surname history. You may wish to study other family association newsletters for money-raising ideas.

In the final chapter I will show you how to complete your ancestor hunt in the most satisfying way—by writing and publishing a book about your family history.

CHAPTER 14

How to Write and Publish a Family History

Most ancestor hunters sooner or later feel the urge to assemble their family findings into a written history, which will pass on the record to all the generations to come. Although publishing a book of family history looks like a monumental job to most people, there are logical and really quite simple steps for doing it.

Pulling Your Research Together

Every family historian begins to compile a mass of ancestral notes, charts, photos, and documents right from the beginning of his search. Soon your one workbook becomes two and then three, and the material you transfer to your personal Family History Book begins to strain the loose-leaf binder. If you're using one of the genealogy computer programs, you can store a great deal of information, but at some time you'll want to see this printed out. This printout or your loose-leaf binder will probably give you something close to a book manuscript.

A good family history requires you to identify the exact sources of your information. Check through your material to make sure your findings have been carefully documented. Good documentation means that you cite your source and where you found it so that another genealogist could locate the same information. If there are conflicts with the sources you have found, and this seems to happen often with dates, simply recognize them in your writing or footnotes and present your reason for resolving them the way you have. Richard S. Lackey's *Cite Your Sources* is a good reference guide for genealogical citations.

Since no family history is ever finished, one of the toughest decisions to make is when to stop collecting and start publishing. Look over your material. If it seems fairly well rounded and well documented, consider it ready.

Don't omit the renegades. Every face discovered—both good and bad—is part of your heritage. Did your ancestor sell horses by day and steal them back by night and was he hanged for it? Put him in! Did one of your forebears start west in a covered wagon and turn back at the first sight of trouble—as one of mine did? Put him in! Was one of your ancestors at Valley Forge in the *summer*—as one of mine was? Put him in! A family history is a mirror of human lives, their triumphs and frailties. We cannot fictionalize or judge the past. So include the scalawags and the fainthearted as well as the saints. There will probably be plenty of both on your family tree.

BEGIN WITH YOUR OWN HISTORY

Include yourself in your Family History Book. Tell your story in a plain, direct, honest manner. A little humor helps.

Some newcomers to the mysteries of genealogy might consider a personal history unnecessary or downright vain. But think with what delight your descendants a hundred years from now will read about your life. Invite your spouse and children to add their personal histories also. A Family History Book should be a family project.

Write as much as you want—what you wish your ancestors had told you about themselves. Put in your vital statistics, your name in full and your nickname. Do the same with your parents and with your siblings and your spouse and your own children. Tell about how your parents earned a living, what your household was like, what the surrounding area was like. Tell about childhood and school memories: diseases, pets, how you earned money, classes, teachers, clubs. Tell about your young adulthood—early jobs, how you met your spouse, your in-laws, military experiences. Then tell about your life today— your work, home, hobbies, religious and political affiliations, and so on. Make a list of ten things you'd like to accomplish in your lifetime. Make five predictions about what the world will be like in a hundred years. Writing your own personal history may look like a great deal of work, and it can be if you try to do it all at once. Just take your time, take it easy, and have fun with it.

You might want to arrange your book something like this, since this is the form that many such books take:

1. Frontispiece—a coat of arms, heraldic description or blazon, photo or portrait of the family progenitor, the old homestead, a map of the travels of your family's immigrant ancestor (my Great-uncle Rowland Barnes, who wrote a most interesting spiritual history, included drawings of his boyhood home, one-room school, and country church)

2. Title page—book title, author's name, printer, date, copyright

3. Foreword—a few pages explaining your numbering system and any unusual or amusing incidents that occurred while you were writing the history, acknowledgment of people who helped, and a dedication

4. Your personal history and the histories of your immediate family

5. Family lineage charts

6. Family name—its origin and meaning

7. Contents—the story of pre-American ancestry, the story of your immigrant ancestor, the family lineage of succeeding generations to the present

8. List of family sayings, recipes, Christmas and Thanksgiving traditions

9. List of abbreviations used or a short dictionary of genealogical terms

10. Bibliography

11. Index of names included

Family histories can be arranged in different ways. The system favored by the New England Historical and Genealogical Society and most other genealogists is the Register Plan which works as follows:

1. In the Contents section of your book, give your first known ancestor the number 1.

2. Give his children lowercase Roman numerals (i, ii, iii, and so on).

3. His sons are also given consecutive numbers (2, 3, 4), if they head their own family unit.

4. Write the personal history of each individual when he or she appears as head of a family; the personal history of children (both males and females) who, as adults, do not head family-surname units should be given when their names first appear.

For a full description of this system, try Joan Ferris Curran's *Numbering Your Genealogy: Sound and Simple Systems.*

PREPARING YOUR MANUSCRIPT

Once you have compiled your material, edit it for spelling errors, capitalization, and the like, and type or print out from your computer a double-spaced manuscript with large margins on all four sides. Have someone whose English grammar skills you trust read your manuscript, too. It's very difficult for the author of a work to catch all errors because we tend to read what we meant to write, not what is actually there. When your manuscript has been proofed, it is then ready for the printer or copier. If you're uncertain about grammar and style see *A Manual of Style*, published by the University of Chicago Press and available in most bookstores or libraries, or go to the Internet at *www.inkspot.com/craft/style.html* for stylistic help.

Some family historians are frankly only interested in a few copies (perhaps as few as ten) to give as Christmas presents to their immediate family. With computer desktop publishing or genealogy programs, it is easier than ever to print your own copies and have them bound. Others, especially those with family association contacts, may want hundreds of copies. I recommend a preorder plan through the family association, in which members order and pay for a certain number of books so that a definite amount can be ordered from your printer. If you aren't using a computer program and want fewer than fifty copies, consult two or three "instant print" shops in your community. They can give you a 100-page book printed on long-lasting paper and bound into binders (even have them imprinted with your title) for as little as ten dollars a book if you don't want color — not a bad price for a gift that will be treasured for generations of your family.

If you want a larger number of books or want the look of a printed book, there are dozens of publishers around the country who solicit your business in genealogical publications and on the Internet. Two such are Heritage Publishing at *www.value-link.com/memories.html* and Genealogy Publishing Service, 573 Beasley Mine Road, Franklin, NC 28734, telephone 704-524-7063 (*www.gpsbooks.com/index.html*). You might try several of these publishers just to see how their bid price compares to printers in your own community. The cost for larger orders, say 500 books of 100 pages, is difficult to determine since there are so many variables—charts, photos, color, hard or soft covers—but expect to pay about ten dollars on up for each hard-covered book and from six dollars on up for each of the same number of soft-covered books. Longer or more complex books, of course, increase the cost. Larger orders decrease the per-book cost.

For more information about how to publish your family history book, read *How to Write and Publish Your Family Book,* by Genealogy Publishing Service (see above), $9.95 postage paid; *To Our Children's Children: Preserving Family Histories for Generations to Come,* by Bob Greene and D. G. Fulford; or Patricia Laws Hatcher's *Producing a Quality Family History.* For help on the Internet, go to the Center for Life Stories Preservation: Easy Ways to Start Preserving Your Family History (*http://members.aol.com/storycntr/easyways.html*). Although it's not a how-to or a genealogical family history, the book *Family,* by Ian Frazier, available in any bookstore, is a loving example of what a special family history book can be.

You will want to copyright your work. Print the proper notice on the title page of your book (for example, "c. 1998 *John Doe*") and that's all you need to do. The book is your artistic property for your lifetime plus fifty years. But there are advantages to registering your work with the U.S. Copyright Office. Registration establishes a public record of your claim and gives you the legal basis for an infringement suit in a court of law. If these protections are important to you, contact the Register of Copyrights, Library of Congress, Washington, DC 20559, telephone 202-707-3000 for a registration Form TX. Registering your copyright carries a fee of twenty dollars and requires you to send two copies of your book. For more information about copyright, go to the Copyright Office's Internet site at *http://lcweb.loc.gov/copyright/*.

If you plan to place your family history in libraries, you will need a Library of Congress catalog card number. Ask for the Request for Preassignment of LCCN Number form from the Copyright Office. Some libraries also require an International Standard Book Number (ISBN). Contact R. R. Bowker, 121 Chanlon Road, New Providence,

NJ 07974, telephone 908-665-6770 (*www.bowker.com*) for their Title Output Information Request Form. The cost is $175.

A TOUCH OF IMMORTALITY

By the time your book is off the press, family members who may have contributed photos or biographical sketches will be clamoring for it. Be sure you advertise in your family association bulletin and in the publication of any genealogical society to which you belong. It is also a good idea to take out an ad in historical or genealogical publications in an area where your family originated.

You will want to see that your Family History Book survives and is available to genealogists and historical researchers. The way to ensure this is to send complimentary copies to your local library, the library in your ancestral hometown, and the LDS library in Salt Lake City. Also send it to Everton Publishers, P.O. Box 368, Logan UT 84323, Attention: Book Review Editor. Your book will be reviewed and reach 200,000 readers of the *Genealogical Helper*. You may also want to make a gift of it to other important genealogical collections.

Carl Sandburg said, "When a society or a civilization perishes, one condition can always be found. They forgot where they came from." With a history of your family in hand, there is no forgetting, no sense of coming to an end. Because there is no end; there is only the sense of continuing.

Bibliography

Allcock, Hubert. *Heraldic Design.* New York: Tudor, 1962.

Banaka, William H. *Training in Depth Interviewing.* New York: Harper & Row, 1971.

Bardsley, Charles Waring. A *Dictionary of English and Welsh Surnames with Special American Instances.* London, 1901.

Begley, Donal F., ed. *Irish Genealogy: A Record Finder.* Dublin: Heraldic Artists, 1981

Bellingham, Mary, et al. *Research Guide to German-American Genealogy.* St. Paul, MN: German Interest Group, MGS, 1991.

Benes, Josef. *O ceskych prijmenich.* Prague: Nakl. Ceskoslovenske Akademie ved, 1962.

Bigwood, A. Rosemary. *Scottish Family History: A Handbook.* Edinburgh, 1993 (self-published).

Black, Dr. George F. *The Surnames of Scotland, Their Origin, Meaning and History.* New York: New York Public Library, 1968.

Blassingame, John. *Slave Testimony: Two Centuries of Letters, Speeches, Interviews, and Autobiographies.* Baton Rouge: Louisiana State University Press, 1977.

Blockson, Charles L., and Ron Fry. *Black Genealogy.* Englewood Cliffs, NJ: Prentice-Hall, 1977.

Boudreau, Dennis M. *Beginning Franco-American Genealogy.* Pawtucket, RI: American-French Genealogical Society, 1986.

Boutell, Charles. *Boutell's Heraldry.* Rev. ed. London: Warne, 1978.

Burke, John. A *General Armory of England, Scotland, and Ireland.* London: Edward Christian, 1842; London: Harrison, 1882.

Chuks-Orji, Ogonna. *Names from Africa, Their Origin, Meaning, and Pronunciation.* New York: Johnson, 1972

Cross, Harold E. *Index to Selected Amish Genealogies.* Baltimore: Division of Medical Genetics, 1970.

Dauzat, Albert. *Dictionnaire Etymologique des Noms de Famille et Prenoms de France.* Paris, 1951.

Doane, Gilbert H. *Searching for Your Ancestors,* Minneapolis: University of Minnesota Press, 1952.

Dobson, David. *Scottish-American Wills, 1650–1900.* Baltimore: Genealogical Publishing Co., 1990.

Falley, Margaret Dickson. *Irish and Scotch-Irish Ancestral Research.* 2 vols. Evanston, IL: Margaret Dickson Falley, 1961–62.

FitzHugh, Terrick V. H. *The Dictionary of Genealogy.* 2nd rev. ed. Totowa, NJ: Barnes & Noble, 1988.

Fucilla, Joseph Guerin. *Our Italian Surnames.* Evanston, IL: Chandler's, 1949.

Gardner, David E., and Frank Smith. *Genealogical Research in England and Wales.* 3 vols. Salt Lake City: Bookcraft Publishers, 1956–1964.

Gottschald, Max. *Deutsche Namenkunde,* Berlin: Dritte Vermehrte Auslage, 1954.

Greenwood, Val D. *The Researcher's Guide to American Genealogy.* Baltimore: Genealogical Publishing Co., 1973.

Jehn, Janet. *Acadian Exiles in the colonies,* Covington, KY, 1977 (self-published).

Johansson, Carl-Erik. *Cradled in Sweden.* Logan, UT: Everton Publishers, Inc., 1977.

Johnson, Arta F., ed. *Bibliography and Source Materials for Researching German-Speaking Ancestry.* Columbus, OH, 1982 (self-published).

Kaminkow, Marion, and Jack Kaminkow. *Original Lists of Emigrants in Bondage from London to the American Colonies, 1719–1744.* Baltimore: Magna Carta Book Co., 1967.

Karp, Abraham. *Golden Door to America: The Jewish Immigrant Experience.* New York: Viking, 1976.

Kirkham, E. Kay. *A Survey of American Church Records.* Logan, UT: Everton Publishers, 1971.

MacLysaght, Edward. *The Surnames of Ireland.* Dublin: Irish Academic Press, 1985.

Mann, Thomas Clifford, and Janet Greene. *Over Their Dead Bodies: Yankee Epitaphs and History.* Brattleboro, VT: Stephen Green Press, 1962.

Meynen, Emil. *Bibliography on German Settlements in Colonial North America, Especially on the Pennsylvania Germans and Their Descendants 1683–1933.* Leipzig: Otto Hrrassowitz, 1937.

Pine, Leslie Gilbert. *Descendants of Norman Ancestry,* Rutland, VT: Charles E. Tuttle Co., 1973.

Rogers, Colin D. *Tracing Your English Ancestors.* New York: St. Martin's, 1989.

Smith, Frank, and Finn A. Thomson. *Genealogical Guidebook and Atlas of Denmark.* Salt Lake City: Thomsen's Genealogical Center, 1969.

Shumway, Gary L., and William G. Hartley. *An Oral History Primer.* Salt Lake City, UT: Deseret Book Co., 1974.

Thode, Ernst. *Address Book of Germanic Genealogy.* 4th ed. Baltimore: Genealogical Publishing, 1991.

Tibon, Gutierre. *Onomastica Hispano Americana.* Mexico, 1961.

Unbegaun, Boros O. *Russian Surnames.* Oxford: Clarendon Press, 1972.

Vance, Lee W. *Tracing Your Philippine Ancestors.* Provo, UT: Stevenson's Genealogical Center, 1980.

Wright, Norman Edgar. *Building an American Pedigree: A Study in Genealogy.* Provo, UT: Brigham Young University Press, 1974.

APPENDIX I

State-By-State
Family History Help List

THE FOLLOWING is a list of specialty libraries, genealogical societies, and other sources of family history information. By no means complete, it is a working list compiled from many sources. As you gather your own addresses, add to this list. Many of the following libraries have free brochures or fact sheets about their collections, so be sure to inquire and send along a SASE. For information about the LDS Family History Library and its branches in almost every state, please check chapter 5.

Alabama

Alabama Archives and History Dept.
World War Memorial Bldg.
Montgomery, 36104

Birmingham Public Library
2020 7th Ave. N.
Birmingham, 35203

Institute of Genealogical and
    Historical Research
Samford University Library
800 Lakeshore Dr.
Birmingham, 35229

Wallace State Community College
    Library
Family and Regional History Program
Hanceville, 35077

Alaska

Alaska Division of State Libraries
Pouch G, State Capitol
Juneau, 99801

Alaska Historical Library
Juneau, 99801

Arizona

Arizona and the West Library
318 University of Arizona
Tucson, 85721

Arizona State Library
Archives and Public Records
Genealogy Library
1700 W. Washington
Phoenix, 85007

M. H. E. Heritage Library
433 S. Hobson
Mesa, 85204

Sun Cities Genealogical Society
Library
12600 113rd Ave., Suite C-6
Youngtown, 85372

Arkansas

Clark County Historical Association
Library
P.O. Box 516
Arkadelphia, 71923

Greene County Library
Arkansas History and Genealogy
Room
120 N. 12th St.
Paragould, 72450

Little Rock Public Library
700 Louisiana St.
Little Rock, 72201

Texarkana Historical Museum
P.O. Box 2343
Texarkana, 75501

California

Augustan Society Library
1510 Cravens Ave.
Torrance, 90501

Bancroft Library
University of California
Berkeley, 94720

California Genealogical Society
Library
300 Brannon St., Suite 409
San Francisco, 94107

California State Archives
1020 O St., Room 200
Sacramento, 95814

California State Library
California Section
914 Capitol Mall, Room 304
Sacramento, 94237

Family History Library
10777 Santa Monica Blvd.
W. Los Angeles, 90025

Genealogical Collection of San
Francisco Public Library
480 Winston Dr.
San Francisco, 94132

Huntington Library
San Marino, 91108

Los Angeles Public Library
630 W. 5th
Los Angeles, 90071

Native Daughters of the Golden West
   Library
555 Baker St.
San Francisco, 94117

San Diego Public Library
820 E St.
San Diego, 92101

Sons of the Revolution Library
Sons of the Revolution Bldg.
600 S. Central Ave.
Glendale, 91204

Whittier College Library
Whittier, 90602

Colorado

Denver Public Library
10 W. 14th Ave. Pkwy.
Denver, 80204

Colorado Historical Society Library
1300 Broadway
Denver, 80203

Stagecoach Library
1840 S. Wolcott Ct.
Denver, 80219

Tutt Library
Colorado College
Colorado Springs, 80903

Connecticut

Beardsley and Memorial Library
Munro Pl.
Winsted, 06098

Connecticut College Library
Mohegan Ave.
New London, 06320

Connecticut State Library
231 Capitol Ave.
Hartford, 06115

Hartford Public Library
500 Main St.
Hartford, 06103

Indian and Colonial Research Center
Old Mystic, 06372

Otis Library
261 Main St.
Norwich, 06360

Simsburg Genealogical and Historical
   Research Library
749 Hopmeadow St.
Simsbury, 06070

Whitney Library of New Haven
Colony Historical Society
114 Whitney Ave.
New Haven, 06510

Yale University Libraries
Box 1603A
New Haven, 06520

Delaware

Division of History
Department of State
Hall of Records
Dover, 19901

The Public Archives
Hall of Records
Dover, 19901

University Library
University of Delaware
Newark, 19711

District of Columbia

Library of Congress
Local History and Genealogy Division
Washington, 20540

National Society Daughters of the
    American Revolution Library
1776 D St. N. W.
Washington, 20006

Martin Luther King Memorial Library
901 G St. N. W.
Washington, 20001

Florida

Keystone Genealogy Library
695 E. Washington
Monticello, 32345

Miami-Dade Public Library
1 Biscayne Blvd. N.
Miami, 33132

Orlando Public Library
101 E. Central Blvd.
Orlando, 32801

Library of Florida History
University of Florida
Gainesville, 32601

Southern Genealogist's Exchange
    Society Library
1580 Blanding Blvd.
Jacksonville, 32203

State Library of Florida
R. A. Gray Bldg.
Tallahassee, 32301

Georgia

Atlanta Public Library
1 Margaret Mitchell Sq.
Atlanta, 30303

Cherokee Regional Library
Georgia History and Genealogy Room
305 S. Duke St.
La Fayette, 30728

Ellen Payne Odom Genealogy Library
c/o Moultrie-Colquitt County Library
204 5th St. S. E.
Moultrie, 31768

Genealogical Center Library
Box 71343
Marietta, 30007

Georgia Department of Archives and
    History
330 Capitol Ave.
Atlanta, 30334

Georgia Historical Society Library
501 Whittaker St.
Savannah, 31401

Georgia State Library
301 State Judicial Bldg.
Capitol Hill Station
Atlanta, 30334

Southwest Georgia Regional Library
Shotwell at Monroe
Bainbridge, 31717

Hawaii

Brigham Young University
Hawaii Campus
55-220 Hulanui St.
Laie, 96762

DAR Memorial Library
1914 Makiki Dr.
Honolulu, 96822

Library of Hawaii
King and Punchbowl Sts.
Honolulu, 96813

Idaho

Boise State University Library
Boise, 83725

Idaho Genealogical Library
325 W. State
Boise, 83702

Idaho State Historical Society Library
and Archives
450 N. 4th St.
Boise, 83702

University of Idaho Library
Moscow, 83843

Illinois

Chicago Public Library
78 E. Washington
Chicago, 60602

Decatur Genealogical Library
356 N. Main St.
Decatur, 62523

Illiana Genealogical Library
19 E. North St.
Danville, 61832

Illinois Regional Archives Depository
Northeastern Illinois University
5500 N. St. Louis Ave.
Chicago, 60625

Illinois State Archives
Archives Building
Springfield, 62756

Illinois State Historical Library
Old State Capitol
Springfield, 62706

Newberry Library
60 W. Walton St.
Chicago, 60610

South Suburban Genealogical and
Historical Society Research Library
Roosevelt Center
320 E. 161st Pl.
South Holland, 60473

University of Illinois Library
Urbana, 61801

Vogel Genealogical Research Library
305 1st St.
Holcomb, 61043

Indiana

Allen County Public Library
P.O. Box 2270
Fort Wayne, 46801

American Legion National
Headquarters Library
700 N. Pennsylvania St.
Indianapolis, 46204

Genealogy Division
Indiana State Library
140 N. Senate Ave.
Indianapolis, 46204

Indiana Historical Society Library
140 N. Senate Ave.
Indianapolis, 46204

Mennonite Historical Library
Goshen, 46526

Saint Joseph County Public Library
Local History/Genealogy Room
304 S. Main St.
South Bend, 46601

Iowa

Iowa Genealogical Society Library
6000 Douglas
Des Moines, 50322

Iowa Historical and Genealogical
  Library
Iowa Dept. of History and Archives
E. 12th St. and Grand Ave.
Des Moines, 50319

Norwegian-American Historical
  Museum
Decorah, 52101

Kansas

Atchison County Kansas Genealogical
  Society Library
c/o Atchison Public Library
401 Kansas Ave.
Atchison, 66002

Kansas Genealogical Society Library
Village Square Mall—Lower Level
2601 Central
Dodge City, 67801

Mennonite Library and Archives
Bethel College
300 E. 27th St.
North Newton, 67117

Topeka Genealogical Society Library
2717 S. E. Indiana St.
Topeka, 66605

Western Kansas Archives
Forsyth Library
Hays, 67601

Kentucky

Breckinridge County Public Library
Hardinsburg, 40143

Kentucky Department for Libraries
  and Archives
Archives Research Room
P.O. Box 537
Frankfort, 40602

Kentucky Historical Society Library
300 W. Broadway
Frankfort, 40621

Kentucky Library
Western Kentucky University
Bowling Green, 42101

Kentucky State Library and Archives
Public Records Division
300 Coffee Tree Rd.
Frankfort, 40602

National Society of the Sons of the
  American Revolution Library
1000 S. 4th St.
Louisville, 40203

Louisiana

Genealogical Library
Louisiana State Archives
3851 Essen La.
Baton Rouge, 70804

Louisiana State Library
State Capitol
Baton Rouge, 70804

New Orleans Public Library
219 Loyola Ave.
New Orleans, 70112

Southwest Louisiana Genealogical
and Historical Library
411 Pujo St.
Lake Charles, 70601

Maine

Bangor Public Library
145 Harlow St.
Bangor, 04401

Bath, Patten Free Library
Maine History and Genealogy Room
333 Summer St.
Bath, 04530

Maine State Library
State House
Augusta, 04330

Maryland

Appalachian Collection
Allegany Community College Library
Willowbrook Rd.
Cumberland, 21502

Enoch Pratt Free Library
400 Cathedral St.
Baltimore, 21201

Jewish Historical Society
Library of Maryland
15 Lloyd St.
Baltimore, 21202

Maryland State Archives
Court of Appeals Bldg.
361 Rose Blvd.
Annapolis, 21401

Massachusetts

(Every library in Massachusetts has a
wealth of historical and genealogical
material.)

American Antiquarian Society Library
185 Salisbury St.
Worcester, 01609

American Portuguese Genealogical
and Historical Society, Inc.
P.O. Box 644
Taunton, 02780

Boston Public Library
P.O. Box 286
Boston, 02117

Essex Institute
132 Essex St.
Salem, 01970

Massachusetts State Library
Beacon Hill
Boston, 02155

New England Historic Genealogical
Society Library
101 Newberry St.
Boston, 02116

Plymouth Public Library
132 South St.
Plymouth, 02360

Michigan

Detroit Public Library
5201 Woodward Ave.
Detroit, 48202

Central Michigan University Library
Mt. Pleasant, 48858

French-Canadian Heritage Society of
    Michigan Library
Mt. Clemens Public Library
150 Cass
Mt. Clemens, 48403

Michigan State Library
Box 30007
Lansing, 48909

Northwestern Michigan Genealogical
    Society
1704 E. Front St.
Traverse City, 49684

Minnesota

Folke Bernadette Memorial Library
Gustavus Adolphus College
St. Peter, 56082

Heart O'Lakes Genealogical Library
714 Summit Ave.
Detroit Lakes, 56501

Minneapolis Public Library
300 Nicollet Ave.
Minneapolis, 55401

Minnesota Genealogical Society
    Library
1650 Carroll Ave.
St. Paul, 55116

Minnesota Historical Society
345 Kellogg Blvd. W.
St. Paul, 55102

Rolvaag Memorial Library
St. Olaf College
Northfield, 55057

University of Minnesota Library
Minneapolis, 55455

Mississippi

Biloxi Public Library
P.O. Box 467
Biloxi, 39533

Department of Archives and History
Archive and History Bldg.
Capitol Green
Jackson, 39205

Historical Trails Library
Rte. 1, Box 373
Philadelphia, 39350

McCain Library and Archives
University of Southern Mississippi
Southern Station, Box 5148
Hattiesburg, 39406

University of Mississippi Library
University, 38652

Missouri

Boone County Historical Society
    Museum
Genealogy and History Library
Nifong Blvd. and Ponderosa Dr.
Columbia, 65201

Cape Girardeau County Genealogical
  Library
Union St.
Jackson, 63755

Joplin Public Library
4th and Main St.
Joplin, 64801

Kansas City Public Library
311 E. 12th St.
Kansas City, 64106

Mid-Continent Public Library
Genealogy and Local History Dept.
317 W. 24 Hwy.
Independence, 64050

Missouri State Library
600 W. Main St.
Jefferson City, 65102

Northwest Genealogical Society
  Library
412 Felix
St. Joseph, 64502

Ozarks Genealogical Society Library
P.O. Box 3494 G. S.
Springfield, 65808

Records and Archives
Office of Secretary of State
Capitol Bldg.
Jefferson City, 65101

St. Louis Public Library
1301 Olive St.
St. Louis, 63101

Springfield Public Library
397 E. Central St.
Springfield, 65801

Montana

Cascade County Historical Museum
  and Archives
1400 1st Ave. N.
Great Falls, 59401

Miles City Public Library
1 S. 10th
Miles City, 59301

Montana State Library
930 E. Lyndale Ave.
Helena, 59601

Montana State University Library
Bozeman, 59717

Public Library
Great Falls, 59401

Nebraska

DAR Genealogical Library
2nd and Washington Sts.
Grand Island, 68801

Nebraska State Historical Society
  Library
1500 R St.
Lincoln, 68508

Omaha Public Library
215 S. 15th St.
Omaha, 68102

Public Library
136 S. 14th St.
Lincoln, 68508

University of Nebraska Library
Lincoln, 68503

Nevada

Las Vegas Public Library
400 E. Mesquite Ave.
Las Vegas, 89101

Nevada State Historical Society
   Library
P.O. Box 1192
Reno, 89501

Northeastern Nevada Genealogical
   Society Library
1515 Idaho St.
Elko, 89801

University of Nevada Library
Reno, 89507

New Hampshire

Dartmouth College Archives
Baker Memorial Library
Hanover, 03755

Exeter Public Library
86 Front St.
Exeter, 03833

New Hampshire State Library
20 Park St.
Concord, 03303

Piscataqua Pioneers "Special
   Collection"
Diamond Library
University of New Hampshire
Durham, 03824

New Jersey

New Jersey State Library
185 W. State St.
Trenton, 08625

Princeton University Library
Princeton, 08540

Rutgers University Library
New Brunswick, 08903

Strickler Research Library
c/o Ocean County Historical Society
26 Hadley Ave.
Toms River, 08654

New Mexico

New Mexico State Library
301 Don Gasper
Santa Fe, 87501

New Mexico State University Library
Las Cruces, 88003

Public Library
423 E. Central Ave.
Albuquerque, 87101

University of New Mexico Library
Albuquerque, 87131

New York

Columbia University
Journalism Library
New York, 10027

Genesee County Library
Department of History
131 W. Main St.
Batavia, 14020

Holland Society of New York Library
122 E. 58th St.
New York, 10022

John M. Olin Library
Cornell University
Ithaca, 14853

Margaret Reaney Memorial Library
and Museum
19 Kingsbury Ave.
St. Johnsville, 13452
(special Palatine German collection)

New York Public Library
5th Ave. and 42nd St.
New York, 10016

New York State Library
Albany, 12224

Onondaga County Public Library
Local History and Special Collections
447 S. Salina St.
Syracuse, 13202

Rochester Public Library
Local History Division
115 South Ave.
Rochester, 14604

Schomburg Center for Research in
Black Culture
515 Malcolm X Blvd.
New York, 10037

Western New York Genealogical
Society Library
P.O. Box 338
Hamburg, 14075

North Carolina

Division of Archives
Office of Archives and History
State Department of Art, Culture, and
History
109 E. Jones St.
Raleigh, 27611

North Carolina State Library
109 E. Jones St.
Raleigh, 27611

Public Library of Charlotte and
Mecklenburg County
310 N. Tryon St.
Charlotte, 28202

University of North Carolina
Drawer 870
Chapel Hill, 27514

North Dakota

Minot Family History Center
c/o Pat Chalcraft
62 Western Village
Minot, 58701

Public Library
Fargo, 58102

Red River Valley Genealogical Society
Library
Manchester Bldg.
112 N. University Dr., Suite L
Fargo, 58106

North Dakota State Library
Bismarck, 58501

University of North Dakota Library
Grand Forks, 58201

Ohio

Akron Public Library
55 S. Main St.
Akron, 44309

American Jewish Archives
Clifton Ave.
Cincinnati, 45220

Cincinnati Historical Society Library
The Museum Center at Cincinnati
Union Terminal
1301 Western Ave.
Cincinnati, 45203

Cincinnati Public Library
800 Vine St.
Cincinnati, 45202

Cleveland Public Library
325 Superior Ave.
Cleveland, 44114

Franklin County Genealogical Society
Library
570 W. Broad St.
Columbus, 43216

Harrison County Genealogical
Chapter Library
45507 Unionvale Rd.
Cadiz, 43907

Hayes Presidential Center Library
1337 Hayes Ave.
Fremont, 43420

Mennonite Historical Library
Bluffton College
Bluffton, 45817

Muskingum County Genealogical
Society Library
P.O. Box 3066
Zanesville, 43702

Ohio Genealogical Society Library
34 Sturges Ave.
Mansfield, 44906

Ohio Historical Society Library
1985 Velma Ave.
Columbus, 43211

Ohio State Library
65 S. Front St.
Columbus, 43215

Toledo Public Library
Local Historical and Genealogical
Dept.
325 Michigan St.
Toledo, 43624

Western Reserve Historical Society
Library
10825 East Blvd.
Cleveland, 44106

Oklahoma

American Heritage Library
P.O. Box 176
Davis, 73030

Metropolitan Library System
131 Dean McGee Ave.
Oklahoma City, 73102

Oklahoma Department of Libraries
200 N. E. 18th
Oklahoma City, 73105

Oklahoma Historical Society Library
2100 N. Lincoln Ave.
Oklahoma City, 73105

Rudsill North Regional Library
1520 N. Hanford
Tulsa, 74106

State DAR Library
Historical Bldg.
Oklahoma City, 73105

University of Oklahoma Library
Norman, 73069

Western Trails Genealogy Library
c/o Southern Prairie Library
421 Hudson St.
Altus, 73521

Oregon

Genealogical Forum of Oregon
  Library
211 Tumwater Dr.
Oregon City, 97045

Oregon Genealogical Society Library
223 N. A St., Suite F
Springfield, 97477

Oregon Historical Society Library
1230 S. W. Park Ave.
Portland, 97201

Oregon State Archives
1005 Broadway N. E.
Salem, 97301

Oregon State Library
State Library Bldg.
Summer and Court Sts.
Salem, 97310

University of Oregon Library
Eugene, 97403

Pennsylvania

Alttoona Public Library
"The Pennsylvania Room"
1600 5th Ave.
Altoona, 16602

Bucks County Historical Society
  Library
84 S. Pine St.
Doylestown, 18901

Carnegie Library of Pittsburgh
Pennsylvania Department
4400 Forbes Ave.
Pittsburgh, 15213

Chester County Archives and Records
  Service
117 W. Gay St.
West Chester, 19380

Free Library of Philadelphia
Logan Sq.
Philadelphia, 19141

Historical Society of Evangelical and
  Reformed Church Archives and
  Libraries
College Ave. and James St.
Lancaster, 17604

Historical Society of Pennsylvania
  Library
1300 Locust St.
Philadelphia, 19107

Lutheran Historical Society Library
Gettysburg, 17325

Mennonite Historical Library
565 Yoder Rd.
Harleysville, 19438

Methodist Historical Center
326 New St.
Philadelphia, 19106

Pennsylvania Historical and Museum
  Commission Division of Archives
  and Manuscripts
Box 1026
Harrisburg, 17108

Pennsylvania State Library
P.O. Box 1601
Harrisburg, 17105

University Library
Pennsylvania State University
University Park, 16802

University of Pennsylvania Library
Central Bldg.
34th St. below Woodland
Philadelphia, 19104

Western Pennsylvania Genealogical
Society Library
4400 Forbes Ave.
Pittsburgh, 15213

Rhode Island

John Hay Library
Brown University
Providence, 02912

Rhode Island Historical Society
Library
121 Hope St.
Providence, 02903

Rhode Island State Archives
314 State House
Providence, 02900

Rhode Island State Library
82 S. State House
Providence, 02903

South Carolina

Faith Clayton Research Center
Rickman Library
Southern Wesleyan University
Central, 29630

Free Library
404 King St.
Charleston, 29407

Old Edgefield District Archives
Chapter
South Carolina Genealogical Society
P.O. Box 468
Edgefield, 29824

South Carolina Archives Dept.
1430 Senate St.
Columbia, 29201

South Carolina State Library
1500 Senate St.
Columbia, 29201

South Dakota

Alexander Mitchell Public Library
519 S. Kline St.
Aberdeen, 57401

Carnegie Free Public Library
10th and Dakota Sts.
Sioux Falls, 57102

State Historical Society Library
Memorial Bldg.
Pierre, 57501

University of South Dakota Library
Vermillion, 57069

Tennessee

Chattanooga-Hamilton County
Bicentennial Library
Genealogy/Local History Dept.
1001 Broad St.
Chattanooga, 37402

Dandridge Memorial Library
Billie R. McNamara, Genealogy
Coordinator
P.O. Box 339
Dandridge, 37725

McClung Historical Collection
East Tennessee Historical Center
314 W. Clinch Ave.
Knoxville, 37902

Memphis Public Library
1850 Peabody
Memphis, 38104

Memphis State University Library
Mississippi Valley Collection
Memphis, 38104

Public Library of Nashville
222 8th Ave. N.
Nashville, 37203

Tennessee Genealogical Library
3340 Poplar Ave.
Memphis, 38111

Tennessee State Library and Archives
403 7th Ave. N.
Nashville, 37219

Texas

Austin History Center
Austin Public Library
810 Guadalupe St.
Austin, 78768

Baylor University Texas Collection
Baylor University
P.O. Box 7142
Waco, 76798

Catholic Archives of Texas
1600 Congress Ave.
Austin, 78811

Confederate Research Center
Harold B. Simpson Hill College
History Complex
112 Lamar Dr.
Hillsboro, 76645

Dallas Public Library
Genealogy Section
1515 Young St.
Dallas, 75201

DAR Museum Library
300 Alamo Plaza
San Antonio, 78295

El Paso Genealogical Library
3631 Douglas
El Paso, 79903

Houston Metropolitan Research
Center
Julia B. Ideson Bldg.
500 McKinney St.
Houston, 77002

Institute of Texan Cultures
Hemisfair Plaza
P.O. Box 1226
San Antonio, 78294

Jewish Holocaust Education Center
and Memorial Museum of Houston
5401 Caroline
Houston, 77004

Redfern Genealogical Research
Center
301 W. Missouri
Midland, 79701

Sam Houston Regional Library and
Research Center
1011 Governor's Rd.
Liberty, 77575

San Jacinto Museum of History
Library
300 Park Rd. N.
La Porte, 77571

Scarborough Library of Genealogy,
History and Biography of South and
Southwest
c/o McMurry Station
Abilene, 79605

Southwest Genealogical Society and
Library
412 W. College St., #A
Carthage, 75633

Texas Land Office Archives and
Records Div.
Stephen F. Austin Bldg.
1700 N. Congress
Austin, 78701

Texas State Library
Genealogy Collection
1201 Brazos St.
Austin, 78711

Waco Public Library
1717 Austin Ave.
Waco, 76701

Utah

American Genealogical Lending
Library
P.O. Box 244
Bountiful, 84011

Brigham Young University Library
Provo, 84601

Everton's Genealogical Library
P.O. Box 368
Logan, 84323

Family History Library of the Church
of Jesus Christ of Latter-Day Saints
35 North West Temple
Salt Lake City, 84150

University of Utah Library
Salt Lake City, 84112

Utah State Historical Society Library
300 Rio Grande
Salt Lake City, 84101

Utah State University Library
Logan, 84321

Vermont

Genealogical Library
Bennington Museum
Bennington, 05201

University of Vermont Library
Burlington, 05401

The Russell Collection
c/o The Dorothy Canfield Library
Main St.
Arlington, 05250

Vermont Department of Libraries
Law and Documents Unit
109 State St.
Montpelier, 05602

Vermont Historical Society Library
Pavillion Bldg.
Montpelier, 05602

Virginia

Alderman Library
University of Virginia
Charlottesville, 22903

Blue Ridge Regional Library
310 E. Church St.
Martinsville, 24112

College of William and Mary Library
Williamsburg, 23185

Commonwealth of Virginia
Virginia State Library
1101 Capitol
Richmond, 23219

Genealogical Society of the Northern
   Neck of Virginia
P.O. Box 511
Heathsville, 22473

James Monroe Museum and
   Memorial Library
908 Charles St.
Fredericksburg, 22401

Jefferson/Madison Regional Library
201 E. Market St.
Charlottesville, 22903

Library of the Albemarle County
Historical Society
220 Court Sq.
Charlottesville, 22903

National Genealogical Society Library
4527 17th St. N.
Arlington, 22207

Virginia Historical Library
P.O. Box 7311
Richmond, 23211

Virginia State Library
11th St. at Capitol Sq.
Richmond, 23219

Washington

Heritage Center Museum and Library
Snohomish County Historical
   Association
P.O. Box 5203
Everett, 98206

Public Library
4th Ave. and Madison
Seattle, 98104
(The genealogical collection of the
   State Library is here.)

Seattle Genealogical Society Library
1405 5th Ave.
Seattle, 98111

Spokane Public Library
Genealogy Room
916 W. Main Ave.
Spokane, 99201

Washington State Historical Society
   Library
State Historical Bldg.
315 N. Stadium Way
Tacoma, 98403

Washington State Library
State Library Bldg.
Olympia, 98501

Washington State University Library
Holland Library
Pullman, 99164

West Virginia

Central West Virginia Genealogical
   and Historical Library and Museum
345 Center St.
Weston, 26452

Division of Archives and History
Cultural Center
Capitol Complex
Charleston, 25305

Huntington Public Library
Huntington, 25701

West Virginia and Regional History
    Collection
Colson Hall
West Virginia University Library
Morgantown, 26506

Wisconsin

Brown County Library
Local History and Genealogy Dept.
515 Pine St.
Green Bay, 54301

Local History and Genealogical
    Library
Racine County Historical Society and
    Museum, Inc.
701 S. Main St.
Racine, 53401

Monroe County Local History Room
    and Library
200 W. Main St.
Sparta, 54656

University Archives
Parkside Library
University of Wisconsin
Kenosha, 53141

Wisconsin Historical Society Library
816 State St.
Madison, 53706

Wyoming

Cheyenne Genealogical Society
Laramie County Library
Central Ave.
Cheyenne, 82001

Laramie County Public Library
Cheyenne, 82001

Western History and Archives Dept.
University of Wyoming
Laramie, 82070

Wyoming State Archives and
    Historical Dept.
State Office Bldg.
Cheyenne, 82001

Wyoming State Library
Supreme Court Bldg.
Cheyenne, 82001

GENEALOGICAL AND HISTORICAL SOCIETIES

Alabama

Alabama Genealogical Society Inc.
AGS Depository and Headquarters
Samford University Library
800 Lakeshore Dr.
Birmingham, 35229

American College of Heraldry
Drawer CG
University of Alabama
Tuscaloosa, 35486

Birmingham Genealogical Society, Inc.
P.O. Box 2432
Birmingham, 35201

Civil War Descendants Society
P.O. Box 233
Athens, 35611

East Alabama Genealogical Society
P.O. Box 2892
Opelika, 36803

Natchez Trace Genealogical Society
P.O. Box 420
Florence, 35631

Society of the Descendants of
    Washington's Army at Valley Forge
Alabama Brigade
Donald W. VanBrunt, Adjutant
7905 Ensley Dr. S. W.
Huntsville, 35802

Southern Society of Genealogists
P.O. Box 295
Centre, 35960

Alaska

Anchorage Genealogical Society
18227 Tonsina Ct.
Eagle River, 99577

Gastineau Genealogical Society
3270 Nowell Ave.
Juneau, 99801

Alaska Genealogical Society
P.O. Box 60534
Fairbanks, 99706

Arizona

Apache Genealogy Society of Cochise
    County
P.O. Box 1084
Sierra Vista, 85636

Arizona Genealogical Advisory Board
P.O. Box 5641
Mesa, 85211

Arizona Genealogical Computer
    Interest Group
2105 S. McClintock
Tempe, 85282

Arizona Pioneer's Historical Society
949 E. 2nd St.
Tucson, 85719

Arizona State Genealogical Society
P.O. Box 42075
Tucson, 85733

Black Family Historical Society of
    Arizona
c/o Larry Lee
P.O. Box 1515
Gilbert, 85299

Cherokee Family Ties
Donna Williams
516 N. 38th St.
Mesa, 85208

Family History Society of Arizona
P.O. Box 63094
Phoenix, 85082

Jewish Historical Society, Arizona
Carlton Brooks
720 W. Edgewood Ave.
Mesa, 85210

Lake Havasu Genealogical Society
P.O. Box 953
Lake Havasu City, 86405

Sun Cities Genealogical Society
P.O. Box 1448
Sun City, 85372

Tucson, Afro-American Historical and
Genealogical Society
Tani Sanchez, President
P.O. Box 58272
Tucson, 85754

Arkansas

Ark-La-Tex Genealogical Assn. Inc.
P.O. Box 4462
Shreveport, 71104

Arkansas Genealogical Research
c/o Rhonda S. Norris
805 E. 5th St.
Russellville, 72801

Arkansas Genealogical Society
P.O. Box 908
Hot Springs, 71902

Arkansas Historical Association
History Dept., Ozark Hall, 12
University of Arkansas
Fayetteville, 72701

Northwest Arkansas Genealogical
Society
P.O. Box 796
Rogers, 72757

Professional Genealogists of Arkansas
P.O. Box 1807
Conway, 72032

Southwest Arkansas Genealogical
Society
c/o Kitty Reeves Jean
1022 Lawton Cir.
Magnolia, 71753

Southwest Arkansas Region Archives
Mary Medaris, Director
Old Washington Historic State Park
Washington, 71862

Tri-County Genealogical Society
(Monroe, Lee and Phillips)
P.O. Box 580
Marvell, 72366

California

African-American Genealogical
Society, California
P.O. Box 8442
Los Angeles, 90008

British Isles Family History Society-
U.S.A.
2531 Sawtelle Blvd., #134
Los Angeles, 90064

California Genealogical Society
P.O. Box 77105
San Francisco, 94107

Califnormia State Genealogical
Alliance
c/o Mrs. Wendy Elliott, President
4808 E. Garland St.
Anaheim, 92807

ComputerRooters
P. O. Box 161693
Sacramento, 95816

German Genealogical Society of
America
2125 Wright Ave., Suite, C-9
La Verne, 91750

Hi Desert Genealogical Society
P.O. Box 1271
Victorville, 92392

Society of Hispanic Historical and
Ancestral Research
P.O. Box 4294
Fullerton, 92635

Leisure World Genealogical Workshop
c/o Leisure World Library
2300 Beverly Manor Rd.
Seal Beach, 90740

Los Angeles Jewish Genealogical
Society
Geraldine Winerman
P.O. Box 55443
Sherman Oaks, 91413

Mayflower Descendants in the State
of California
405 14th St., Terrace Level
Oakland, 94612

Native Daughters of the Golden West
555 Baker St.
San Francisco, 94117

Palm Springs Genealogical Society
P.O. Box 2093
Palm Springs, 92263

Polish Genealogical Society of Cali-
fornia
P.O. Box 713
Midway City, 92655

Sacramento Genealogical Association
P.O. Box 292145
Sacramento, 95829

Santa Barbara County Genealogical
Society
P.O. Box 1303
Santa Barbara, 93116

Southern California Genealogical
Society
P.O. Box 4377
Burbank, 91503

Colorado

Aspen Historical Society
620 W. Bleeker St.
Aspen, 81611

Black Genealogical Research Group
4605E Kentucky Ave., 5F
Denver, 80222

Boulder Genealogical Society
P.O. Box 3246
Boulder, 80307

Colorado Council of Genealogical
Societies
P.O. Box 24379
Denver, 80224

Colorado Genealogical Society
P.O. Box 9218
Denver, 80209

Eastern Colorado Historical Society
(Cheyenne County)
c/o Karlene McKean
43433 Road CC
Cheyenne Wells, 80810

Southeastern Colorado Genealogical
Society, Inc.
P.O. Box 4207
Pueblo, 81003

Connecticut

Connecticut Ancestry Society, Inc.
P.O. Box 249
Stamford, 06904

Connecticut Historical Commission
59 S. Prospect St.
Hartford, 06106

Connecticut Professional
Genealogists Council
P.O. Box 4273
Hartford, 06147

Connecticut Society of Genealogists,
Inc.
P.O. Box 435
Glastonbury, 06033

French-Canadian Genealogical
Society of Connecticut
P.O. Box 45
Tolland, 06084

Jewish Genealogical Society of
Connecticut
Jonathan Smith
394 Sport Hills Rd.
Easton, 06612

Polish Genealogical Society of
Connecticut
c/o Jonathan D. Shea, President
8 Lyle Rd.
New Britain, 06053

Society of Mayflower Descendants in
Connecticut
36 Arundel Ave.
Hartford, 06107

Stamford Historical Society
1508 High Ridge Rd.
Stamford, 06903

Delaware

Delaware Genealogical Society
505 Market St. Mall
Wiilmington, 19801

Historical Society of Delaware
Old Town Hall
Wilmington, 19801

District of Columbia

Afro-American Historical and
Genealogical Society, Inc.,
National
Barbara D. Walker, President
P.O. Box 73086
Washington, 20056

Jewish Genealogy Society of Greater
Washington
Diane Goldman
P.O. Box 412
Vienna, Virginia 22183

National Genealogical Society
4527 17th St. N.
Arlington, Virginia 22207

National Society Daughters of
American Colonists
2205 Massachusetts Ave. N.W.
Washington, 20008

National Society Daughters of the
American Revolution
Memorial Continental Hall
1776 D. St. N.W.
Washington, 20006

White House Historical Association
740 Jackson Pl. N.W.
Washington, 20506

Florida

Brevard Genealogical Society
P.O. Box 1123
Cocoa, 32922

Broward County Genealogical Society
P.O. Box 485
Ft. Lauderdale, 33302

Broward County Jewish Genealogical
Society
Bernard I. Kouchel
P.O. Box 17251
Ft. Lauderdale, 33318

Central Florida Afro-American
Historical and Genealogical Society
Mary J. Fears, President
P.O. Box 5742
Deltona, 32728

Descendants of the Knights of the
Bath
James D. Partin, Registrar
P.O. Box 7062 GH
Gainesville, 32605

Florida Genealogical Society, Inc.
P.O. Box 18624
Tampa, 33679

Florida Society of Genealogical
Research, Inc.
8415 122nd St. N.
Seminole, 34642

Florida State Genealogical Society
P.O. Box 10249
Tallahassee, 32302

Greater Miami Genealogical Society
P.O. Box 162905
Miami, 33116

Greater Miami Jewish Genealogical
Society
Arthur Chassman
8340 S.W. 151 St.
Miami, 33158

International Genealogy Fellowship of
Rotarians
I.F.R. Genealogy
c/o Charles D. Townsend
5721 Antietam Dr.
Sarasota, 34231

Jacksonville Genealogical Society, Inc.
P.O. Box 60756
Jacksonville, 32236

Palm Beach Jewish Genealogical
Society
Albert Silberfeld
6037 Pointe Regal Cir., #205
Delray Beach, 33484

Sarasota Genealogical Society, Inc.
P.O. Box 1917
Sarasota, 34230

Southern Genealogist's Exchange
Society, Inc.
P.O. Box 2801
Jacksonville, 32203

St. Augustine Genealogical Society
St. Johns County Public Library
1960 N. Ponce de Leon Blvd.
St. Augustine, 32084

Georgia

African-American Family History
  Association, Inc.
P.O. Box 115268
Atlanta, 30310

Ancestors Unlimited, Inc.
P.O. Box 1507
Jonesboro, 30336

Atlanta Historical Society
130 W. Paces Ferry Rd., N.W.
Atlanta, 30305

Augusta Genealogical Society
P.O. Box 3743
Augusta, 30914

Central Georgia Genealogical
  Society, Inc.
P.O. Box 2024
Warner Robins, 31099

Georgia Genealogical Society
P.O. Box 54575
Atlanta, 30308

Jewish Genealogical Society of
  Georgia
Peggy Freedman
245 Dalrymple Rd.
Atlanta, 30328

Northwest Georgia Historical and
  Genealogical Society
P.O. Box 5063
Rome, 30161

Savannah Area Genealogical Society
P.O. Box 15385
Savannah, 31416

South Georgia Genealogical Society
P.O. Box 246
Ochlocknee, 31773

Hawaii

Hawaii County Genealogical Society
P.O. Box 331
Keaau, 96749

Hawaiian Historical Society
560 Kawaiahao St.
Honolulu, 96813

Sandwich Islands Genealogical
  Society
1116 Kealaolou Ave.
Honolulu, 96816

Idaho

Bonneville County Historical Society
P.O. Box 1784
Idaho Falls, 83401

Idaho Genealogical Society, Inc.
4620 Overland Rd., Room 204
Boise, 83705

Idaho Historical Society
325 State St.
Boise, 83702

Pocatello Branch Genealogical
  Society
156½ S. 6th Ave.
Pocatello, 83201

Upper Snake River Valley Historical
  Society
P.O. Box 244
Rexburg, 83440

Illinois

Afro-American Historical and
  Genealogical Society
12516 S. Lowe St.
Chicago, 60628

Chicago Genealogical Society
P.O. Box 1160
Chicago, 60690

Chicago Historical Society
North Ave. and Clark St.
Chicago, 60614

Decatur Genealogical Society
P.O. Box 1548
Decatur, 62525

Du Page County Genealogical
  Society
P.O. Box 133
Lomard, 60148

Fayette County Genealogical Society
P.O. Box 177
Vandalia, 62471

Illiana Genealogical and Historical
  Society
P.O. Box 207
Danville, 61834

Illinois State Genealogical Society
P.O. Box 10195
Springfield, 62791

Jewish Genealogical Society of Illinois
Belle Holman
P.O. Box 515
Northbrook, 60065

Kankakee Valley Genealogical Society
304 S. Indiana Ave.
Kankakee, 60901

Lithuanian American Genealogy
  Society
Balzekas Museum of Lithuanian
  Culture
6500 S. Pulaski Rd.
Chicago, 60629

Mennonite Historical and
  Genealogical Society, Illinois
P.O. Box 819
Metamora, 61548

North Central Illinois Genealogical
  Society
P.O. Box 4635
Rockford, 61110

Palatines to America, Illinois Chapter
P.O. Box 3448
Quincy, 62305

Polish Genealogical Society
984 Milwaukee Ave.
Chicago, 60622

Rock Island County Historical Society
P.O. Box 632
Moline, 61265

Sons of Union Veterans of the Civil
  War, Illinois Department
c/o D. C. Bailey
P.O. Box 2314
Naperville, 60567

Southern Illinois Genealogy Society
c/o John A. Logan College
Rte. 2, Box 145
Carterville, 62918

Indiana

African-American Historical and
Genealogical Society, Indiana
502 Clover Terr.
Bloomington, 47404

Allen County Genealogical Society of
Indiana
P.O. Box 12003
Fort Wayne, 46862

Boone County Historical Society
P.O. Box 141
Lebanon, 46052

DeKalb County Genealogy Society
c/o Eckhart Public Library
603 S. Jackson St.
Auburn, 46706

Elkhart County Genealogical Society
1812 Jeanwood Dr.
Elkhart, 46514

Family Tree and Crests
6233 Carrollton Ave.
Indianapolis, 46220

Illiana Jewish Genealogical Society
Henry Landauer
404 Douglas
Park Forest, 60466

Indiana Genealogical Society
P.O. Box 10507
Fort Wayne, 46852

Indiana Historical Society
315 W. Ohio St.
Indianapolis, 46202

Northwest Indiana Genealogical
Society
c/o Valparaiso Public Library
103 Jefferson St.
Valparaiso, 46383

Northwest Territory Genealogical
Society
Lewis Historical Library
Vincennes University
Vincennes, 47591

Palatines to America, Indiana Chapter
1801 N. Duane Rd.
Muncie, 47304

South Bend Area Genealogical
Society
P.O. Box 1222
South Bend, 46624

Southern Indiana Genealogical
Society
P.O. Box 665
New Albany, 47151

Wabash Valley Genealogical Society
P.O. Box 85
Terre Haute, 47808

Iowa

Adair County Anquestors
Genealogical Society
c/o Greenfield Public Library
P.O. Box 328
Greenfield, 50849

Central Iowa Genealogical Society
Box 945
Marshalltown, 50158

Daughters of Union Veterans, Iowa
Dept.
c/o Sherry Foresman
R1, Box 23
Menlo, 50164

Des Moines County Genealogical
Society
P.O. Box 493
Burlington, 52601

German American Heritage Center
P.O. Box 243
Davenport, 52805

Greater Sioux County Genealogical
Society
c/o Sioux Center Public Library
327 1st Ave., N.W.
Sioux Center, 51250

Iowa City Genealogical Society
Darrell M. Wilkins
403 S. Walnut
Mt. Pleasant, 52641

Northeast Iowa Genealogical Society
c/o Grout Museum of History and
Science
503 South St.
Waterloo, 50701

Northwest Iowa Genealogical Society
c/o LeMars Public Library
46 1st St., S. W.
LeMars, 51031

State Historical Society of Iowa
600 E. Locust
Des Moines, 50319

Kansas

Atchison County Kansas Genealogical
Society
c/o Atchison Library
401 Kansas Ave.
Atchison, 66002

Fort Hays, Kansas Genealogical
Society
c/o Forsyth Library
FHS University
Hays, 67601

Kansas Council of Genealogical
Societies, Inc.
P.O. Box 3858
Topeka, 66604

Kansas Genealogical Society, Inc.
P.O. Box 103
Dodge City, 67801

Kansas State Historical Society
6425 S.W. 6th Ave.
Topeka, 66615

Leavenworth County Genealogical
Society
P.O. Box 362
Leavenworth, 66048

North Central Kansas Genealogical
Society
Box 251
Cawker City, 67430

Northwest Kansas Genealogical and
Historical Society
700 W. 3rd
Oakley, 67748

Santa Fe Trail Genealogical Society
P.O. Box 1048
Syracuse, 67878

Kentucky

Eastern Kentucky Genealogical
  Society
Box 1544
Ashland, 41101

Harlan County Genealogical Society
P.O. Box 1498
Harlan, 40831

Kentucky Genealogical Society
P.O. Box 153
Frankfort, 40602

Kentucky Historical Society
P.O. Box H
Frankfort, 40602

Kentucky Society of Pioneers
c/o Sam McDowell, President
1129 Pleasant Ridge Rd.
Utica, 42376

Louisville Genealogical Society
P.O. Box 5164
Louisville, 40255

National Society of the Sons of the
  American Revolution
National Headquarters
1000 S. 4th St.
Louisville, 40203

Southern Historical Association
c/o University of Kentucky
Lexington, 40506

South Central Kentucky
Historical/Genealogical Society
P.O. Box 80
Glasgow, 42141

Southern Kentucky Genealogical
  Society
P. O. Box 1782
Bowling Green, 42102

West-Central Kentucky Family
  Research Association
(Nineteen counties of west-central
  Kentucky)
P.O. Box 1932
Owensboro, 42302

Louisiana

Ark-La-Tex Genealogical Association
P.O. Box 4462
Shreveport, 71134

Baton Rouge Genealogical and
  Historical Society
P. O. Box 80565 S. W. Station
Baton Rouge, 70898

Central Louisiana Genealogical
  Society
P.O. Box 12206
Alexandria, 71315

Evangeline Genealogical and
  Historical Society
P.O. Box 664
Ville Platte, 70586

Friends of Genealogy
P.O. Box 17835
Shreveport, 71138

Genealogy West, Inc.
(West Bank of the Mississippi River)
5644 Abby Dr.
New Orleans, 70131

Louisiana Genealogical and Historical
Society
P.O. Box 82060
Baton Rouge, 70884

Mississippi Memories Society
P.O. Box 18991
Shreveport, 71138

Natchitoches Genealogical and
Historical Association
c/o Henrietta Breedlove
P.O. Box 1349
Natchitoches, 71458

New Orleans Genealogical Research
Society
P.O. Box 71791
New Orleans, 70150

New Orleans, Jewish Genealogical
Society of Jacob and Vicki Karno
23 Waverly Pl.
Metairie, 70003

North Louisiana Genealogical Society
P.O. Box 324
Ruston, 71270

Plaquemines Parish Genealogical
Society
203 Hwy. 23
South Buras, 70041

Southwest Louisiana Genealogical
Society Inc.
P.O. Box 5552
Lake Charles, 70606

Maine

Bath Historical Society
Sagadahoc History and Genealogy
Room
Patten Free Library
33 Summer St.
Bath, 04530

Maine Genealogical Society
P.O. Box 221
Farmington, 04938

Maine Historical Society
485 Congress St.
Portland, 04111

Maryland

Anne Arundel Genealogical Society
P.O. Box 221
Pasadena, 21122

Baltimore Afro-American Historical
and Genealogical Society
P.O. Box 10085
Baltimore, 21218

Baltimore County Genealogical
Society, Inc.
P.O. Box 10085
Towson, 21285

Central Maryland, Afro-American
Historical and Genealogical Society
P.O. Box 2774
Columbia, 21045

Frederick County Historical Society
24 E. Church St.
Frederick, 21701

Jewish Historical Society of Maryland
  Carol Rider
2707 Moores Valley Dr.
Baltimore, 21209

Maryland Genealogical and Historical
  Society
201 W. Monument St.
Baltimore, 21201

Prince George's County Genealogical
  Society
Box 819
Bowie, 20718

Queene Anne's County Historical
  Society
Wright's Chance
Commerce St.
Centreville, 21617

United Methodist Historical Society
Lovely Lane United Methodist
  Church
2200 St. Paul St.
Baltimore, 21218

Massachusetts

American Jewish Historical Society
2 Thornton Rd.
Waltham, 02154

Berkshire Family History Association
P.O. Box 1437
Pittsfield, 01201

Cape Cod Genealogical Society
P.O. Box 1394
E. Harwich, 02645

Congregational Christian Historical
  Society
14 Beacon St.
Boston, 02108

Essex Institute
132 Essex St.
Salem, 01970

Essex Society of Genealogy
P.O. Box 313
Lynnfield, 01940

Greater Boston, Jewish Genealogical
  Society
Gary R. Rachins
P.O. Box 366
Newton Highlands, 02161

Irish Ancestral Research Association
P.O. Box 619
Sudbury, 01776

Massachusetts Genealogical Council
P.O. Box 5393
Cochituate, 01778

Massachusetts Historical Society
1154 Boylston St.
Boston, 02215

Massachusetts Society of Genealogists,
  Inc.
P.O. Box 215
Ashland, 01721

Massachusetts Society of Mayflower
  Descendants
376 Boylston St.
Boston, 02116

New England Historic Genealogical
  Society
101 Newbury St.
Boston, 02116

Plymouth Colony Genealogists
60 Sheridan St.
Brockton, 02402

Western Massachusetts Genealogical
Society
P.O. Box 206, Forest Park Station
Springfield, 01108

Michigan

Dearborn Genealogical Society
P.O. Box 1112
Dearborn, 48121

Detroit Society for Genealogical
Research
Detroit Public Library
5201 Woodward Ave.
Detroit, 48202

Genealogical Society of Flemish
Americans
18740 Thirteen Mile Rd.
Roseville, 48066

Flint Genealogical Society
P.O. Box 1217
Flint, 48501

French-Canadian Heritage Society of
Michigan
c/o Mt. Clemens Public Library
P.O. Box 10028
Lansing, 48901

Holland Genealogical Society
Herrick Public Library
300 River Ave.
Holland, 49423

Jewish Genealogical Society of
Michigan
David Sloan
8050 Lincoln Dr.
Huntington Woods, 48070

Michigan Genealogical Council
P.O. Box 80953
Lansing, 48908

Michigan Historical Commission
505 State Office Bldg.
Lansing, 48913

Michigan Society, Order of Founders
and Patriots of America
Charles K. Field, Councilor General
2961 Woodcreek Way
Bloomfield Hills, 48304

Midland Genealogical Society
c/o Grace A. Dow Library
1710 W. St. Andrews Dr.
Midland, 48640

Mid-Michigan Genealogical Society
P.O. Box 16033
Lansing, 48901

Northeast Michigan Genealogical
Society
c/o Jesse Besser Museum
491 Johnson St.
Alpena, 49707

Palatines to America, Michigan
Chapter
868 Beechwood St. N.W.
Grand Rapids, 49505

Polish Genealogical Society of
Michigan
c/o Burton Historical Collections
5201 Woodward Ave.
Detroit, 48202

Saginaw Genealogical Society
c/o Saginaw Public Library
505 Janes Ave.
Saginaw, 48507

Southwestern Michigan Genealogical
Association
Box 573
St. Joseph, 49085

Western Michigan Genealogical
Society
c/o Grand Rapids Public Library
Library Plaza
Grand Rapids, 49503

Minnesota

American Swedish Institute
2600 Park Ave.
Minneapolis, 55407

Association for Certification of
Minnesota Genealogists, Inc.
c/o Shirley Rodman Lewison,
Applications Secretary
330 S. Park
Mora, 55051

Czechoslovak Genealogical Society
International
P.O. Box 16225
St. Paul, 55116

English Interest Group
Minnesota Genealogical Society
9009 Northwood Cir.
New Hope, 55427

MinnKota Genealogical Society
c/o Janet Smith
126 East
Grand Forks, 56721

Nicollet County Historical Society
and Museum
P.O. Box 153
St. Peter, 56082

Northwest Territory Canadian and
French Heritage Center
P.O. Box 29397
Brooklyn Center, 55429

Norwegian-American Genealogical
Association
c/o Minnesota Genealogical Society
P.O. Box 16069
St. Paul, 55116

Norwegian-American Historical
Association
Northfield, 55057

St. Cloud Area Genealogists, Inc.
P.O. Box 213
St. Cloud, 56302

Mississippi

Mississippi Coast Genealogical and
Historical Society
P.O. Box 513
Biloxi, 39530

Mississippi Genealogical Society
P.O. Box 5301
Jackson, 39216

Northeast Mississippi Historical and
Genealogical Society
P.O. Box 434
Tupelo, 38801

South Mississippi Genealogical
Society
Box 15271
Hattiesburg, 39401

Vicksburg Genealogical Society, Inc.
P.O. Box 1161
Vicksburg, 39181

Missouri

American Family Records Association
P.O. Box 15505
Kansas City, 64106

Baptist Historical Society, Missouri
William Jewell College Library
Liberty, 64068

Cape Girardeau County, Missouri
Genealogical Society
204 S. Union Ave.
Jackson, 63755

Daughters of Union Veterans of the
Civil War, Missouri Department
c/o Mrs. Sue Ladage
2615 Porter Ave.
Brentwood, 63144

Heart of America Genealogical
Society
c/o Public Library
311 E. 12th St.
Kansas City, 64106

Missouri Historical Society
Jefferson Memorial Bldg.
Forest Park
St. Louis, 63112

Missouri State Genealogical
Association
P.O. Box 833
Columbia, 65205

Missouri Territorial Pioneers
3929 Milton Dr.
Independence, 64055

State Historical Society of Missouri
Hitt and Lowry Sts.
Columbia, 65201

Union Cemetery Historical Society
2727 Main St., Suite 120
Kansas City, 64108

Montana

Big Horn County Genealogical
Society
Box 51
Hardin, 59034

Gallatin Genealogy Society
P.O. Box 1783
Bozeman, 59715

Great Falls Genealogy Society
Paris Gibson Sq.
1400 1st Ave. N.
Great Falls, 49401

Miles City Genealogical Society
c/o Miles City Public Library
P.O. Box 711
Miles City, 59301

Montana Historical Society
225 N. Roberts St.
Helena, 59620

Montana State Genealogical Society
P.O. Box 555
Chester, 59522

Western Montana Genealogical
Society
P.O. Box 2714
Missoula, 59806

Yellowstone Genealogy Forum
c/o Parmly Billings Library
510 N. Broadway
Billings, 59101

Nebraska

American Historical Society of
Germans from Russia
631 D. St.
Lincoln, 68502

Custer County Historical Society, Inc.
P.O. Box 334
Broken Bow, 68822

Fort Kearny Genealogical Society
Box 22
Kearney, 68847

Greater Omaha Genealogical Society
P.O. Box 4011
Omaha, 68104

Omaha Family History Center
c/o Cherie Mierzejewski
617 S. 153rd Cir.
Omaha, 68154

Nebraska State Genealogical Society
P.O. Box 5608
Lincoln, 68505

North Platte Genealogical Society
P.O. Box 1452
North Platte, 69101

Northeastern Nebraska Genealogical
Society
P.O. Box 249
Lyons, 68038

Northwest Genealogical Society
503 Morehead
Chadron, 64337

Omaha Family History Center
c/o Paul Brown
6601 Lafayette Ave.
Omaha, 68132

South Central Genealogical Society
c/o Jensen Memorial Library
443 N. Kearney
Minden, 68959

Southeast Nebraska Genealogical
Society
P.O. Box 562
Beatrice, 68301

Southwest Nebraska Genealogical
Society
P.O. Box 156
Beatrice, 68301

Nevada

Clark County, Nevada, Genealogical
Society
P.O. Box 1929
Las Vegas, 89125

Las Vegas Jewish Genealogical Society
Carole Montello
P.O. Box 29342
Las Vegas, 89126

Nevada State Genealogical Society
P.O. Box 20666
Reno, 89515

Northeastern Nevada Genealogical
Society
1515 Idaho St.
Elko, 89801

New Hampshire

Acadian Genealogical and Historical
Association
P.O. Box 668
Manchester, 03105

American-Canadian Genealogical
Society
P.O. Box 668
Manchester, 03105

New Hampshire Society of
Genealogists
P.O. Box 633
Exeter, 03833

New Hampshire Historical Society
30 Park St.
Concord, 03301

North Country Genealogical Society
c/o Elva Reeg
P.O. Box 618
Littleton, 03561

New Jersey

Afro-American Historical and
Genealogical Society, New Jersey
Lloyd E. Washington, President
18 Lindsley Ave.
Maplewood, 07040

Association of Jewish Genealogical
Societies
155 N. Washington Ave.
Bergenfield, 07621

Camden County Historical Society
Euclid Ave. and Park Blvd.
Camden, 08103

Descendants of Founders of New
Jersey
c/o Mrs. William A. Smith
850-A Thornhill Ct.
Lakewood, 08701

Genealogical Society of New Jersey
P.O. Box 1291
New Brunswick, 08903

New Jersey Historical Society
230 Broadway
Newark, 07104

New Mexico

Albuquerque Public Library
Genealogy Club
423 Central Ave. N.E.
Albuquerque, 87102

Los Alamos Family History Society
P.O. Box 900
Los Alamos, 87544

New Mexico Genealogical Society
P.O. Box 8283
Albuquerque, 87198

Roswell New Mexico Genealogical
Group
2604 N. Kentucky
Roswell, 88201

Southern New Mexico Genealogical
Society
P.O. Box 2563
Las Cruces, 88004

Southwestern New Mexico
Genealogical Society
P.O. Box 5725
Hobbs, 88240

New York

Adirondack Genealogical-Historical
Society
100 Main St.
Saranac Lake, 12983

Albany Jewish Genealogical Society
Rabbi Don Cashman
P.O. Box 3850
Albany, 12208

Brooklyn Historical Society
128 Pierrepont St.
Brooklyn, 11201

Capital District Genealogical Society
P.O. Box 2175, Empire State Plaza
Station
Albany, 12220

Central New York Genealogical
Society
Box 104, Colvin Station
Syracuse, 13205

Colonial Dames of America
421 E. 61st St.
New York, 10021

Colonial Wars Genealogical Society
122 E. 58th St.
New York, 10022

Creole-American Genealogical
Society, Inc.
P.O. Box 2666, Church St. Station
New York, 10008

Finger Lakes Genealogical Society
P.O. Box 47
Seneca Falls, 13148

German Genealogical Group
24 Jonquill La.
Kings Park, 11754

Greater New York, Afro-American
Historical and Genealogical Society
Antonia C. Martin, President
P.O. Box 022340
Brooklyn, 11202

Huguenot Historical Society
14 Forest Glen Rd.
New Paltz, 12561

Irish Family History Forum, Inc.
P.O. Box 351
Rockville Centre, 11571

Italian Genealogical Group of New
York
7 Grayon Dr.
Dix Hills, 11746

Jewish Genealogical Society, Inc.
Marsha Saron Dennis
P.O. Box 6398
New York, 10128

Jewish Research Institute
1048 5th Ave.
New York, 10028

Leo Baeck Institute, German-Jewish
Families
129 E. 73rd St.
New York 10021

New York Genealogical and
Biographical Society
122 E. 58th St.
New York, 10022

New York Historical Association
170 Central Park W.
New York, 10024

New York State Council of
Genealogical Organizations
P.O. Box 2593
Syracuse, 13220

New York State Historical Association
Fenimore House, Lake Rd.
Cooperstown, 13326

Northern New York American-
Canadian Genealogical Society
P.O. Box 1256
Plattsburgh, 12901

Schenectady County Historical
Society
32 Washington Ave.
Schenectady, 12305

Tioga County Historical Society
110–112 Front St.
Oswego, 13827

Westchester County Genealogical
Society
P.O. Box 518
White Plains, 10603

Western New York Genealogical
Society
P.O. Box 338
Hamburg, 14075

North Carolina

Afro-American Heritage Society,
North Carolina
P.O. Box 26334
Raleigh, 27611

Alamance County, North Carolina,
Genealogical Society
P.O. Box 3052
Burlington, 27215

Albemarle Genealogical Society
P.O. Box 87
Currituck, 27929

Carolinas Genealogical Society
604 Craig St.
Monroe, 28110

Eastern North Carolina Genealogical
Society
P.O. Box 395
New Bern, 28560

Loyalist Descendants (American
Revolution)
P.O. Box 848, Desk 120
Rockingham, 28379

Mecklenburg Genealogical Society
P.O. Box 32453
Charlotte, 28232

North Carolina Genealogical Society
P.O. Box 1492
Raleigh, 27602

Presbyterian and Reformed Churches,
Historic Foundation
Montreat, 28757

Randolph County Genealogical
Society
Randolph County Public Library
201 Worth St.
Asheboro, 27203

VA-NC Piedmont Genealogical
Society
P.O. Box 2272
Danville, Virginia 24541

Wilkes Genealogical Society, Inc.
P.O. Box 1629
North Wilkesboro, 28659

North Dakota

Bismarck-Mandan Genealogical
Society
c/o Karen Williams, President
P.O. Box 485
Bismarck, 58502

Central North Dakota Genealogical
  Society
c/o Marlene Ripplinger
Harvey Public Library
119 E. 10th
Harvey, 58341

Germans from Russia Heritage
  Society
P.O. Box 1671
Bismarck, 58501

North Dakota State Genealogical
  Society
c/o John Mogren, President
P.O. Box 485
Bismarck, 58502

Red River Valley Genealogical Society
c/o Alice Ellingsberg, President
P.O. Box 9284
Fargo, 58106

Southwestern North Dakota
  Genealogical Society
c/o Patricia Hartman, HCR 01
Box 321
Regent, 58650

State Historical Society of North
  Dakota
Liberty Memorial Bldg.
Bismarck, 58501

Ohio

Cincinnati Historical Society
The Museum Center at Cincinnati
Union Terminal
1301 Western Ave.
Cincinnati, 45203

Cleveland, Afro-American Historical
  and Genealogical Society
P.O. Box 200382
Cleveland, 44120

Cleveland, Jewish Genealogical
  Society
Arlene Blank Rich
996 Eastlawn Dr.
Highland Heights, 44143

Daughters of Union Veterans of the
  Civil War, Ohio Department
Shirleen Howard
31927 U.S. Rte. 30
Hanoverton, 44423

Erie County Chapter, Ohio
  Genealogical Society
P.O. Box 1301
Sandusky, 44871

Franklin County Genealogical Society
P.O. Box 44309
Columbus, 43204

Greater Cincinnati Jewish
  Genealogical Society
Nancy Felson Brant
Bureau of Jewish Education
1580 Summit Rd.
Cincinnati, 45237

Greater Cleveland Genealogical
  Society
P.O. Box 40254
Cleveland, 44140

Greater Cleveland, Polish
  Genealogical Society
906 College Ave.
Cleveland, 44113

Greene County Chapter, Ohio
 Genealogical Society
P.O. Box 706
Xenia, 45385

Marion Area Genealogical Society
P.O. Box 844
Marion, 43301

Muskingum County Chapter, Ohio
 Genealogical Society
220 N. 5th St.
Zanesville, 43702

Ohio Genealogical Society
P.O. Box 2625
Mansfield, 44906

Palatines to America, Ohio Chapter
Capital Univ., Box 101D
Columbus, 43209

Richland County Chapter, Ohio
 Genealogical Society
P.O. Box 3823
Mansfield, 44907

Ross County Genealogical Society
P.O. Box 6352
Chillicothe, 45601

Sons of Union Veterans of the Civil
 War, Ohio Department
Keith D. Ashley, Historian
34465 Crew Rd.
Pomeroy, 45769

Southern Ohio Genealogical Society
P.O. Box 414
Hillsboro, 45133

Western Reserve Historical Society
10825 East Blvd.
Cleveland, 44106

Oklahoma

Broken Arrow Genealogical Society
P.O. Box 1244
Broken Arrow, 74013

Federation of Oklahoma Genealogical
 Societies
P.O. Box 26151
Okalhoma City, 73126

Logan County Genealogical Society
P.O. Box 1419
Guthrie, 73044

Muskogee County Genealogical
 Society
801 W. Okmulgee
Muskogee, 74401

Northwest Oklahoma Genealogical
 Society
P.O. Box 834
Woodward, 73801

Oklahoma City LDS Stake
 Genealogical Group
c/o Dorothy Hollinsworth
3108 Windsor Terr.
Oklahoma City, 73122

Oklahoma Genealogical Society
P.O. Box 12986
Oklahoma City, 73157

Oklahoma Historical Society
Historical Bldg.
Oklahoma City, 73105

Pocahontas Trails Genealogical
 Society
(Oklahoma-Texas Regional Chapter)
c/o Susan Bradford
Rte. 2, Box 40
Mangum, 73554

Sons and Daughters of the Cherokee
Strip Pioneers
P.O. Box 465
Enid, 73702

Southwest Oklahoma Genealogical
Society
P.O. Box 148
Lawton, 73502

Tulsa Genealogical Society
P.O. Box 585
Tulsa, 74101

Oregon

Adoptive Rights Association of Oregon
P.O. Box 882
Portland, 97207

Bend Genealogical Society
P.O. Box 8254
Bend, 97708

Clackamas County Family History
Society
P.O. Box 995
Oregon City, 97045

Coos Bay Genealogical Forum
P.O. Box 1067
North Bend, 97459

Deschutes County Historical and
Genealogical Society
P.O. Box 5252
Bend, 97708

Genealogical Council of Oregon, Inc.
P.O. Box 15169
Portland, 97215

Genealogical Forum of Oregon, Inc.
2130 S.W. 5th Ave., Suite 220
Portland, 97201

Genealogical Heritage Council of
Oregon
P.O. Box 628
Ashland, 97520

Grants Pass Genealogical Society
P.O. Box 1834
Grants Pass, 97720

Jewish Genealogical Society of
Oregon
Lorraine Greyson
5437 S.W. Wichita St.
Tualatin, 97062

Mennonite Historical and
Genealogical Society of Oregon
675 Elma Ave. S.E.
Salem, 97301

Oregon Genealogical Society, Inc.
223 N. A St., Suite F.
Springfield, 97477

Rogue Valley Genealogical Society,
Inc.
133 S. Central Ave.
Medford, 97501

Scandinavian Genealogical Society of
Oregon
1123 7th St. N.W.
Salem, 97304

Tillamook County Historical Society
Genealogy Study Group
P.O. Box 123
Tillamook, 97141

Willamette Valley Genealogical
Society
P.O. Box 2083
Salem, 97308

Pennsylvania

African American Genealogy Group
Gene Stackhouse
P.O. Box 1798
Philadelphia, 19105

Allegheny Foothills Historical Society
Boyce Park Adm. Bldg.
675 Old Franklin Rd.
Pittsburgh, 15239

American Swedish Historical
    Foundation
1900 Pattiso Ave.
Philadelphia, 19145

Ancient Order of Hiberians
McKeesport Heritage Center
c/o Timothy Cox
180 W. Schwab Ave.
Munhall, 15120

Berks County Historical Society
940 Centre Ave.
Reading, 19605

Bucks County Genealogical Society
P.O. Box 1092
Doylestown, 18901

Central Pennsylvania Genealogical
    Pioneers
Northumberland, 17857

Evangelical and Reformed Historical
    Society
Phillip Schaff Library
Lancaster Theological Seminary
555 W. James St.
Lancaster, 17603

Friends Historical Association
Haverford College
Haverford, 19041

Genealogical Society of Pennsylvania
1305 Locust St., 3rd Floor
Philadelphia, 19107

German Society, Pennsylvania
P.O. Box 397
Birdsboro, 19508

Historical Society of Pennsylvania
1300 Locust St.
Philadelphia, 19107

Lancaster Mennonite Historical
    Society
2215 Millstream Rd.
Lancaster, 17602

Northeast Pennsylvania Genealogical
    Society, Inc.
P.O. Box 1776
Shavertown, 18708

Palatines to America
Pennsylvania Chapter
P.O. Box 280
Strasburg, 17579

Pennsylvania Genealogical Society
1300 Locust St.
Philadelphia, 19107

Philadelphia Jewish Genealogical
    Society
Jon E. Stein
332 Harrison Ave.
Elkins Park, 19117

Pittsburgh Jewish Genealogical
    Society
Julian Falk
2131 5th Ave.
Pittsburgh, 15219

Schuylkill County Historical Society
14 N. 3rd St.
Pottsville, 17901

Scottish Historical and Research
Society of the Delaware Valley, Inc.
102 St. Paul's Rd.
Ardmore, 19003

South Central Pennsylvania
Genealogical Society
P.O. Box 1824
York, 17405

Southwestern Pennsylvania
Genealogical Society
P.O. Box 894
Washington, 15301

Western Pennsylvania Genealogical
Society
c/o Carnegie Library
4400 Forbes Ave.
Pittsburgh, 15213

Western Pennsylvania Historical
Society
4338 Bigelow Blvd.
Pittsburgh, 15213

Rhode Island

American-French Genealogical
Society
P.O. Box 2113
Pawtucket, 02861

Black Heritage Society of Rhode
Island
46 Alborn St.
Providence, 02903

Mayflower Descendants of Rhode
Island
128 Massasoit
Warwick, 02888

Newport Historical Society
82 Touro St.
Newport, 02840

Rhode Island Genealogical Society
507 Clark's Row
Bristol, 02809

Rhode Island State Historical Society
52 Power St.
Providence, 02906

South Carolina

Charleston Chapter, South Carolina
Genealogical Society
P.O. Box 20266
Charleston, 29413

Huguenot Society of South Carolina
138 Logan St.
Charleston, 29401

Orangeburg German-Swiss
Genealogical Society
P.O. Box 974
Orangeburg, 29119

Piedmont Historical Society
P.O. Box 8096
Spartanburg, 29305

South Carolina Genealogical Society
c/o Bonnie Glasgow
2910 Duncan St.
Columbia, 29205

South Carolina Historical Society
100 Meeting St.
Charleston, 29401

South Dakota

Aberdeen Area Genealogical Society
P.O. Box 493
Aberdeen, 57402

Lake County Genealogical Society
c/o Karl Mundt Library
Dakota State College
Madison, 57042

Pierre-Ft. Pierre Genealogical Society
P.O. Box 925
Pierre, 57501

Rapid City Society for Genealogical
Research
P.O. Box 1495
Rapid City, 57701

Sioux Valley Genealogical Society
200 W. 6th St.
Sioux Falls, 57104

South Dakota Genealogical Society
P.O. Box 1101
Pierre, 57501

Tri-State Genealogical Society
905 5th St.
Belle Fourche, 57717

Tennessee

Claiborne County Historical Society
P.O. Box 32
Tazewell, 37879

East Tennessee Historical Society
500 W. Church Ave.
Knoxville, 37902

Jefferson County Genealogical
Society
P.O. Box 267
Jefferson City, 37760

Jonesborough Genealogical Society
c/o Washington County–Jonesborough
Library
200 Sabine Dr.
Jonesborough, 37659

Marion County Genealogical Group
6611 Old Dunlap Rd.
Whitwell, 37397

Middle Tennessee Genealogical
Society
P.O. Box 190625
Nashville, 37219

Mid-West Tennessee Genealogical
Society
P.O. Box 3343
Jackson, 38301

Signal Mountain Genealogical
Society, Inc.
103 Florida Ave.
Signal Mountain, 37377

Tennessee Genealogical Society
P.O. Box 247
Brunswick, 38014

Van Buren County Historical Society
P.O. Box 126
Spencer, 38585

Texas

Amarillo Genealogical Society
c/o Amarillo Public Library
300 E. 4th
Amarillo, 79189

Austin Genealogical Society
P.O. Box 1507
Austin, 78767

Austin County Historical Commission
206 S. Masonic St.
Bellville, 77418

Beaumont Heritage Society
(Jefferson County)
2985 French Rd.
Beaumont, 77706

Brazos Genealogical Association
P.O. Box 5493
Bryan, 77805

Central Texas Genealogical Society
Waco McLennan County Library
1717 Austin Ave.
Waco, 76701

Clan McLaren Society of North
   America, Ltd.
c/o Banks McLaurin, Jr.
5843 Royal Crest Dr.
Dallas, 75230

Czech Heritage Society of Texas
c/o Thomas Novosad
7411 Kite Hill
Houston, 77041

Dallas Genealogical Society
P.O. Box 12648
Dallas, 75225

Dallas Jewish Historical Society
Jewish Genealogy Division
David Chapin
7900 Northaven Rd.
Dallas, 75230

El Paso Genealogical Society
c/o El Paso Main Public Library
501 N. Oregon St.
El Paso, 79901

Forth Worth Genealogical Society
P.O. Box 9767
Fort Worth, 76147

German-Texan Heritage Society
507 E. 10th St.
Austin, 78768

Gulf Coast Ancestry Researchers
(Chambers County)
P.O. Box 157
Wallisville, 77597

Heart of Texas Genealogical Society
P.O. Box 133
Rochelle, 76872

High Plains Genealogical Society
1807 Ennis St.
Plainview, 79072

Hispanic Genealogical Society
2932 Baksdale
Houston, 77093

Houston, Afro-American Historical
   and Genealogical Society
Eleanor F. Caldwell, President
302 Harbor Dr.
Houston, 77062

Houston Area Genealogical
   Association
2507 Tannehill
Houston, 77008

Houston Genealogical Forum
P.O. Box 271466
Houston, 77277

Houston Jewish Genealogical Society
c/o Myra T. Ephross
11727 Riverview Dr.
Houston, 77077

Lubbock Heritage Society
P.O. Box 5443
Lubbock, 79417

Methodist Historical Society
Fondren Library
Southern Methodist University
Dallas, 75222

North Texas Genealogical and
Historical Association
P.O. Box 4602
Wichita Falls, 76308

San Antonio Genealogical and
Historical Society
P.O. Box 17461
San Antonio, 78217

South Texas Genealogical Society
P.O. Box 754
Beeville, 78104

Southeast Texas Genealogical and
Historical Society
c/o Tyrrel Historical Library
P.O. Box 3827
Beaumont, 77704

Southwest Texas Genealogical Society
P.O. Box 295
Uvalde, 78802

Texas-Oklahoma Panhandle
Genealogical Society
c/o Sue Morgan
1010 S. Harvard
Perryton, 79070

West Texas Genealogical Society
P.O. Box 2307
Abilene, 79604

Utah

Cuban Genealogical Society
P.O. Box 2650
Salt Lake City, 84110

Everton's International Genealogical
Society
P.O. Box 368
Logan, 84323

Genealogical Society of Utah
35 North West Temple
Salt Lake City, 84150

Salt Lake City Jewish Genealogical
Society
Thomas W. Noy
3510 Fleetwood Dr.
Salt Lake City, 84109

Utah Genealogical Association
P.O. Box 1144
Salt Lake City, 84110

Vermont

Genealogical Society of Vermont
Westminster West
RFD 3
Putney, 05346

Vermont Genealogical Society
P.O. Box 422
Pittsford, 05763

Vermont Historical Society
Pavillion Office Bldg.
109 State St.
Montpelier, 05602

Welsh-American Genealogical Society
c/o Llyn Mawr
Lewis Rd., RR2, Box 516
Poultney, 05764

Virginia

Albermarle County Historical Society
220 Court Sq.
Charlottesville, 22901

Central Virginia Genealogical
Association
P.O. Box 5583
Charlottesville, 22905

Culpeper Historical Society, Inc.
P.O. Box 785
Culpeper, 22701

Cumberland County Historical
Society
Box 88
Cumberland, 23040

Fairfax Historical Society
P.O. Box 415
Fairfax, 22030

Fredericksburg Regional Genealogical
Society
P.O. Box 42013
Fredericksburg, 22404

Genealogical Research Institute of
Virginia
P.O. Box 29178
Richmond, 23242

Hampton Roads, Afro-American
Historical and Genealogical Society
Zach H. Lewis, President
P.O. Box 2448
Newport News, 23609

Norfolk Genealogical Society
P.O. Box 12813, Thomas Corner
Station
Norfolk, 23502

Palatines to America, Virginia Chapter
3249 Cambridge Ct.
Fairfax, 22032

Prince William County Genealogical
Society
P.O. Box 2019
Manassas, 20108

Southwestern Virginia Genealogical
Society
P.O. Box 12485
Roanoke, 24026

Southwest Virginia Historical Society
Wise, 24293

Tidewater, Afro-American Historical
and Genealogical Society
Esther Lloyd, President
2200 Crossroad Tr.
Virginia Beach, 23456

Tidewater Genealogical Society
P.O. Box 7650
Hampton, 23666

Tidewater Jewish Genealogical
Society
Jewish Community Center
7300 Newport Ave.
Norfolk, 23505

VA-NC Piedmont Genealogical
Society
P.O. Box 2272
Danville, 24541

Washington

Chehalis Valley Historical Society
c/o Kelle A. Davis
268-11 Oak Meadows Rd.
Oakville, 98568

Eastern Washington Genealogical
Society
P.O. Box 1826
Spokane, 99210

Ft. Vancouver Historical Society
P.O. Box 1834
Vancouver, 98663

Italian Interest Group of the Eastside
Genealogical Society
P.O. Box 374
Bellevue, 98009

Jewish Genealogical Society of
Washington
Jerome Becker
14222 N.E. 1st La.
Bellevue, 98007

Lower Columbia Genealogical
Society
P.O. Box 472
Longview, 98632

Northeast Washington Genealogical
Society
c/o Colville Public Library
195 S. Oak
Colville, 99114

Puget Sound Genealogical Society
(Kitsap and North Mason Counties)
1026 Sidney Ave., Suite 110
Port Orchard, 98366

Seattle Genealogical Society
8511 15th Ave. N.E.
Seattle, 98115

State Capitol Historical Association
211 W. 21st Ave.
Olympia, 98501

Stillaguamish Valley Genealogical So-
ciety of North Snohomish County
P.O. Box 34
Arlington, 98223

Tacoma-Pierce County Genealogy
Society
P.O. Box 1952
Tacoma, 98401

Walla Walla Valley Genealogy Society
P.O. Box 115
Walla Walla, 99362

Washington State Historical Society
Library
State Historical Bldg.
315 N. Stadium Way
Tacoma, 98403

Yakima Valley Genealogical Society
P.O. Box 445
Yakima, 98907

West Virginia

Boone County Genealogical Society
P.O. Box 295
Madison, 25130

Hacker's Creek Pioneer Descendants,
Inc.
c/o Central West Virginia
Genealogical and History Library
Rte. 1, Box 238
Jane Lew, 26378

Logan County Genealogical Society
P.O. Box 1959
Logan, 25601

Marion County Genealogical Club,
Inc.
Marion County Library
Monroe St.
Fairmont, 26554

Mingo County Genealogical Society
Box 2581
Williamson, 25661

Palatines to America
West Virginia Chapter
572 Plymouth Ave.
Morgantown, 26505

Taylor County Historical and
Genealogical Society, Inc.
P.O. Box 522
Grafton, 26354

West Augusta Historical and
Genealogical Society
2515 10th Ave.
Parkersburg, 26101

West Virginia Historical Society
Cultural Center
Capitol Complex
Charleston, 25305

Wetzel County Genealogical Society
P.O. Box 464
New Martinsville, 26155

Wisconsin

Bay Area Genealogical Society
P.O. Box 283
Green Bay, 54305

Eau Claire Genealogical Research
Society
c/o Chippewa Valley Museum
P.O. Box 1204
Eau Claire, 54702

Fond du Lac County Genealogical
Society
c/o Spillman Library
719 Wisconsin Ave.
North Fond du Lac, 54937

Fond du Lac County Historical
Society
P.O. Box 1284
Fond du Lac, 54935

French-Canadian/Acadian
Genealogists of Wisconsin
P.O. Box 414
Hales Corners, 53130

Heart O'Wisconsin Genealogical
Society
c/o MacMillan Memorial Library
490 E. Grand Ave.
Wisconsin Rapids, 54494

Irish Genealogical Society of
Wisconsin
P.O. Box 13766
Wauwatosa, 53213

Jewish Genealogical Society, Wisconsin
Penny Deshur
9280 N. Fairway Dr.
Milwaukee, 53217

Kenosha County Genealogical Society
c/o Lois R. Stein
4902 52nd St.
Kenosha, 53142

Lower Wisconsin River Genealogical
and Historical Research Center
P.O. Box 202
Wauzeka, 53826

Milwaukee, Afro-American
Genealogical Society
Carol J. Calvin, President
2620 W. Center St.
Milwaukee, 53206

Milwaukee County Genealogical
Society
P.O. Box 27326
Milwaukee, 53227

Milwaukee County Historical Society
910 N. 3rd St.
Milwaukee, 53203

Polish Genealogical Society of
Wisconsin
c/o Ray Supersynski
3731 Turnwood Dr.
Richfield, 53076

Pommerscher Verein Freistadt
Rundschreiben
(Pomeranian Society of Freistadt)
P.O. Box 204
Germantown, 53022

Seventh Day Baptist Historical Society
P.O. Box 1678
Janesville, 53547

Sheboygan County Historical
Research Center
518 Water St., #3
Sheboygan Falls, 53085

State Historical Society of Wisconsin
University of Wisconsin
816 State St.
Madison, 53706

Waukesha County Genealogical
Society
P.O. Box 1541
Waukesha, 53187

Wisconsin Genealogical Council, Inc.
N9307 Abitz La.
Luxemburg, 54217

Wisconsin State Genealogical Society,
Inc.
2109 20th Ave.
Monroe, 53566

Wyoming

Cheyenne Genealogical Society
Laramie County Library
Central Ave.
Cheyenne, 82001

Laramie Peak Genealogy Society of
Platte County
c/o Cindy Anderson
1108 21st St.
Wheatland, 82201

Sheridan County Genealogical
Society
Wyoming Room
335 W. Alger St.
Sheridan, 82801

Sublette County Genealogy Society
P.O. Box 1186
Pindale, 82941

Genealogical Publishers and Bookstores

THE GROWTH OF interest in genealogy has stimulated publishing on the subject as well as the opening of bookstores with specialties in this area. The following list contains the names of some of the more established bookstores and genealogical publishers by geographical area. Most of the stores specialize in genealogical works that have a strong regional appeal, although their collections frequently contain more extensive material. As with other aspects of genealogy, letter of inquiry (containing a SASE of course) and a little detective work will uncover surprising treasures in many of these places. Most of the publishers and bookstores listed supply catalogs on request. Many are free; some have a small charge, which is usually waived with an order.

Northeast

Closson Press
1935 Sampson Dr.
Apollo, PA 15613
Telephone: 412-337-4482
($2 for catalog)

Family Line Publications
Rear 63 E. Main St.
Westminster, MD 21157
Telephone 800-876-6103
http://pages.prodigy.com/Strawn/family.htm
(Free catalog)

Genealogical Publishing Co., Inc.
1000 N. Calvert St.
Baltimore, MD 21202
Telephone: 800-296-6687

Heritage Books, Inc.
1540-E Pointer Ridge Pl., Suite 201
Bowie, MD 20716
Telephone: 800-398-7709
(Free catalog)

Higginson Book Company
148 Washington St.
Salem, MA 01970
Telephone: 508-745-7170
(Catalog $4; 7,200 local and family
histories)

New England Historic and
Genealogical Society
101 Newbury St.
Boston, MA 02116

Picton Press
P.O. Box 250
Rockport, ME 04856
Telephone: 207-236-6565
(German-Swiss books)

Scholarly Resources, Inc.
104 Greenhill Ave.
Wilmington, DE 19805
Telephone: 800-772-8937

Tuttle Antiquarian Books, Inc.
28 S. Main St.
Rutland, VT 05701
Telephone: 802-773-8229
(Catalog $7.50, postpaid; lists
thousands of family histories)

John F. Walter
79-13 67 Dr.
Middle Village, NY 11379

Telephone: 718-894-3164
(Over 7,500 Civil War unit histories at
$15 per unit)

Hoenstine Book Mart
P.O. Box 208
Hollidaysburg, PA 16648

District of Columbia

U.S. Government Printing Office
Washington, DC 20402
(Many brochures including *Where to
Write for Birth, Death, Divorce and
Marriage Records*)

South

Appleton's Fine Used Bookseller and
Genealogy
Tower Pl. Mall
8700 Pineville-Mathews Rd., #610
Charlotte, NC 28226
Telephone: 800-777-3601
www.appletons.com
(Free genealogy catalog)

Boyd Publishing Company
P.O. Box 367
Milledgeville, GA 31061
($2 for 68-page catalog)

National Archives Trust Fund
NEPS Dept. 735
P.O. Box 10093
Atlanta, GA 30384
(Publications about National Archives
collections)

National Genealogical Society
4527 17th St. N.
Arlington, VA 22207

T.L.C. Genealogy Books
P.O. Box 403369
Miami Beach, FL 33140
Telephone: 800-858-8558
www.tlc-gen.com

Southern Historical Press, Inc.
P.O. Box 1267
Greenville, SC 29602
Telephone: 864-233-2346

Midwest

Beckers Bookshelf
1314 Prospect Ave.
Norfolk, NE 68701
(Books for rent; send SASE for details)

Gale Research Company
Book Tower
Detroit, MI 48226
Telephone: 313-961-6810
http://galenet.gale.com
(On-line searchable databases)

Madigan's Books
P.O. Box 62
Charleston, IL 61920
www.advant.com/madigan

Storebecks
P.O. Box 510062
New Berlin, WI 53151
Telephone: 800-360-3555
(German genealogy books)

Southwest

Frontier Press
P.O. Box 3715
Galveston, TX 77552

Telephone: 800-772-7559
www.doit.com/frontier
($1 for catalog)

The Memorabilia Corner
1312 McKinley Ave.
Norman, OK 73072
(Native American books)

West

Brigham Young University
205 University Press Bldg.
Provo, UT 84602

Dutch Family Heritage Society
2463 Ledgewood Dr.
West Jordan, UT 84084
Telephone: 801-967-8400
(Specializes in Dutch books; free
catalog)

Everton Publishers, Inc.
P.O. Box 368
Logan, UT 84323
Telephone: 800-443-6325
www.everton.com
(Publishers of *Genealogical Helper*
magazine, many books and supplies,
also CDs)

Family History Books
404 Tule Lake Rd. S.
Tacoma, WA 98444

Parker Research and Publishing
2463 Ledgewood Dr.
West Jordan, UT 84084
Telephone: 801-967-8400
(Specializes in Scandinavian books)

Stemons Publishing
Box 612
West Jordan, UT 84084
(Specializes in Pennsylvania books)

Yates Publishing FGSE
P.O. Box 67
Stevensville, MT 59870
Telephone: 406-777-3797
(Sells family group sheets for
hundreds of surnames)

Miscellaneous

Ancestry, Inc.
P.O. Box 990
Orem, UT 84059
www.ancestry.com
(Books, CDs, audiotapes)

APPENDIX III

Map Sources
for Genealogists

Northeast

Historical Ink Company
Secret Lake
Phillipston, MA 01331
http://members.aol.com/oldmapsne
(Old maps of New England; catalog
$2)

Jonathan Sheppard Books
Box 2020, Plaza Station
Albany, NY 12220
(European maps before 1800; send 64
cents in stamps for complete
description)

Quintin Publications
28 Felsmere Ave.
Pawtucket, RI 02861
Telephone: 401-723-6797
www.quintinpublications.com
(Ordnance maps of the British Isles—
1884)

District of Columbia

United States Government Printing
Office
Superintendent of Documents
Washington, DC 20402
(*The Geography and Map Division:
A Guide to Its Collections and
Services*; specify stock number
030-004-00015-9)

Geography and Map Division
Library of Congress
Washington, DC 20540
(Two free brochures: *Geography and
Map Division, the Library of Congress
and List of Publications, Geography
and Map Division*)

United States Geological Survey
523 National Center
Reston, VA 20192
Telephone 703-648-4544

http://mapping.usgs.gov/mac/isb/pubs/
booklets/genealogy/genealogy.html)
(Copies of maps of the United States,
its territories, and outlying areas may
be ordered as photo blowups. To
order, call 1-800-USA-MAPS.)

Midwest

Travel Genie Maps
3815 Calhoun Ave.
Ames, Iowa 50010
Telephone: 515-232-1070
www.netins.net/showcase/travelgenie
(Free brochure of detailed maps of
Britain, Denmark, Germany, Ireland,
Norway, Poland, and Sweden)

Omega Translation Services
P.O. Box 745
Iowa City, IA 52244
(European maps; send SASE)

Southwest

Texas State Historical Maps
Drawer 3885
San Angelo, TX 76901

Slocum Books
Box 10998C
Austin, TX 78766
Telephone: 800-521-4451
(Historic maps)

West

AGLL Genealogical Services
P.O. Box 329
Bountiful, UT 84011
Telephone: 800-769-AGLL
www.agll.com
(Map guide to American migration
routes)

Ancestry, Inc.
P.O. Box 990
Orem, UT 84059
www.ancestry.com/ancestry/maps.asp
(On-line ordering)

Miscellaneous

Department of Highways
State Capitol
Each State
(State maps with cemeteries)

Special Immigrant Passenger Lists

Because passenger lists are so valuable for genealogical purposes, many have been published privately by genealogical and historical societies or by publishers who specialize in such research books, and they can be found in most genealogical library collections. Among the most important are the following:

Charles Browning, *Welsh Settlement of Pennsylvania*

David Dobson, *Directory of Scots Banished to the American Plantations, 1650–1775*

John Evjen, *Scandinavian Immigrants in New York, 1630–1674*

John Farmer, *A Genealogical Register of the First Settlers of New England*

Ira A. Glazier, *The Famine Emigrants: Lists of Irish Immigrants Arriving at the Port of New York, 1846–1851*

Ira A. Glazier and P. William Filby, *Germans to America: Lists of Passengers Arriving at U.S. Ports, 1850–1887*

John Hotten, *The Original List of Persons of Quality Who Went from Great Britain to the American Plantations, 1600–1700*

Samuel Joseph, *Jewish Immigration to the United States from 1881 to 1910*

Jack Kaminkow, A *List of Emigrants from England to America, 1719–1759*

Nils William Olsson, *Swedish Passenger Arrivals in New York 1820–1850*

Israel Rupp, A *Collection of Thirty Thousand Names of German, Swiss, Dutch, French, and Other Immigrants in Pennsylvania from 1727 to 1776*

Ralph Strassburger, *Pennsylvania German Pioneers: Port of Philadelphia from 1727 to 1808*

Donald Yoder, *Emigrants from Wyer Hemberg; the Adolf Gerber Lists*

Major Ports of Entry for Immigrants

Passenger lists for these ports are available in the National Archives in Washington, DC, and its branches (see chapter 8).

Name of Seaport or District	Passenger Lists
Alexandria, Virginia	1820–52
Annapolis, Maryland	1849
Baltimore, Maryland	1820–1909
Bangor, Maine	1848
Barnstable, Massachusetts	1820–26
Bath, Maine	1825–32, 1867
Boston, Massachusetts	1820–1943
Bristol and Warren, Rhode Island	1820–24, 1828, 1843–71
Charleston, South Carolina	1820–29, 1906–45
Galveston, Texas	1846–71
Jacksonville, Florida	1804–45
Kennebunk, Maine	1820–27, 1842

Key West, Florida	1837–68, 1898–1945
Marblehead, Massachusetts	1820–52
Miami, Florida	1899–1945
Mobile, Alabama	1820–62, 1904–45
Nantucket, Massachusetts	1820–62
New Bedford, Massachusetts	1823–99, 1902–42
New Orleans, Louisiana	1820–1945
New York, New York	1820–1942
Newport, Rhode Island	1820–75
Plymouth, Massachusetts	1821–43
Providence, Rhode Island	1820–67, 1911–43
Richmond Virginia	1820–44
St. Augustine, Florida	1820–27, 1870
Savannah, Georgia	1820–68, 1906–45

List of *Mayflower* Passengers

THE SPELLING is true to the passenger list; asterisks denote the passengers whose family line has been traced by modern genealogists. If you think you have a *Mayflower* ancestor, you should check with the New England Historic and Genealogical Society (see chapter 6).

John Carver and his wife, Katherine
Desire Minter
John Howland* and Roger Wilder, two manservants
William Latham, a boy
Jasper More, a child
William Brewster* and his wife, Mary,* with two sons, Love* and Wrasling
Richard More, a boy
Edward Winslow* and his wife, Elizabeth, with two manservants, George Sowle* and Elias Story; also a little girl called Ellen More
William Bradford* and his wife, Dorothy
Isaak Allerton* and his wife, Mary, with three children, Bartholomew, Remember,* and Mary,* and a servant boy, John Hooke

Samuel Fuller* and a servant called William Butten

John Crakston and his son John Crakston

Captain Myles Standish* and his wife, Rose

Christopher Martin and his wife, and two servants, Salamon Prower and John Langemore

William Mullines and his wife, and two children, Joseph and Priscilla,* and a servant, Robart Carter

William White and Susana,* his wife, and a son called Resolved,* one other son born on the ship called Peregriene* and two servants named William Holbeck and Edward Thomson

Steven Hopkins* and his wife, Elizabeth,* and two children, Giles* and Constanta* by a former wife; and Damaris and Oceanus by this wife; and two servants called Edward Doty* and Edward Litster

Richard Warren*

John Billinton* and his wife, Elen,* and two sons, John and Francis*

Edward Tillie and his wife, Ann, and two children that were their cousins, Henery Samson* and Humility Coper

John Tillie and his wife and their daughter Eellizabeth*

Francis Cooke* and his son John*

Thomas Rogers and his son Joseph*

Thomas Tinker and his wife and a son

John Rigdale and his wife, Alice

James Chilton and his wife and their daughter Mary*

Edward Fuller and his wife and Samuell*, their son

John Turner and two sons

Francis Eaton* and his wife, Sarah, and Samuell,* their son

Moyses Fletcher

John Goodman

Thomas Williams

Digerie Preist

Edmond Margeson

Peter Browne*

Richard Britterige
Richard Clarke
Richard Gardenar
Gilbert Winslow
John Alden,* a cooper hired at Southhampton
John Allerton and Thomas English, both seamen

Index

Place names:
  Scottish, 152
  as surnames, 13, 14
    German, 18
    Japanese, 18
    Jewish, 19
    Russian, 20
    Spanish, 21
POINT (Pursuing Our Italian Names Together), 171–72
Poland, 183–85, 234
  immigrants from, 26, 34, 82
  Jewish records, 175
  LDS library records, 68
  occupational surnames, 15
Polynesian ancestry records, 101
Population Census Schedules, 115
Ports of entry, for immigrants, 319–20
Portugal, 234
  immigrants from, 37
Postal Reply Coupons, 138
Postmarks, 59
Primary records, 84
Printers, for computers, 200
Privacy Act of 1974, 112
Private cemeteries, 92
Private libraries, 71, 81–82
Probate records, 84, 87
  England, 146
  France, 162
  Greece, 168
  Italy, 171
  Native American, 129
  New York, 78
  Northern Ireland, 149
  Norway, 180–81
  Scotland, 151
Procedures in genealogical search, 72–74
Professional genealogists, 126–28
Property records:
  Canada, 155
  Denmark, 160
  France, 162
  Mexico, 178
  Norway, 181
  Sweden, 192
Protestants, and names, 8
Psychohistory of family, 240–45
Public libraries, xv–xvi, 70, 74–79
Public records, local, 84–103
Publications:
  family association, 250
  family history, 252–58
  genealogical societies, 79–80
Publishers, genealogical, 311–14

Puerto Ricans, 36
Puerto Rico, National Archives, 106
Puritans, 30

Quakers, 88–89, 147
Questionnaires, family history, 43, 48

Rad, Shirley Linder, 249
Railroads, 40
  passenger lists, 123
Rasmussen, Louis J., 123
Recording of interviews, 53
Record-keeping system, 71–72
Redford, Robert, 108
Re-emigration, of Italians, 33
Regional archives:
  Norway, 179–81
  Sweden, 191–92
Relationships within families, 242–45
  census information, 113
Relatives, 2–3
  interviews with, 41, 50–57
Religious records. *See* Church records
Research, genetic, 238
Researchers, to hire, England, 146
Research locale, 72–73
Research reminder list, 72
Reu-Net, 96
Reunion (software), 215
Reunions, family, xvi, 3, 247
Revolutionary War records, 118–20
Rhode Island, 106, 275, 303
  French immigrants, 31
Richard III, King of England, 222
Righter, Peter, 105
Roads, 37–40
Roman Catholics:
  England, 147
  Irish records, 169
  Scotland, 150
Roosevelt, Theodore, 17
Roots, Haley, 4, 28, 98
Roots-L (newsgroup), 206
Royal ancestry, 4–5, 224–25
Royal College of Arms, London, 222
Ruoff, W. H., 195
Russia, 185–87, 235
  immigrants from, 26, 35
  LDS library records, 68
Russian names, 19–20

Saints' names, 8
Salt Lake City, Utah, genealogical records, 61–69
Samoa, National Archives, 107

About the Author

JEANE EDDY WESTIN has pursued a lifelong interest in history, which has helped her research several of her familial lines back to the 1600s and one even to the thirteenth-century kings of Scotland and England. She is just as proud of the far more plentiful farmers and millers in her family tree but admits to mixed feelings about the scarcely lawful horse trader and the army deserters she has uncovered. She lives with her husband in Sacramento.